Geopolitics in Central Europe

Geopolitics in Central Europe
Superpower Competition and Regional Dynamics

Csaba Moldicz

BLOOMSBURY ACADEMIC
LONDON • NEW YORK • OXFORD • NEW DELHI • SYDNEY

BLOOMSBURY ACADEMIC

Bloomsbury Publishing Plc, 50 Bedford Square, London, WC1B 3DP, UK
Bloomsbury Publishing Inc, 1385 Broadway, New York, NY 10018, USA
Bloomsbury Publishing Ireland, 29 Earlsfort Terrace, Dublin 2, D02 AY28, Ireland

BLOOMSBURY, BLOOMSBURY ACADEMIC and the Diana logo are trademarks of
Bloomsbury Publishing Plc

First published in Great Britain 2023
Paperback edition published 2025

Copyright © Csaba Moldicz, 2023

Csaba Moldicz has asserted his right under the Copyright, Designs and Patents Act, 1988,
to be identified as Author of this work.

For legal purposes the Acknowledgements on p. xii constitute an extension of this
copyright page.

Series design by Adriana Brioso

All rights reserved. No part of this publication may be: i) reproduced or transmitted
in any form, electronic or mechanical, including photocopying, recording or by means
of any information storage or retrieval system without prior permission in writing from
the publishers; or ii) used or reproduced in any way for the training, development or
operation of artificial intelligence (AI) technologies, including generative AI technologies.
The rights holders expressly reserve this publication from the text and data mining
exception as per Article 4(3) of the Digital Single Market Directive (EU) 2019/790.

Bloomsbury Publishing Plc does not have any control over, or responsibility for, any
third-party websites referred to or in this book. All internet addresses given in this
book were correct at the time of going to press. The author and publisher regret any
inconvenience caused if addresses have changed or sites have ceased to exist,
but can accept no responsibility for any such changes.

A catalogue record for this book is available from the British Library.

A catalog record for this book is available from the Library of Congress.

ISBN: HB: 978-1-3503-2672-9
PB: 978-1-3503-2676-7
ePDF: 978-1-3503-2674-3
eBook: 978-1-3503-2673-6

Typeset by Deanta Global Publishing Services, Chennai, India

For product safety related questions contact productsafety@bloomsbury.com.

To find out more about our authors and books visit www.bloomsbury.com and
sign up for our newsletters.

Contents

List of illustrations	viii
Preface: The 'Great Game' in Central Europe	x
Acknowledgements	xii

1 A geopolitical report on Central Europe ... 1
   1.1. 'Through a glass darkly': The definition of Central Europe ... 2
   1.2. From hope to disillusionment: The period from 1989 until 2008 ... 3
   1.3. Rising from the ashes: The geopolitical consequences of China's rise (2008–20) ... 6
   1.4. Fault lines in Europe: Different interpretations of China's rise ... 10
   1.5. Diversification in the spotlight ... 15
      1.5.1. Trading with the Chinese dragon? ... 15
      1.5.2. China buying up Central Europe? ... 18
      1.5.3. Yuan replacing dollar in Central Europe? ... 19
   1.6. Straddling the divide? The current geopolitical environment of Central Europe ... 21

2 From reluctant to assertive player? US foreign policy in Central Europe policy ... 25
   2.1. The tragic failure: Downgrading Europe ... 26
      2.1.1. The alliance of the giant and the dwarf? An asymmetry of power ... 26
      2.1.2. Mission impossible? Strategic autonomy of the EU ... 27
      2.1.3. Why the pivot to Asia? ... 29
      2.1.4. From honeymoon to divorce? Milestones of American–European relations ... 30
      2.1.5. The grand American strategy and Europe's role in it ... 34
   2.2. The confrontation of giants: Consequences for CE region ... 37
      2.2.1. China going global? ... 37
      2.2.2. Locked in a triangle? China, the CEE region and the United States ... 40

	2.3.	US Confrontation with Russia: Consequences for CE region	42
		2.3.1. Rosy beginnings and overt hostilities: From the 1990s to the annexation of Crimea	42
		2.3.2. Locked in a triangle? Russia, the CEE region and the United States	46
3	The newcomer in the region: China		49
	3.1.	From 'open door policies' to 'dual circulation'	54
	3.2.	China policy in the EU and its nuances	57
	3.3.	China policy in Central Europe	61
		3.3.1. The Belt and Road Initiative and the 16 + 1 cooperation	61
		3.3.2. The yuan's digitalization	67
	3.4.	Disillusionment over China	69
4	Russia: Behind the new Iron Curtain?		75
	4.1.	From the collapse to a more assertive foreign policy: Russia's foreign policy	75
	4.2.	Russia and China standing together, and its consequence for Central Europe	82
	4.3.	Central Europe in the world of emerging economic blocs	87
		4.3.1. Trading blocks	88
		4.3.2. Technological sovereignty	90
		4.3.3. Parallel financial infrastructures	91
		4.3.4. Parallel brands, and supply chains	93
5	Germany and its European Union: Central European aspects		99
	5.1.	EU on collision course with Central Europe?	99
		5.1.1. The controversial idea of an 'ever closer Union'	99
		5.1.2. Cultural, social gap between the West and East?	102
	5.2.	Germany in Central Europe: Drive to the East?	109
		5.2.1. Germany in Central Europe: The rise of an economic hinterland	113
		5.2.2. Resilience from Central Europe	114
	5.3.	Poland's foreign policy and German reactions	116
	5.4.	Hungary's foreign policy in the EU and German reactions	119
		5.4.1. The case of Hong Kong	119
		5.4.2. The case of EU's Africa–Pacific Trade and Development Deal	120

	5.4.3. The case of the Israel-Palestine ceasefire	121
	5.4.4. The case of Belarus	122
5.5.	Summary	123

6 The region as a pray of superpowers? 125
    6.1. The ideal EU for Central Europe 126
    6.2. Central Europe's catch-22? Catching up with the West 129
        6.2.1. *Central Europe depending on others: The 'dependent model'* 131
        6.2.2. Overreliance on external sources 132
        6.2.3. Overreliance on foreign companies 133
        6.2.4. Weak overall and corporate research and development performance 136
        6.2.5. Weak labour bargaining power 137
        6.2.6. Development traps expressed in figures: The Hungarian example 137
    6.3. Different foreign policy strategies in Central Europe 139
        6.3.1. Foreign policies based on values? The case of Estonia ... 139
        6.3.2. Foreign policies based on interests? The case of Hungary ... 143

7 Summary: Central Europe in the 'Heartland'? 145
    7.1. A geopolitical report on Central Europe 146
    7.2. From reluctant to assertive player? US foreign policy in Central Europe policy 149
    7.3. The newcomer in the region: China 152
    7.4. Russia: Behind the new Iron Curtain? 157
    7.5. Germany and its European Union: Central European aspects ... 161
    7.6. The region as a pray of superpowers? 166

Bibliography 171
Index 190

Illustrations

Graph

2.1	US Share in World GDP (PPP, %)	35

Tables

1.1	Ownership of 5G Patent Families in October 2021 (%)	8
1.2	Merchandise Trade with China in 1999 and 2019 (%)	8
1.3	Chinese FDI as % of GDP, Ranking Based on the Relative Size of Chinese FDI to GDP	15
1.4	Who Is More Important in Export and Import? China's and the United States' Shares in 2019	16
1.5	Foreign Direct Investment Stock without Special Vehicle Entities (2020)	17
2.1	NATO Defence Expenditure (Estimated of NATO Countries and Share of GDP in 2021)	27
3.1	Chinese Direct Investment in the EU and the United Kingdom 2000–21 (billion euros)	71
3.2	Chinese FDI in the EU and the United Kingdom between 2000 and 2021 (as of GDP, %)	73
4.1	Export in terms of GDP (%, 2020)	89
4.2	Factors of Russia–CEE region relations	96
4.3	Relations of pro and con arguments in Russia relations	96
5.1	Number of Infringement Cases in the European Union	107
5.2	Germany's Export and Import by Country and Region (2019, %)	114
6.1	GDP Per Capita (EU = 100%, in Purchasing Power Parity)	129
6.2	GDP Per Hour Worked (EU28 = 100%)	130
6.3	Current Account Balance as of GDP in Central Europe (%)	132
6.4	Foreign Firms in Hungary (%)	134

6.5 Share of Value-added in Foreign-controlled Enterprises in EU (%)   134
6.6 The Share of Foreign Companies in Revenues (Per Cent, 2018)   135
6.7 Research and Development Expenditures (%, in Terms of GDP)   136
6.8 Trade Union Density   137

Preface

The 'Great Game' in Central Europe

Until the political and economic transition of the early 1990s, the history of Central Europe seemed to be a collection of unfulfilled dreams. Neither the revolutions of 1848 nor the uprisings (in Poland, Hungary and Czechoslovakia) against Soviet rule were successful, but with the collapse of the communist bloc in Europe, this curse of history seemed to reverse itself, opening the gates to democratization, greater sovereignty and a market economy. While the region's reintegration into the West brought partial successes, it also revealed two catch-22 situations facing these countries. The first pitfall was the asymmetrical dependence on the West for capital, technology and trade. While this dependence led to success in the early stages of catching up with the West, this asymmetry has hindered the continuation of this process in the later stages of development.

The other 'catch' was the contradiction between the need for more integration and more sovereignty, which led to dissatisfaction with the EU in the region and an opening to East Asia. The latter strategic move occurred for two reasons. While economic integration and embeddedness in European supply chains made the countries successful, this very integration and embeddedness made them more vulnerable to economic shocks and increasingly dependent on Western capital and technology. The 2008–9 crisis was a rude awakening for these countries. This disillusionment coincided with the economic rise of China and the more assertive posture of Russian foreign policy. The region turned to the East, in some cases in the form of official strategies (such as in Poland, Slovakia and Hungary).

Around 2018 and 2019, pressure on Central Europe to change its policy of opening up to the East came from the European Commission and the United States, which have considerable weight in the region. In response, some countries altered the course of their foreign policy, while others did not. At the same time, the European Union also slowly changed its policy towards China, toughening its tone to the point that China went from being a strategic partner to an all-out competitor in the eyes of the EU. The question arises how the EU's strategic autonomy in foreign policy can be maintained when it does not have its own voice or develop its own strategies on various issues of world politics. The unified strategy towards China is complicated by the EU's diversity, and similar differences can be seen in the Central European region as well.

Contrary to mainstream thinking, the differences between countries regarding China do not originate in different approaches to democracy, not to mention the rise of so-called 'illiberal regimes'. The difference in attitudes towards China originates in an economic model, the 'dependent model', which these countries would like to get rid of. This process is not a win-win situation for Western multinational companies in Central Europe, because it means more competition and a more centralized state with a more efficient bureaucracy that cracks down on the extra profits of these companies and puts national economic interests front and centre, whereas before 2008–9 most Central European governments served the interests of these companies. It is no surprise that Western European political and economic elites do not welcome these changes, as they run counter to their interests.

Obviously, the war in Ukraine is a turning point in many ways because the war has brought the United States back to Europe. So we have all the players in Central Europe – Germany, China, Russia and the United States – at the table and these players seem to be playing the 'Great Game', which seems to be bringing the region to the brink of chaos.

This book illustrates the 'Great Game' of the great powers in Central Europe, from which the countries of the region will most likely not emerge as winners. They can only lose in this process if they do not resolutely defend their own national interests.

Acknowledgements

The completion of this book would not have been possible without the professional help and support of my colleague Dean Karalekas, who happens to be my very best friend.

1

A geopolitical report on Central Europe

The geopolitical landscape of Central Europe has changed tremendously in the last two decades. While the period before the Global Financial Crisis was about restoring relations with the Western world (see the 'big bang' enlargement of the EU in 2004, or the expansions of NATO starting in the late 1990s), the post-crisis period was more about rethinking the goals of foreign policy and economic development strategy in these countries. The realization that reintegration, in addition to its economic benefits, also meant a growing asymmetric dependence on the West for technology and capital, and the EU's economic problems (see the Eurozone crisis after 2010) led to a reorientation towards Asia. This reorientation fortunately coincided with the economic and political rise of Eurasian countries, more specifically China, which launched the Belt and Road Initiative and the 16+1 cooperation scheme. For about a decade, the revision of foreign policy strategy was driven by increased cooperation between Central Europe and China within the 16+1 format and the Belt and Road Initiative. However, the results were moderate, slow and unevenly distributed regionally, and the perception of the results was influenced by different cultural backgrounds, as well as the time frame in which we interpret them.

At the same time, Central European countries soon had to realize that cooperation with China also had geopolitical implications. The growing cooperation between China and Central Europe was increasingly viewed with suspicion by the United States, France and Germany, leading some of them to relent and change course again in their foreign policies. The chapter not only reports on these foreign policy changes but also defines the concept of Central Europe as used in this book.

1.1. 'Through a glass darkly': The definition of Central Europe

Concepts such as Central Europe, Eastern Europe and Central and Eastern Europe are extremely vague, and they are not so much geographically as politically motivated. The first concept of 'Mittel Europa' (Central Europe) to reach a wider audience was promulgated by Friedrich Naumann, but the first theorization of the concept was attempted by Karl Ludwig von Bruck and Lorenz von Stein. Naumann published the concept in his book *Mittel Europe*, in which he subjected the region to German rule and argued that this German-dominated region would achieve harmony. On pages 286 and 287 he writes: 'The Nibelungen faith of the Emperor Wilhelm II shall be raised to the formation of a state. Ancient disputes about development, for us already settled, must begin afresh in this connection. But does not this great war say to us all that we cannot remain where we are? We shall emerge from it other than what we were when we entered upon it. We shall emerge from the war as Mid-Europeans (Naumann, 1917: 286–7).' The concept argued along the lines of federalism but had (German) nationalism in mind, although this did not distinguish it from other concepts of the time. Several analysts interpret it as a clear manifestation of the interests of German capitalists, who saw Central Europe as the region of their potential expansion (see Irinyi (1973) or Galántai (1974)). The irony of this interpretation is that the Central European region was modernized by German companies after 1990, and the dominance of German capital is still a prevalent feature of this region.

In this book, however, we use the term 'Central Europe' in a very different way for several reasons:

- First, the term 'Central Europe' does not mean that we are advocating a federalist solution for the region or the entire European region, because nation states are still the building blocks of the EU.
- Second, the use of the term does not mean that we forget the existing differences between the Central European countries, although they form more or less a relatively homogeneous region.
- Third, we narrow down the original concept to the countries that are both EU members and former socialist countries.
- Other relevant aspects are the level of economic development of the country and its geographical location.

The logic behind this selection of criteria is to find a group of countries that is relatively homogeneous in terms of economic development, geographic location, historical experience and recent period of catching up with the West. Therefore, the concept of Central Europe proposed in this book includes the Baltic countries (Estonia, Latvia and Lithuania), the Visegrad countries (Poland, Czechia, Slovakia and Hungary) and Croatia and Slovenia, which were part of the former Yugoslavia, but at the same time, historically, were always more part of Central Europe. Our story does not begin after 1989, but it makes sense to start there, since the political and economic conditions for the entire region were redefined with the so-called transformation in the early 1990s.

1.2. From hope to disillusionment: The period from 1989 until 2008

The collapse of the Soviet bloc was followed by enthusiasm in the region and hope that the Cold War would never return. Today, the division of the world into trading blocs and/or independent technological ecosystems (see the term 'technological sovereignty')[1] seems to be a real threat. Experts vigorously debate the possibilities of a new Cold War, and even its modalities are discussed. Brands and Gaddis summarize this situation this way: 'It's no longer debatable that the United States and China, tacit allies during the last half of the last Cold War, are entering their own new cold war: Chinese President Xi Jinping has declared it, and a rare bipartisan consensus in the United States has accepted the challenge' (Brands & Gaddis, 2021: 10). The other side of the story is the ongoing struggle between the United States and Russia. The difference between China and Russia as opponents of American

---

[1] Torreblanca summarizes the reasons why the issue of technological sovereignty has attracted so much attention recently: 'Great powers have realised that access to new technologies can be critical to their sovereignty, prompting them to engage in a fierce competition to develop their technological capabilities. After massively embracing globalisation due to its positive economic impact, these powers now regard the interdependence associated with it as a dangerous vulnerability that they need to constrain and, eventually, reduce' (Torreblanca, 2021). We must add that peaceful cooperation would reduce fears related to the loss of sovereignty associated with technology, but the increasing geopolitical competition between superpowers continues to fuel the debate.

hegemony is significant because China has been advancing economically and technologically for decades while Russia was not.²

The question is how we got to a system where China and Russia are challenging the world order created after 1989 and dominated by the United States since then, from Fukuyama's 'the end of history' approach, which predicted the end of ideological struggle and competition between political and economic systems.

The optimistic but naïve approach was based on the belief that free market neoliberal capitalism and the Western version of democracy were the only path to long-term economic prosperity and peace. Looking at the failure of the Soviet bloc, this conclusion seemed obvious to contemporary observers. Today, the rise of China, with the implementation of Chinese economic reforms, relative economic prosperity, and the survival of authoritarian regimes challenges the zeitgeist of the 1990s for two reasons:

- *The question of the economic model.* We do not yet know whether China's economic and technological rise is an inexorable trend or whether further development will also require additional social and political reforms in China that will bring it close to the West, as many argue,³ but we do know that the very existence of these regimes and their success call into question the values and solutions that the West has long believed to be the only correct ones. And there may be another path to success. This belief was reflected in the so-called Washington Consensus, which laid out the path for how developing and emerging countries should build their economic institutions if they were to succeed. Since following this advice proved counterproductive for these countries – especially the Central European countries – the concept was challenged. On the other hand,

---

[2] Nevertheless, Russia was able to challenge US dominance militarily because it got away with annexing Crimea. Russian arguments emphasize that the wave of NATO expansion since the 1990s is a breach of earlier promises not to expand NATO. Whether these promises were made or not does not matter; what was more important was that Russia really felt encircled by NATO allies and threatened in this way. And that was basically the main reason for the invasion of Ukraine in early 2022.

[3] Rosen focuses on the lack of economic reform in modern China. He argues that even under Xi, China has tried to implement these reforms but has basically failed (Rosen, 2021: 20). Others emphasize that China's rise has a certain pace, and that the country's rise is slowly coming to a halt. The argument is that there are several reasons for the well-predicted relapse: resource scarcity, demographic collapse, private enterprises suffering from lack of capital and declining productivity (Beckley & Brands, 2021).

there is no Beijing Consensus[4] in the sense of a strict or clear proposal for an economic model. The idea of intervening more directly and forcefully in the economy resonated with many Central European policymakers because it was the economic chaos of the Global Financial Crisis (2008–9) and then the recession triggered by the global pandemic in 2020 that provided incentives to intervene more directly in the economy than neoliberal economic doctrine would ever suggest. The other reason Beijing's model may have appealed to Central European countries is Beijing's multilateralist approach as opposed to Washington's increasingly unilateralist stance.

- *Shifting economic power.* The shift of economic power to the East also opens up new opportunities for Central European countries. Whereas in 1980 the G-7 countries accounted for more than half of global GDP (measured in purchasing power parity [PPP]), today the ratio is less than one-third, while the share of emerging and developing Asia[5] grew from 8 per cent in 1980 to more than one-third of global GDP in 2020. China is another excellent example, as its share of global GDP (PPP) was 2.3 per cent in 1980 and rose to 17 per cent by 2020. India has also experienced similar, though somewhat less rapid, growth over the same period. Its share of global GDP was 2.8 per cent in 1980 and will be 6.8 per cent by 2020.[6] The IMF predicts that the rise of these countries is not over yet; emerging and developing economies will continue their rapid growth and reach about 36 per cent.

While we can observe these shifts in political and economic power, we can also see how foreign policy and economic development strategy in the Central European region are also changing, albeit very slowly. Eastern bloc countries,

---

[4] The term 'Beijing Consensus' a clear allusion to the Washington Consensus was invented by Joshua Ramo, who emphasized three crucial elements of Chinese success: the value of innovation, the rejection of the GDP-per-capita approach and self-determination (Ramo, 2004: 11–12). Although the term became popular for a short time, it failed to reflect many other features of Chinese economic development and to compare the Chinese experience with the example of Japan, South Korea, Taiwan and Singapore.

[5] Based on the classification of IMF: Bangladesh, Bhutan, Brunei Darussalam, Cambodia, China, Fiji, India, Indonesia, Kiribati, Lao P.D.R., Malaysia, Maldives, Marshall Islands, Micronesia, Mongolia, Myanmar, Nauru, Nepal, Palau, Papua New Guinea, Philippines, Samoa, Solomon Islands, Sri Lanka, Thailand, Timor-Leste, Tonga, Tuvalu, Vanuatu and Vietnam.

[6] The data are from the database of IMF World Economic Outlook, October 2020.

especially those that joined NATO in the 1990s[7] and the European Union in the 2000s,[8] believed that membership in these organizations was a (foreign policy) goal that would allow them to achieve greater political sovereignty and economic prosperity. However, as institutional integration was completed in Central Europe, it became clear that these elements were necessary but not sufficient to effect a catching-up with the West.

1.3. Rising from the ashes: The geopolitical consequences of China's rise (2008–20)

The rise of China and the debate surrounding it is not new. Since the late 1990s, economists have debated the question of how long China's catch-up process can continue, or whether it will eventually stall before China reaches the living standards of advanced economies. Opinions range from the overly optimistic to those who have been predicting the imminent collapse of the Chinese state and economy for many years. Kristóf argued in 1993 that '(t)he rise of China, if it continues, may be the most important trend in the world for the next century' (Kristóf, 1993). Gordon G. Chang, on the other hand, predicted several times the imminent collapse of China's economic and political system (Chang, 2001), updating the year of the expected collapse by several years. Indeed, despite conflicting views of China's future, Bernstein and Munro could accurately see in 1997 that China was the great power rivalling the United States in the Pacific (Bernstein & Munro, 1997). From a Central European perspective, these two issues – the sustainability of China's rise and the competition between the two powers – seemed less important as long as China offered economic opportunities for these countries. However, before assessing the record of economic cooperation with China, let us briefly review some main points of China's rise, focusing on economic indicators, because China is not and will not be a major military and geopolitical power in Central Europe.

---

[7] Poland, Hungary and Czechia became members of NATO in 1999, while the Baltic countries (Estonia, Latvia, Lithuania), Slovakia, Slovenia, Bulgaria and Romania joined the organization in 2004.
[8] The Baltic countries, the Visegrad countries (Poland, Czechia, Slovakia, Hungary) and Slovenia joined the EU in 2007, while Romania and Bulgaria joined in 2007. The last country from this region to join was Croatia (2013).

- *Gross Domestic Product.* In 1980, China's share of world GDP (measured in PPP) was 2.3 per cent, while the same figure was 17 per cent in 2021, and the International Monetary Fund predicts it will exceed 20 per cent in 2026.
- *Trade.* More than 80 per cent of countries traded more with the United States than with China in 2002, while the situation was completely reversed in 2020, when 70 per cent of countries traded more with China than with the United States, with the exception of the Baltic countries where the United States is still more important in trade than China (National Bank of Canada, 2021).
- *Foreign Direct Investment (FDI).* In 2020, China was the world's largest foreign investor, with invested FDI totalling US$154 billion, bringing the stock of FDI in China to US$2.5 trillion (Global Times, 2021).
- Technology.
  - Patents. According to the World Intellectual Property Organization (WIPO), China led the world in patent filing with 2.5 million applications. China's performance was two and a half times better than that of the United States. We had the same situation with trademarks, as China registered 9.3 million trademark applications, compared to 900,000 in the United States (World Intellectual Property Organization, 2021).
  - *5G technology.* We should add that the improvement in technology indicators can only be partly explained by the sheer size of the market indicators such as the number of mobile users, science and engineering graduates and number of publications. But there is another area where Chinese companies have the upper hand in terms of market share and number of patents: that is in 5G. According to the market and consumer data firm Statista, as of October 2021, China had a 41.3 per cent share of patent families, while Korea was second with 19.8 per cent, and the United States was third on the list (see Table 1.1!).
  - *Education.* China overtook the United States in the production of science, technology, engineering and mathematics (STEM) PhDs. China graduated 39,830 students in 2019, while the number of STEM PhDs in the United States was 30,609. According to the Center for Security and Emerging Technology (CSET), this number will increase to nearly

Table 1.1 Ownership of 5G Patent Families in October 2021 (%)

China	41.3
Korea	19.8
United States	15.3
Japan	8.9
Finland	8.3
Sweden	4.7

Source: Statista database

Table 1.2 Merchandise Trade with China in 1999 and 2019 (%)

	Export share to China (%)		Import share from China (%)		Difference between export and import share	
Year	1999	2019	1999	2019	1999	2019
Hungary	0.28	1.36	2.18	6.10	−0.90	−4.74
Czechia	0.21	1.24	1.96	15.8	−1.75	−14.56
Poland	0.49	1.00	2.66	12.3	−2.17	−11.30
Slovakia	0.06	2.10	1.28	6.40	−1.22	−4.30
Estonia	0.11	1.13	1.17	8.10	−1.06	−6.97
Latvia	0.01	1.24	0.51	3.21	−0.50	−1.97
Slovenia	0.15	0.79	1.34	6.12	−1.19	−5.33

Source: World Bank WITS database

60,000 in the case of China, while it is expected to be around 35,000 in the United States (Zwetsloot et al., 2021: 5). Based on future scenarios, Zwetsloot et al. conclude: 'Given the scale of Chinese investment in higher education and the technological competition between the United States and China, with much at stake, the gap in STEM doctoral production could undermine the long-term economic and national security of the United States' Zwetsloot et al., 2021: 10). What is a threat to the United States is a potential opportunity for Central Europe.

Another important trend that emerges from Table 1.2 is the growing dominance of the East Asian region, from which 72 per cent of patent families originate. The table vividly shows the shift of global economic growth and technological development to Asia. While there are voices that disagree with this trend, those who focus on long-term trends predict the rise of the East Asian region, and that is now the mainstream. At the same time, we do not know the future. Uncertainty is always there, and this rise cannot be taken for granted. Loong articulated this uncertainty in August 2020: 'Asia has prospered because Pax Americana, which has held since the end of World War II, provided a favorable strategic context. But now, the troubled US.-Chinese relationship raises profound questions about Asia's future and the shape of the emerging international order' (Loong, 2020: 52).

Despite the uncertainty about Asian economic growth, a crucial question for Central European countries is from which region exactly within the Eurasian continent the growth impetus might come, that is, which economies will exceed the world and regional averages. We see that the G-7 countries, an informal grouping of advanced countries (Canada, France, Germany, Italy, Japan, the United Kingdom, the United States and the European Union) accounted for more than half of world GDP in 1980, measured in purchasing power parity (IMF data). Their share of global GDP has declined significantly in recent decades and now stands at just over one-third. On the other hand, the Asian emerging and developing countries have caught up with the G-7 countries.

The question of whether this growth of Asian emerging and developing countries will catch up with the West is irrelevant to the Central European countries. Business opportunities emerge not only due to growing income levels in the catching-up Asian countries, but they are mainly created by the size of these economies, and the potential trade and investment matter for Central European countries. Asian flagship companies are able to invest, create jobs and increase technology transfer. In the latter, Chinese companies can be significant contributors.

If classifying Eurasian nations based on the economic interests of Central European states, we can distinguish three groups of countries:

- *In the first circle of countries,* we see Asian countries that are not only growing faster than the world average, but also have economic growth rates far above the regional average. In addition to China, India has also experienced similar, if somewhat less rapid, growth in recent decades. According to the IMF, the country's share of world GDP (PPP) will be around 8 per cent. Higher GDP growth rates than the world and regional averages are seen in Malaysia and Vietnam, but China's role will also remain significant. The role of India and China may also be important in technology transfer.
- The *second group* of Asian countries consists of those that are not growing as fast, but whose technology-intensive investments are nevertheless

important for Central European countries. Japanese and Korean direct investments have been crucial for Hungary's modernization, but they play a similar role in other Central European countries as well. The change in the wind can be seen in the investment data. Hungary's FDI stock is still dominated by Germany, but in 2019 (HIPA, 2020, 11 February) and 2021, South Korea (HIPA, 2021, 31 December), and in 2020, China, were the largest foreign investors in Hungary (HIPA, 2021, 25 January).

- We can put countries (Russia, Kazakhstan) *in the third circle,* whose share in the world GDP has shrunk in recent decades, and according to the IMF this trend will continue, but these countries supply the Central European region with energy and raw materials. This was the point where we can see that the perception of Russia was different in these countries, which led to different foreign policy strategies until the invasion of Ukraine in 2022. Poland is a good example, as the country, due to its historical experience and geographical location, has always been more concerned about Russia's intentions and ambitions. Consequently, the country has been more willing to consider US arguments regarding Russia. The United States is able to provide security guarantees to Poland, probably for the same reason that the country is more willing to heed US advice and follow through on issues related to China. When Russia invaded Ukraine, Hungary, as a member of NATO and the EU, followed with sanctions, as it did after the annexation of Crimea.

Of course, this classification system is not completely clear: China belongs simultaneously to the first and to the third circle of Eurasian countries, and India could belong to the third circle given time. Still, these categories are useful in that they show us the evolution of political and economic relations with these countries, and even the changing nature of these relations.

1.4. Fault lines in Europe: Different interpretations of China's rise

Despite the potential benefits of economic cooperation with China, Russia and other Eurasian countries, most Central European countries have made a U-turn in their foreign policies in recent years. As geopolitical tensions between the

United States and China or Russia have increased since 2016, these countries are siding with the United States and arguing against Russia and/or China, even though their economic interests would dictate that they do the opposite. It should be noted that these countries have similar motivations for Eurasian cooperation, but their different geopolitical situations and economic development have led to different outcomes in their foreign policies. With the exception of Hungary, the Central European countries are adopting a more unfriendly tone than they used to. The cooperation with Russia was always more about securing energy and raw materials, and not the diversification of trade and investment relations. We will revisit this topic in the chapter 'Russia: Behind the new iron curtain?' Now, we focus solely on the question of how Central European efforts of diversification evolved in the context of China relations.

The break with the previous policy of US engagement with China came with the administration of US president Donald Trump, which first launched a so-called trade war and later added new layers to the competition between the two powers. The policy of engagement was replaced by a comprehensive policy of containment, reminiscent of the 'Zeitgeist' of the Cold War. There is a growing literature on the question of whether we can use that term in the current context, and the answer seems to be 'not yet'. But asking the question also gives us an opportunity to see the differences between this contest and the struggle between the Soviet Union and the United States. One clear difference is the lack of an ideological component, although we can find these hints in US communications, but unlike the Soviet Union, China is not spending significant financial resources in other countries to get them to copy the Chinese model. It does spend money in other countries to gain influence, but that is not the same thing. As Mearsheimer puts it, 'But there is an "ism" that China has in spades, one that is likely to exacerbate its rivalry with the United States: nationalism. Normally the world's most powerful political ideology, nationalism had limited influence in the Soviet Union because it was at odds with communism. Chinese nationalism, however, has gained strength since the early 1990s' (Mearsheimer, 2021: 57). The quote also reveals another commonality between China and the Central European region. Nationalism, sovereignty and the nation state have a higher status in both regions than in Western Europe.

The similarity between the struggle in the 1950s and 1960s and the geopolitical contest of today is that the two superpowers are looking for allies.

This is the reason why fault lines have emerged in Central Europe, and several countries have turned away from Beijing while others have pursued friendly China policies. Another reason is economic cooperation with China, which has been less successful than expected.

Kavalski outlines four reasons for the poor outcome of cooperation with China:

- unfulfilled promises made by China;
- pressure from the United States and the European Union;
- the negative Central European perception of the Hong Kong demonstrations, reminiscent of events before the fall of the Berlin Wall; and
- last but not least, Chinese public opinion is concerned about the costly Belt and Road Initiative and 16+1 cooperation projects. He summarizes this as follows: 'Central and eastern [sic] European countries used to be buoyant about benefiting from China's economic largesse, but now – like the EU itself – many view Beijing as a threat. It's unlikely that a Chinese government that is increasingly preoccupied with its own regime stability will be able to make up, let alone repair, the damage done by the multiple opportunities missed over the past eight years' (Kavalski, 2020).

Kavalski essentially summarizes the push factors that are in play right now. Let us find the pull factors that can explain a different approach to China.

(1) *China's economic development policy is more intertwined with its foreign policy than America's.* This argument is complex, but it helps to understand the nature of the competition between the two powers. US economic development changed after 2008–9, but it is still less interventionist than Chinese development policy. In this case, we refer specifically to the version that directly or indirectly guides Chinese companies in technology investments abroad, that is, where they invest or do not invest. This approach does not ignore profitability, but the final investment decision is tied to a green light from political leaders. This setup of Chinese politics also means that good Chinese business relationships imply good political ties with China, while US foreign policy moves do not directly influence the investment decisions of American companies. Ironically, this is the main reason why Central European countries can enjoy the 'luxury' of having the best of both worlds and being on good terms with China.

(2) *Nationalism and sovereignty are more reflected in the foreign policies of China and Central Europe than in Western Europe.* Nationalism and sovereignty in Central Europe can be traced to historical experiences that underscore the importance of sovereignty, statehood and self-government. It took several decades for the landscape of Central Europe to emerge with the borders we know, while French, British and even German statehood was never questioned. Nationalism and sovereignty are also important for China, but for different reasons. With the emergence of the modern Chinese state, the empire became obsolete, and with the decline of communist ideology, nationalism is more important than ever in holding China together. It is clear that Chinese and Central European nationalisms have different roots and goals. Westad points out the threats that Chinese nationalism embodies. He says,

> Making this nationalism even more sinister is the particular view of history endorsed by the Chinese leadership, which sees the history of China from the mid-nineteenth century to the Communists' coming to power in 1949 as an endless series of humiliations at the hands of foreign powers. . . . Another troubling aspect of nationalism in China today is that the country is a *de facto* empire that tries to behave as if it were a nation-state. (Westad, 2019: 88)

There are clear differences between China and Central Europe in terms of perceptions of sovereignty and the nation state, but Western Europe, which makes the Western European approach indisputable, highlights the similarities between Central Europe and China. Hungary and Poland's debates with the European Commission revolve around the rule of law, migration, LGBTQ rights, Europe's energy supply and relations with China and Russia. These seemingly random topics can easily be linked to the question of how the countries see the future of Europe. The nation state and national identity seem to be much more important for Central European countries than for Western and Northern European countries. Understandably, they have a very different historical heritage and economic and social development. The concept of a 'United States of Europe' and 'ever closer union' is hardly acceptable for these countries, while the concept of a 'Europe of nations' is easily accepted. The problem is that the two parts of Europe seem to be at different stages of development, and these conflicts will only continue in the long run. The Hungarian prime minister has summed up this contradiction:

'Instead of a Europe of nations, they in Brussels build a European super state to which they don't have any mandate for' (Orban, 2021, 19 June, cited by Portfolio).

The 'Europe of nations' concept is the exact opposite of the European super state, because in the latter concept, the process weakens the sovereignty of nation states, dooming them to disappear, or at least to weaken to a point where there is no turnaround possible in the integration process. The 'Europe of nations' concept, on the other hand, emphasizes that only strong nations can make Europe strong again. This is the point we need to make clear: that this concept of 'Europe of nations' is different from that of the nineteenth century, which included nationalism and eventually led to world war in Europe. Andrén has made this distinction explicit:

> a Europe of nations must be a Europe without nationalism. In this, this group of intellectuals represent the direction for the mainstream of Europeanist thinking in the postwar era. That is, the idea that a unification must build on the nations and nation states rather than erase them; that the nations will not cease to exist within a shared community; that nationhood and national culture can be and should be separated from nationalism. (Andrén, 2020)

Central European countries share a distaste for the idea of a 'United States of Europe'; however, they differ in the extent to which they are willing to protect their sovereignty. The reason for this difference in approach lies in the small details. Poland, Slovakia and the Czech Republic have more strained relations with Russia, while Hungary places more emphasis on economic relations with Russia, although in this case its historical past is not free of problems that were never fully resolved.

In summary, Central Europe's diversification efforts are often portrayed in Western Europe and the United States as being contrary to the West's interests, so we foresee long-term tensions in this regard. The irony of the situation is that Central European countries are interested in strengthening Europe, not weakening it, but this can only be achieved if the sovereignty of Central European countries is also strengthened. In the next chapter, we will take a look at how the diversification of trade, investment relations and other economic relations took place and whether it can be seen as a success story or not (Table 1.3).

Table 1.3 Chinese FDI as % of GDP, Ranking Based on the Relative Size of Chinese FDI to GDP

	Chinese FDI stock between 2005 and 2020 (billion US$)	GDP (billion US$, 2019)	Chinese FDI as % of GDP (%)
Slovenia	2.18	54	4.04
Hungary	5.88	161	3.65
Czechia	0.96	246	0.39
Poland	2.28	592	0.39
Latvia	0.10	34	0.29

Source: Own calculation based on World Bank data and the AEI's China Global Investment Tracker (American Enterprise Institute, 2020)

1.5. Diversification in the spotlight

As far as the Eurasian region is concerned, diversification in trade and investment comes mainly from China, so the next part focuses on trends in this relationship. At the same time, we must emphasize that both South Korea and Japan, as well as the Taiwanese economy, can be major sources of diversification for Central European countries, especially when it comes to direct investment and technology-intensive investment in this region.

1.5.1. Trading with the Chinese dragon?

If there is one relationship where there is room for trade diversification, it is trade with China. We should remember that 80 per cent of countries traded more with the United States than with China in 2002, but that pattern has changed, with 70 per cent of countries now trading more with China than with the United States. Of the sixteen countries, only the Baltic countries were in the group of countries that traded more with the United States than with China in 2018 (National Bank of Canada, 2021). (Even Latvia and Lithuania traded more with China than with the United States in 2019, see Table 1.4, though these ratios may change slightly due to growing tensions between China and Lithuania.)[9]

---

[9] Lithuania withdrew from 17+1 cooperation in 2021, then allowed Taiwan to open an office called the 'Taiwanese Representative Office'. These offices in Europe are normally named 'Taipei Representative Office' to comply with each country's one-China policy. This move angered Beijing, which downgraded diplomatic relations and, according to Lithuania, prevented the import of goods to China, although China denies this move. To show its solidarity, the EU initiated a case against China at the World Trade Organization (European Commission, 27 January 2022).

Table 1.4 Who Is More Important in Export and Import? China's and the United States' Shares in 2019

	Export share to China and the United States (%)		More important export partner	Import share from China and the United States (%)		More important import partner	More important overall trade partner
	United States	China		United States	China		
Hungary	2.80	1.36	US	2.13	6.10	China	China
Czechia	2.49	1.24	US	2.62	15.8	China	China
Poland	2.91	1.07	US	3.21	12.33	China	China
Slovakia	3.14	2.11	US	1.18	6.36	China	China
Estonia	6.84	1.13	US	1.94	8.10	China	China
Latvia	1.58	1.24	US	0.95	3.21	China	China
Slovenia	1.76	0.79	US	2.14	6.12	China	China

Source: World Bank WITS database

Table 1.5 Foreign Direct Investment Stock without Special Vehicle Entities (2020)

	United States	China and Hong Kong	More important partner
Poland	4,240 million US$	286+507 million US$	United States
Czechia	7,942 million US$	705+15.2 million US$	United States
Hungary	1,591 million Euro	375+1,173 million euro	United States
Estonia	403 million euro	46+66 million euro	United States
Slovenia	66 million euro	2+126 million euro	China

Source: Databases of the respective central banks

Trade with China has increased in the region over the past two decades. However, a look at trade data shows that the relationship with China is far from the most important, and at the same time trade with China is unbalanced. In 2019, Poland had a trade deficit with China of US$ 2.7 billion, while the country as a whole enjoyed a trade surplus of US$ 5.2 billion. The Czech Republic has the worst trade balance with China. In Table 1.5, we see China's share of exports and imports in 1999 and 2019 (columns 2 and 3) and the difference between China's exports and imports in each country's trade in 1999 and 2019 (column 4).

In the latter case, the negative numbers represent a larger import share with China than an export share. In other words, there is no country in the region that would have a surplus in trade with China, and there is no country in the region where the deficit would not have increased between 1999 and 2019. Yet, there are big differences between these countries, as we see double-digit deficits in Poland and the Czech Republic, and a very small trade deficit in the case of Latvia.

This comparison shows us why Poland is more cautious in deepening trade with China. At the same time, we must add that these data might be somewhat misleading, as they do not indicate how many of the Chinese goods are re-exported to other EU member states.

Since we have to analyse the data amid increasing political tensions between the United States and China, it is convenient to ask which superpower is more important for these countries in terms of trade and investment, and even the question of the reserve currency can be raised.

A look at the table shows that the United States is still more important than China as an export destination for these countries. There is no country where China would be a more important export destination than the United States. On the other hand, China is the most important import partner for all Central European countries. We also have to pay attention to the ratios. If we add the export and import shares, it is clear that China is a bigger trading partner than the United States. Estonia is almost the only exception in the group, but even in this case China is a more important trading partner than the United States.

1.5.2. China buying up Central Europe?

While the *New York Post* and *Forbes* have run headlines such as 'China seeks influence in Europe, one deal at a time' (Barboza, Santora & Stevenson, 2018, 12 August) or 'China's Bid to Buy Eastern Europe on the Cheap: The "16+1" Group' (Babones, 2017, 27 November), the reality is far from this depiction. Hutt and Turcsányi sum it up this way: 'Rather than being a "gateway" for Chinese investment into Europe, as Czech President Milos Zeman boasted of his country, Beijing more often bypassed the region altogether – taking its investments straight into wealthier Western Europe' (Hutt & Turcsányi, 2020, 27 May).

When it comes to investments, evaluation is difficult because the data is less reliable. The main reason is that, in the case of direct investment, the balance of payments often does not reflect the countries of origin. Very often, other countries are used to channel capital to the destination country in order to minimize taxes. In Central European countries, Germany, Austria and the Netherlands are usually the main investors. In Poland and Czechia, the Netherlands; in Slovenia, Austria; and in Hungary, Germany are the main investors. Sweden is the largest investor in Latvia. The most important point, however, is that neither China nor the United States is an important source of direct investment in this region. If we compare the relative influence of these two superpowers, the United States is still more influential in the region. This situation cannot change, as the US positions are the result of thirty years of long-term investments in the region, while at the same time China seems to be gaining power in this regard.

There are significant differences in the extent to which Central European countries have been able to attract Chinese investment to the region. It would be too simplistic to reduce China policy in these countries to a business decision. However, if we look at the countries at the lower end of the scale, we can see that these countries seem to have changed their attitude towards China recently, while Hungary is developing increasingly friendly relations with China. Because of the Russian threat, the Baltic countries and Poland are bowing to the goals of US foreign policy. Countries that are more dependent on the United States and Chinese economic and security support because of their size or for other economic and geopolitical reasons are more willing to accept attempts at geopolitical influence and take sides in the intensifying contest between the United States and China. While China offers the BRI and 17+1 cooperation to these countries, it does not appear to have a security policy in the region.

1.5.3. Yuan replacing dollar in Central Europe?

Another aspect is the importance of currency. The internationalization of the yuan also depends on the development of relations between China and America. Due to the increasing tensions between the two powers, Central European countries that choose to use the yuan in trade transactions may also face pressure from the American side. In other words: If the Central European countries use the yuan in trade, they must have serious reasons to partially replace the US$ with the Chinese yuan.

Under current conditions, the United States dominates the global financial system. Not only is the US dollar the key currency for central bank reserves, foreign exchange and international trade transactions, but the United States can also impose sanctions on countries that do not comply. The vehicle for sanctions is the Society for Worldwide Interbank Financial Telecommunications (SWIFT), the world's largest clearinghouse for cross-border payments, which is dominated by the United States. One need only look at the case of Russia to see how this works. When sanctions are imposed on a country, it is extremely difficult for that country to trade with the rest of the world.

- According to the latest IMF data, 54.7 per cent of global central bank reserves are held in US$, while the Chinese yuan accounts for 2.7 per cent of reserves (2022Q1).
- The United States dominated currency trading with 88.3 per cent in 2019 (National Bank of Canada, 2021).
- According to Bansal and Singh, US financial institutions are involved in at least one leg of the trading transactions conducted globally (Bansal & Singh, 2021: 3).

In a world where political tensions between the United States and China are increasing, it is a logical step for Beijing to reduce the influence of the United States on China in this area. It is not only the challenge of the US dollar, but also the internationalization of the yuan that are important aspects for China.

We can also raise the question of why China is bound to challenge the existing global financial system.

- First, there is a stark discrepancy between China's role in trade and the role of its currency in global foreign reserves. While China is the world's largest trading nation, the yuan's role as a global reserve is almost non-existent.
- Second, China will always be in an unfavourable position in a trade war as long as it relies on the US dollar for transactions.
- Third, the United States can impose sanctions on countries that do not comply. The SWIFT system can be used to achieve this goal. The list of sanctioned countries is relatively long. More importantly, most sanctions are imposed unilaterally by the United States, meaning it does not need the support of other major economies to have leverage. This is not new, but the use of SWIFT first took clear shape when the United States sought to choke off funds from terrorist organizations after the 2001 attack on the World Trade Center, and since then sanctions have become a regular tool of US foreign policy.
- Fourth, attempts to meet needs in emerging markets serve as pull factors for new solutions.

The case of Russia shows us that replacing the dollar is not an impossible challenge. The share of the Chinese yuan in bilateral trade between China and Russia has increased from 3.1 per cent in 2014 to 17.5 per cent in 2020 (Chinese Ambassador to Russia Hanhui, cited by *Global Times* 2021). Moreover, the yuan accounts for 30.4 per cent of the holdings of the Russian National Wealth Fund and 12.8 per cent of Russia's foreign exchange reserves. What we can see here fits with the internationalization of the yuan. Internationalization efforts can be seen on several levels:

- Offshore renminbi market in Hong Kong foreign exchange market,
- Bilateral swap agreements,
- The use of China's version of SWIFT, the Cross-Border Inter-Bank Payments System (CIPS),
- The issuance of Panda bonds,
- Loans from Chinese development banks.

What still stands in the way of the internationalization of the currency is the non-convertibility of the yuan. Pivak summarized this problem as follows:

'One of the main reasons for the yuan's lack of progress is that it is not freely convertible. Instead, the People's Bank of China sets a daily reference rate for the yuan against the dollar, from which trading via interbank currency markets cannot diverge by more than 2 per cent. There are also restrictions on moving capital out of China, including for foreign companies' (Pivak, 2021). The real effect of the yuan, of course, would be the convertibility of the currency, making the use of the yuan more attractive to Central European countries.[10]

1.6. Straddling the divide? The current geopolitical environment of Central Europe

We have seen in this chapter how the geopolitical position of Central Europe has evolved from the early 1990s to recent times. We have focused on the rise of China and its consequences as a long-term trend in the geopolitical relations of the region, but the war in Ukraine, see Chapter 3 on Russia's role in the region in detail, has rapidly changed these relations. In this summary, we address the challenges posed by the changing world order.

The world order is no longer stable, it is floating, and hence unable to provide adequate and coherent responses to international challenges. The last time it was more or less able to deal with a challenge was during the joint steps taken by major countries to avoid a Great Depression in the wake of the 2008–9 credit crunch. Even the measures taken to deal with global warming and the global pandemic were feeble, and nowhere near as powerful or targeted enough to prevent disaster. It is ironic that while humanity has the necessary knowledge and technology to combat these problems, the will to do so seems

---

[10] According to Tachikava, the next pros and cons influencing the internationalization of the Chinese currency can be found: (1) The value of the currency is not necessarily determined by the market, as the exchange rate is managed by the central bank, it is called a managed floating rate system. (2) At the same time, the digital yuan would enable emerging economies to carry out payment and settlement operations swiftly and conveniently at low cost. (3) A pro element is that the Chinese yuan creates stability. We should bear in mind that, before the collapse of the Lehman Brothers in 2008, China had a vast amount of dollar reserves. It was only afterwards that China sped up its internationalization efforts regarding the yuan. (We should add, if China had continued this policy, it would have faced massive write-downs as the dollar was significantly devalued after the crisis.) (4) If China would consequently mandate the yuan in the China-led economic zone, the use of the Chinese currency would spread easily. The term 'China-led economic zone' here stands for Southeast-Asian, African and other Eurasian countries that participate in the Belt and Road Initiative and the 16+1 cooperation. This region accounts for around one-third of world GDP (Tachikava, 2021).

to be waning. And this problem seems to derive from the simple fact that fewer and fewer countries support the current world order as it was readjusted after the collapse of the Soviet Union in 1991. In the period from 1991 to 2009, the United States maintained order and behaved as a global leader, referring to the system as 'open, rules-based, and liberal', and putting democracy and free markets at the centre of attention.

Strikingly, this self-justification could be sold among experts and scholars of international theory for many years, but world order – this one is no exception – relied on American military, economic and political power. Contrary to those who argue for a change in the word order, we do not find the current way of maintaining power reprehensible; rather, it reflects the true nature of power. Offensive realism asserts that 'states are disposed to competition and conflict because they are self-interested, power maximizing, and fearful of other states. Moreover, it argues that states are obliged to behave this way because doing so favors survival in the international system' (Johnson, Phil & Thayer, 2016: 1). The proponents of classical realism – Hans Morgenthau, E. H. Carr, George Kennan and Henry Kissinger – laid the groundwork for realism, but unlike them, offensive realists use insights from the life sciences to factor in human nature. The desire for power, 'animus dominandi', as Morgenthau put it, is the common characteristic of the major countries that want to shape the world order and adjust it to suit their needs. Chinese, Russian and American foreign policies do not differ from each other in this respect.

The attempt to change the world order can take many forms: (a) territorial disputes; (b) military buildup; (c) challenging free trade, and suchlike. As a result, none of the major powers is truly satisfied with the current world order: The United States has turned away from the UN and the WTO; Russia's invasion of Ukraine and Russian arguments for this justification of war are obviously clear signs of dissatisfaction; China's initiatives (the Belt and Road Initiative, the launch of 16+1 cooperation, the Asian Infrastructure Investment Bank, etc.) are steps designed to return China to the centre of the world, and also to show that Beijing is not satisfied with its current role in the world. The growing importance of multilateral forms of cooperation such as the Quadrilateral Security Dialog, the Shanghai Cooperation and the BRICS also provide clues to the new institutional framework on which the new multilateral world order will be based.

The birth pangs of the new world are in no way mitigated by US president Joe Biden's 'everything doctrine'. As Shapiro summarized it,

So far, the Biden administration has, at least rhetorically, insisted that it can pursue all its objectives without making sacrifices or encountering tensions. Such a foreign policy of broad commitment is no longer sustainable. Indeed, the administration's recent decision to withdraw US forces from Afghanistan implies that it understands the need to limit its commitments. The key question for an emerging Biden doctrine is whether it will succeed in reducing US responsibilities or become tangled in its excessive promises. (Shapiro, 2021, 22 April)

Shapiro wrote these sentences before the Ukraine war, and since then it has become clear that the United States has not succeeded in reducing American responsibilities in the world.

The logical response of the Central European countries to the growing anarchy and uncertainty in the world order is to seek a balance with the great powers, or straddle divides. This is not a regional but a global phenomenon. Balancing of ASEAN countries, and the resistance of many African, Asian and South American countries against joining the economic sanctions regime against Russia, are part of the emerging balance and hedging strategies.[11]

As we shall see later, the reaction of Central European countries is not uniform, with strategies ranging from bandwagoning to balancing. Hungary,[12] however, seems to be the best example of the search for a balance between

---

[11] In foreign policy, the spectrum of countries' behaviour is usually put between bandwagoning and balancing, where balancing means using political, economic and military means to prevent a rising power from becoming a hegemon, and bandwagoning means striking an alliance with the rising power. For the definition of hedging, we rely on Koge, who maintains that it means 'an insurance policy against opportunism' (Lake, 1996: 15). Koge argues that hedging strategies include deeper economic cooperation and preparation for confrontation (Koge, 2018: 2).

[12] During the COVID-19 pandemic, the resilience of the Chinese economy was astonishing by international standards, seeing as China's GDP – the only one among major economies – could rise in 2020. Not only during the previous year, but for the last decades, China's relevance in Hungarian trade and investment has been increasing while the American economic influence has been dwindling for many years, which means that now there is no going back to the Obama era for Hungary's economic relations. This rapid growth of China coincides with Hungary's need for trade and investment diversification. This need became very clear after the Global Financial Crisis (2008–9), when the asymmetric dependence of the Hungarian economy on the West backfired and made Hungarian decision-makers aware of the threat of asymmetric dependence in terms of financing and technology. For this reason, Hungary has been pursuing a hedging strategy between China and the United States, Russia, and the United States, and in some cases the European Commission, since 2010. Due to the Biden administration's priorities, Hungary needed to rethink its US strategy, not only because the Hungarian government rooted for Trump in the election, but more importantly because Biden set his emphasis on so-called shared democratic values upon which Washington intends to stand up against China. Before this debate can be resolved, however, there are two (in our opinion) core questions where Hungary and the United States disagree, and solutions are difficult to find: (1) energy supplies from Russia; and (2) growing economic relations with China.

competing superpowers, while the strategies of the Baltic countries seem to be in line with US foreign policy interests. The position of Central Europe differs from other regions seeking balance in that the region sits on the dividing line between the West and the East, so the countries of the region are more immediately forced to choose between the two camps. The main interest of the countries lies in not being forced to choose, since any choice they would make would limit their development path and deprive them of natural resources, technology, capital and markets. This is of no concern to the competing powers in the region – the United States, China, Russia and even Germany – because for these countries, survival is at stake. As Mearsheimer, a theorist of offensive realism, puts it, 'Great powers must be forever vigilant and never subordinate survival to any other goal, including prosperity' (Mearsheimer, 2001: 371).

2

From reluctant to assertive player?
US foreign policy in Central Europe policy

With the exception of Croatia, the economies of the Central European region are among the high-income countries according to the World Bank's classification, but primarily because of its size, this region is not important to the United States. Moreover, the region is highly integrated into Western European supply chains, with the specialization of these economies mostly being assembly, as European multinationals have located their production capacity in this region, attracted by relatively cheap yet skilled labour. Proximity to major markets was another key factor. Therefore, the region cannot be characterized by technology-intensive manufacturing. There is one factor that has made the region important to US foreign policy in recent years. US relations with Russia are the key factor in whether or not the Central European region is important to the United States. In the 1980s, the democratization of Poland, Hungary and, later, Czechoslovakia and Estonia was an important foreign-policy tool for the United States, and thus contributed to the weakening of the Soviet Union. Later, the power vacuum left by the 1991 dissolution of the Warsaw Pact was filled by NATO. The Baltic countries, the Visegrad countries, and Croatia and Slovenia joined NATO. At the same time, Russia perceived the continued expansion of NATO as a threat, and the relative strengthening of Moscow and stabilization of the political regime in Russia led to a more assertive Russian foreign policy. In the US interpretation, Russia is a threat to the US presence in Europe. An EU independently pursuing its own foreign-policy goals is something American foreign-policy thinkers and planners would like to avoid. In short, keeping Central Europe under American influence is part of the US Grand Strategy.

China's economic rise gave it the motivation to expand globally. China's globalization strategy included the launch of the Belt and Road Initiative (BRI)[1] and the 16+1 cooperation framework. While the BRI extends to all continents and stands for expensive infrastructure construction projects that are intended to improve the routes connecting China to the rest of the world, like the ancient Silk Road, the 16+1 Cooperation Framework[2] focuses on cooperation with the Baltic countries, the Visegrad countries and the countries of the former Yugoslavia, as well as other Balkan countries such as Albania, Romania, Bulgaria and Greece. From a global perspective, we can see that globalization between 1990 and 2008 included many regions and sectors; however, if we wanted to find countries and sectors that were least affected by globalization, then this region would be Central Asia. The two main economic centres of the world, Europe and China, cooperate with each other without having fast connections, the sea route still being the main trade route. The heart of the BRI is to improve connectivity, especially between Europe and China. In a global context, we can interpret China's BRI as a logical step, as China has realized that it is still less powerful than the United States in the Pacific–Oceanic region, and its trade routes can be easily blocked by the United States in the event of a military conflict. (In addition, it should be mentioned that the developmental needs of Western China also require better connectivity with the West.)

2.1. The tragic failure: Downgrading Europe

2.1.1. The alliance of the giant and the dwarf? An asymmetry of power

There is a fixed element in the relationship between the United States and the European Union, and that is the asymmetry of political and military

---

[1] The Belt and Road Initiative was proposed by the Chinese President in 2010, and its interpretations range from being the largest and widest globalization and modernization project of humankind in the twenty-first century to being a Chinese geopolitical tool to expand Chinese influence in the participating countries. As of December 2021, the number of participating countries who signed a memorandum of understanding with China was 141. Basically, it was just Western Europe, North America, Australia and Brazil that did not join the initiative.

[2] The '16+1' mechanism was introduced in 2012 with China and sixteen CEE countries. Typically, a summit was held in a different capital every year: Warsaw, Poland (2012); Bucharest, Romania (2013); Belgrade, Serbia (2014); Suzhou, China (2015); Riga, Latvia (2016); Budapest, Hungary (2017); Sofia, Bulgaria (2018); and Dubrovnik, Croatia (2019). When Greece joined the 16+1 in 2019, the name of the cooperation was changed to '17+1 cooperation', and it was changed back to '16+1' cooperation when Lithuania left the cooperation. At the time of writing, the members are Latvia, Estonia, Poland, Czechia, Slovakia, Hungary, Croatia, Slovenia, Bulgaria, Romania, Serbia, Albania, North-Macedonia, Montenegro, Greece and Bosnia and Herzegovina.

Table 2.1 NATO Defence Expenditure (Estimated of NATO Countries and Share of GDP in 2021)

Country	Billion US dollars	Share of GDP in 2021	Share of GDP change compared to 2017
United States	811	3.52	+0.10
United Kingdom	73	2.29	+0.15
Germany	65	1.53	+0.15
France	59	2.01	+0.17
Italy	30	1.41	+0.19
Poland	13	2.10	+0.10
Romania	6	2.02	+0.02
Czechia	4	1.42	+0.23
Hungary	3	1.60	+0.39
Slovakia	2	1.73	-0.01
Croatia	2	2.79	+1.10
Lithuania	1	2.03	0.00
Latvia	0.9	2.27	+0.26
Estonia	0.8	2.28	+0.14
Slovenia	0.7	1.28	+0.24

Source: NATO

power. This asymmetry does not go unnoticed by partners; one could even say that it is, as Poyakova and Haddad observe, a cultivated asymmetry between partners. The break came with Donald Trump, who denounced the asymmetrical burden-sharing in NATO and demanded more of an effort from NATO members on military spending. By 2021, one-third of members had reached the 2 per cent of GDP that had been agreed on in 2014. In terms of GDP and absolute spending, NATO members have increased their military spending. Table 2.1 shows spending by the United States, the larger European countries and the Central European countries. However, this imbalance will not disappear in the medium term. Moreover, we can argue that the United States is more interested in maintaining this imbalance because it can better 'control' the foreign policy of European countries.

2.1.2. Mission impossible? Strategic autonomy of the EU

At the same time, an increase in military spending would not lead to 'strategic autonomy' for the European Union, a goal that has long been called for. Achieving 'strategic autonomy' requires a political vision that leads to agreement on a unified defence and foreign policy. However, the Ukraine crisis in 2021–2 has shown that the members of NATO are not on the same page when it comes to de-escalating the crisis. The term 'strategic autonomy' was first used by the European Council in 2014 and conceptualized in the 'Council Conclusions on implementing the EU Global Strategy in the area of Security and Defence' (Foreign Affairs Council, 2016). The proposal of the High Representative of the Union for Foreign Affairs and Security Policy further elaborated on this concept, stating as follows: 'In carrying forward its actions, the EU will work with partners and actively enhance its partnerships, while strengthening its own ability to take responsibility and share the burden with our partners in security and defence. Europe's strategic autonomy entails the ability to act and cooperate with international and regional partners wherever possible, while being able to operate autonomously when and where necessary' (High Representative of the Union for Foreign Affairs and Security Policy, 2016: 17). Macron also uses the concept frequently, but his statements are contradictory, as he wants to speak for a united Europe and take a leading role in shaping foreign policy. Gavin and Polyakova also caution against the approach, which misses the point that there is no strategic coherence or unified strategy among members' foreign-policy goals. As they put it,

> This vision assumes that a continent with a long history of divisions is now united on its defense and foreign policy. But a cursory look at the recent debates on Russia, China, and even the United States shows a lack of strategic coherence among European states. Macron's vision, in short, could splinter Europe and dilute its capabilities and focus, all while playing into the United States' worst instincts to disengage from the transatlantic alliance to focus on China. (Gavin & Polyakova, 2022, 19 January)

To sum it up, there are three main reasons for the lack of a unified strategy:

- The economic development goals of Central European countries differ from those of Western Europe, and these differences are – according to our interpretation – permanent rather than superficial, from which one can conclude that foreign-policy goals will also differ in the long run. (See the diversification efforts of these countries in Chapter 1!)
- The interpretation of sovereignty in these countries also differs from that in Western Europe, and this discrepancy will not disappear soon.
- The United States seems to have no interest in developing a more sovereign Europe. Moreover, we can argue that the abovementioned asymmetrical relationship after the Second World War was not only accepted but also cultivated by both sides (Polyakova & Haddad, 2019: 109–20).

2.1.3. Why the pivot to Asia?

The concept of 'pivot to Asia' has shifted the focus of US foreign policy from MENA to Asia. The Iraq wars, the war in Afghanistan, the intervention in Somalia, the involvement in the civil war following the break-up of the former Yugoslavia, all led the United States to focus on other regions, but as the war in Iraq came to an end and Americans began to withdraw troops from Afghanistan, the United States found itself at a 'pivot point', to paraphrase the first sentence of Hillary Clinton's famous 2011 article. Clinton concluded, 'The future of politics will be decided in Asia, not Afghanistan or Iraq, and the United States will be right at the center of the action' (Clinton, 2011).

The reduced attention to Europe lasted only a few years, until the annexation of Crimea and the launch of the Belt and Road Initiative and the 16+1 cooperation, which made Europe more important to the United States again, but the return of the United States to Europe – we must understand – took place in a global context and not because of the EU. One could argue that the United States downgraded its relationship with Europe because of its diminishing economic and political influence in the world. Let us look at the element of growing weakness point by point:

- The EU's share of world GDP fell dramatically between 1980 (25.9 per cent) and 2021 (14.9 per cent). The decline in this share was more than 10 percentage points. (These data are based on purchasing power parity.) (IMF, 2021).
- In 1960, the EU27 population accounted for about 12 per cent of the world's population, and in 2019, this share had fallen to 6 per cent. The EU's share of the world's population is expected to fall below 4 per cent by 2070 (European Commission, 2020).
- EU military spending has also fallen dramatically. The EU27 spent 3.8 per cent of its GDP on the military in 1960. This ratio declined until 2015, when it reached its lowest point at 1.32 per cent of GDP. The decline was understandable after the political change in Europe in 1990, but we can say that the decline was also continuous during the second Cold War, since 1980, which is quite surprising (World Bank database). This trend, coupled with the EU's shrinking share of world GDP, makes the EU a dwarf when it comes to hard power.

- According to the OECD database, the EU spent US$ 393 billion on R&D in 2019, while the United States and China spent US$ 613 and US$ 515 billion, respectively, on R&D in the same year. Japan alone spent nearly half of what the 27 EU countries spent on R&D. According to Statista, China was the largest donor of research and development activities in 2021, spending US$ 621 billion, while the United States ranked second for the first time since the Second World War, spending US$ 599 billion.
- When it comes to intellectual property, the World Intellectual Property Organization (WIPO) records filing activity worldwide and publishes it every year. According to this ranking, Germany and France are the only European countries that play a significant role in this field. In 2019, Germany ranked fifth for patents, seventh for trademarks and third for designs, while France ranked sixth for patents and for trademarks and fifth for designs (WIPO, 2021: 9).

Based on this trend, the decline in the relative economic and political power of the Europeans is a clear case, but this is not the only reason why the United States has refocused its foreign policy on Asia. The rise of Asian economies is a factor per se, especially that of China, which since the collapse and break-up of the Soviet Union is the only country that can challenge the United States as a global hegemonic power.

2.1.4. From honeymoon to divorce? Milestones of American–European relations

2.1.4.1. What to do with Europe? From the 1950s to the 1980s

While the United States and the European Union appeared to be uneasy allies before the war in Ukraine, the United States welcomed the idea of a united Europe in the 1950s and 1960s. Its support became less enthusiastic, however, because a united Europe could also threaten US global leadership or at least become an independent actor and not an agent complying with American foreign-policy objectives. The waning enthusiasm was recognized by Brzezinksi in 1970, who wrote: 'But whatever the merit of my analysis, for Europeans contemporary America is doubtless a less certain protector, a less committed partner' (Brzezinski, 1970: 14). He also referred to Nixon's annual message, in which the American president argued that it was time to change

American policy from one of 'preponderance' to one of genuine partnership. In particular, the American war in Vietnam was a financial burden on the United States, and more (financial) commitment from the Western European side was demanded – in vain – by the Americans. The United States solved the problem of the financial burden – at least for a while – by ending the convertibility of the dollar into gold in August 1971. The already simmering tensions in the global financial system, the end of dollar-to-gold convertibility, and the devaluation of the dollar led to the collapse of the Bretton Woods system[3] and created the floating exchange rates that form the basis of today's global financial order.

2.1.4.2. The troubled 1980s

The 1980s were marked by the following major events and trends:

- The invasion of Afghanistan (December 1979), which led to the denunciation of the SALT II Treaty and the decision to deploy nuclear missiles in Western Europe;
- The nuclear crisis in West Germany triggered massive public demonstrations against the plans (Tagliabue, 1983: 9) and ultimately led to the strengthening of NATO and relations between the United States and Western Europe (Shea, 2009);[4]
- The debt crisis that affected both Western and Eastern European countries;
- The spread and activities of leftist terrorist organizations;[5]

---

[3] Certain elements of the Bretton Woods systems – the International Monetary Fund, the World Bank – are still with us; however, the core of this system was the fixed exchange rate of the American dollar, which was given up after 1973. After the Second World War, the United States committed itself to issuing only that amount of money that can be backed by the gold reserves of the FED. That allowed the maintenance of the fixed exchange rate of the US$ and contributed to a stable global financial system. At the same time, this system did not allow the free flow of capital and became a burden later. But the real reason why the system collapsed was that the United States had to choose between two options to finance its costly wars: maintain the system and tax the American economy more, or simply issue more money than they had in gold reserves. The choice was evident.

[4] Shea said in a video lecture about this element: 'NATO was helped though, despite the fact that we suddenly had for the first time since the end of the Cold War the collapse of the pro-NATO political consensus between right and left, NATO was helped by some unlikely Allies: President Mitterrand of France. He went to the Bundestag in January 1983 and he gave a very famous speech where he said to people, hey, as he said in French "les missiles sont à l'est, les pacifistes sont à l'ouest Missiles are in the East, peace campaigners in the West." (Shea, 2009).

[5] Action Directe (AD) in France, Communist Combatant Cells (CCC) in Belgium, First of October Anti-Fascist Resistance Groups (GRAPO) in Spain, Irish National Liberation Army (INLA) in

- The imposition of martial law in Poland in 1981 (Milewski, Pomian & Zielonka, 1985: 337–59);
- The period of so-called Eurosclerosis in the early 1980s, which ended with the adoption of the Single Market Program (1986–92).

As we can see from the aforementioned list, during this period the American presence on the continent was no problem for Western European countries, and so the question of unequal burden-sharing was much less relevant than the threat posed by the Soviet Union.

2.1.4.3. *The beginning of the long American withdrawal: Europe after the collapse of Eastern European communist regimes*

After the fall of the Berlin Wall and the collapse of the Eastern European socialist bloc, the US presence was increasingly being questioned by allies as Europe was less threatened (or more to the point, not threatened) by the Soviet successor state, Russia. Not only was the world order unilaterally shaped by the United States over the next decade, but the American economy was much like the Roaring 1920s that led to the Great Depression. The economic policy missteps of the 1990s led to the Great Recession (2008–9), but at the same time, American companies conquered the world, shaping our present with technological innovations and creating the Internet communications technology on which our world depends.

At the end of the decade, relations between Americans and Europeans became strained again, as Wallace and Zielonka put it, 'Eurobashing is back in fashion in the United States.' They continued, 'The European visitor to Washington now encounters American economic triumphalism mixed with contempt for Europe's sluggish growth and social protection. American critics castigate Europe for not contributing to regional and global order while demanding that Europeans shoulder more of the cost of leadership. For Europeans in Washington, *Newsweek*'s Michael Hirsh recently noted, "it's hard to get respect"' (Wallace & Zielonka, 1999: 65).

We can find the next causes for a negative perception of Europe:

> Although more European integration seems in many ways a logical response to Europe's problems, Americans are hesitant about where to

Ireland, Popular Forces 25 April (FP-25) in Portugal, Red Army Faction (RAF) in Germany, Red Brigades in Italy.

stop supporting it because they do not want to create a global rival. This fits very well with the global long-term strategy of US foreign policy. As Brzenzinski put it, 'In the short run, the United States should consolidate and perpetuate the prevailing geopolitical pluralism on the map of Eurasia. This strategy will put a premium on political maneuvering and diplomatic manipulation, preventing the emergence of a hostile coalition that could challenge America's primacy, not to mention the remote possibility of any one state seeking to do so.' We must not misunderstand or misinterpret the meaning of the sentence, because the premise applies to West Europe as well. (Brzezinski, 1997: 51). He writes, 'A larger Europe will expand the range of American influence without simultaneously creating a Europe so politically integrated that it could challenge the United States on matters of geopolitical importance, particularly in the Middle East' (Brzezinski, 1997: 53). The United States followed the introduction of the common currency, the euro, with skepticism. The euro had the potential – at least in theory – to challenge the American dollar in the global financial system: its role as foreign reserves, as the main currency for commercial transactions and foreign exchange market transactions. None of this has come to pass; the Global Financial Crisis and the eurozone crisis have put an end to those dreams. Wallace and Zielonka point to Americans' disdain or misunderstanding of European social systems. They write, 'American denunciation of Europe's costly welfare systems, extensive social regulation, and sluggish labor mobility also project on Europe the domestic American debate' (Wallace & Zielonka, 1999: 70). The final reason for the negative interpretation of the EU was its role in the break-up of Yugoslavia. Although the Maastricht Treaty created the so-called Common Foreign and Security Policy in 1992, the disagreements between Germany on one side and France and the United Kingdom on the other side showed that the common policy was not working properly. The main reason is that the European Union still consists of sovereign countries. And if you want to find a core element of sovereignty, it is independent foreign policy. Giving this up means the end of the concept of a Europe of nation states. The debate about the ultimate goal of European integration has never been settled. Until this work is done, it will be difficult to work out a functioning version of the common foreign policy.

Americans may be wrong on other points, but this last point and the criticism of the single currency are the ones in which the institutional shortcomings of European integration become very clear.

2.1.4.4. US supporting the break-up of the EU? After the Great Recession until the Ukraine crisis in 2021–22

The Eurozone crisis that developed in the wake of the Great Recession (2008–9) took place between 2010 and 2012. Not only did the crisis call into question the very existence of the Eurozone, but several analyses also did not rule out the break-up of the European Union. Clearly, the crisis did not convey the image of a solid partner to the Americans, who became more involved in the Arab Spring and, later, in the Syrian civil war starting in 2011. Moreover, from the start of Operation Enduring Freedom in 2001 until the American withdrawal in 2021, the US commitment in Afghanistan cost 2,400 troops and US$ 2.3 billion (Shortridge, 2021).

In 1989, the number of US troops stationed in Europe was 315,000, which declined significantly over the next three decades. In 1995, there were only 115,000 American troops in Europe. The next major decrease occurred in 2008, when the number was reduced to 64,000 soldiers. Since then, the number of American troops stationed there has remained more or less the same. Allen et al. summarize this process, 'The Sept. 11, 2001, attacks in particular marked a dramatic shift in where the U.S. focused its troop deployments and security concerns. The beginning of the war in Afghanistan in 2001 and the 2003 invasion of Iraq brought massive changes in the United States' military position globally as it shifted focus to Central Asia and the Middle East' (Allen, Machain & Flynn, 2022). Clearly, the invasion of Georgia in 2008, the annexation of Crimea and Russian recognition of the Donetsk and Luhansk republics in 2022 may mark a turning point in the long-term trend of this decade. (The deployment of 7000 troops in Poland, Romania and the Baltic countries is not significant, but instructive [Smitt, 2022]).

2.1.5. The grand American strategy and Europe's role in it

At this point we argue that power cannot be understood apart from its economic basis. The greatest challenge facing any hegemonic power is that it must spend significant resources globally, internationalize its currency and diffuse its technology in order to maintain its hegemonic position (Schutte, 2022). This idea aligns very well with Gilpin's proposal. He saw relative economic decline as a fact. Since decline is a slow and gradual process, it is difficult to identify and predict when the hegemonic power will overstretch its economic and military capabilities. While the US GDP accounted for 21 per cent of world GDP in 1980 and still 21 per cent ten years later, that share has shrunk to 15 per cent. (See Chart 1!). The trend line is not free of fluctuations. There are periods – the period after the second oil crisis and the period before the dot-com bubble – when the bubble appears to reverse, but the long-term trend appears to be downwards. The dot.com bubble phenomenon is easier to explain because the bubble itself and the technological innovation that preceded it put the US economy on a rapid growth path. The post-1982 period is more interesting, as the global economy was on the verge of recession (0.5 per cent GDP growth in 1985) and political tensions between the two major blocs were on the rise again. What the United States did in a different way during the second oil crisis was to implement a money-tightening neoliberal monetary policy, which had the effect of taking money out of the world economy and bringing US dollars back to the United States and putting them to work. The point I want to make here is that in the 1980s, the United States had the political and economic power and the moral high ground to directly influence the world economy and policy, while after the Global Financial Crisis, China was also needed to revive the world economy (Graph 2.1).

We see another dilemma in the design and formulation of an American Grand Strategy. American society is increasingly riven by growing income inequality, racial tensions and the hollowing out of the middle class. In early

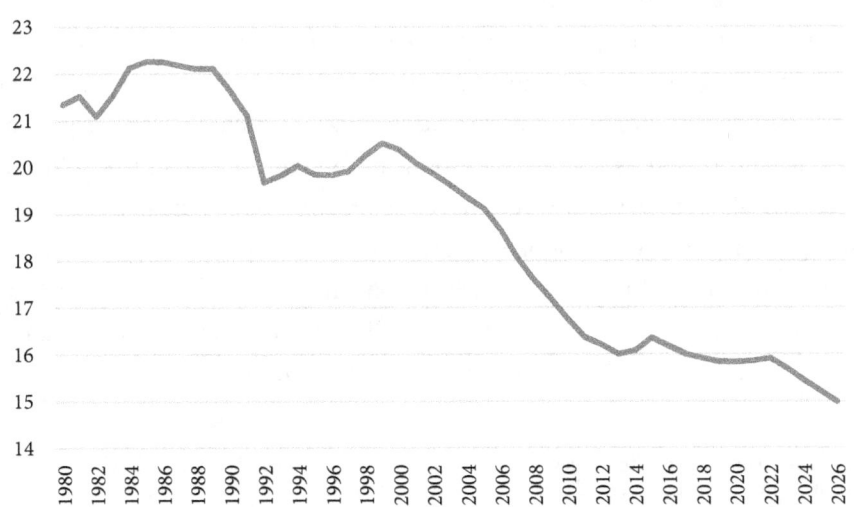

Graph 2.1 US Share in World GDP (PPP, %). *Source*: World Bank. World Economic Outlook 2021, October.

2021, US president Joe Biden linked foreign and domestic policy: 'There's no longer a bright line between foreign and domestic policy. Every action we take in our conduct abroad, we must take with American working families in mind. Advancing a foreign policy for the middle class demands urgent focus on our domestic economic renewal' (Biden, 2021). The question is how to balance economic renewal (see the American Rescue Plan) and a comprehensive modernization of the American economy with a foreign policy that does not prioritize but pursues all goals simultaneously. In other words, America's economic decline would not be a problem per se, just as it was never a problem for Russia when it invaded Ukraine and achieved its foreign-policy goals.

In the same speech, Biden also mentioned the need to confront the new moment of 'advancing authoritarianism, including China's growing ambitions to rival the United States and Russia's determination to damage and disrupt our democracy' (Biden, 2021). Being present on all fronts will overwhelm US economic and military capabilities. Moreover, if this problem is met with a new wave of US isolationism, the United States could turn its back on the world, as has happened in part during the Trump administration. The 'America first policy' launched by then president Donald Trump was a return to a foreign policy that has a very long tradition in the United States and resonates with many American voters, especially the middle class, whose relative income position has deteriorated since the 1990s and who do not believe the promises of the so-called American dream.[6]

The 'America first' approach is not pure isolationism, of course, nor can it be in an age of globalization and interconnectedness, but the roots of the 'America first' policy go back to isolationism, which, as Hooker puts it, 'had always existed as a strain in American foreign policy [and] would not disappear altogether, but it would never again contend for primacy in grand strategy' (Hooker, 2014). Hooker wrote this sentence in 2014, and two years later Trump refuted the claim that isolationism could never regain primacy in grand strategy. Trump's decision to withdraw from several international commitments was ended by Biden, whose 'America is back' foreign policy

---

[6] Petersen summarizes the process thus: 'Forty years ago, the term "middle class" referred to Americans who had successfully obtained a version of the American dream: a steady income from one or two earners, a home, and security for the future. It meant the ability to save and acquire assets. Now, it mostly means the ability to put your bills on autopay and service debt. The stability that once characterized the middle class, that made it such a coveted and aspirational echelon of American existence, has been hollowed out' (Petersen, 2021).

seemed to have halted that trend. But the question remains whether the United States still has the capacity to maintain its global superpower position and unilaterally settle issues of global order.

2.2. The confrontation of giants: Consequences for CE region

2.2.1. China going global?

The Shanghai Communiqué was signed by the United States and China in 1972, the year bilateral relations between the two countries were restored, marking the beginning of a long period in which US policy towards China was more or less friendly. In December 1978, the two countries normalized their relations and a One China policy was adopted by the United States. Beijing could also rely on American capital and technology in its modernization process. The break with the Soviet alliance offered China the opportunity to gradually integrate its economy into the world economy. The long period, however, was not free of political tensions between the two countries, the most obvious of which was the suppression of demonstrations in Tiananmen Square (June 1989). Despite the embargo imposed by the United States following the massacre, it did not take long for the economic interests of US corporations to override the moral aspects of foreign policy. Tensions also increased with the Third Taiwan Strait Crisis in 1995–6, which began with Republic of China president Lee Teng-hui's private visit to the United States and ended with a joint US–China statement in October 1997 (Frost, 1997).

The collapse of the Soviet empire made a reconceptualization of US foreign policy inevitable. After 1989, the term engagement also became associated with the concept that economic transformation would sooner or later lead to reform of the political system in China and eventually to a process of democratization. Neil argues that while the policy of engagement has produced significant results (Neil, 2019), China has not evolved into a Western-style democracy.[7]

---

[7] It is a question how we assess a society regarding its democratic values. Western-based non-governmental organizations measure democracy by whether political institutions correspond to Western norms. Obviously, China does not meet these requirements; however, it must be added that these reports do not include the aspect of economic progress. Economic progress for the broad layers of the society is important in societies where leaders of the society are accountable for social and economic trends. The Chinese system's performance is better than many other developing and democratic countries.

It is very difficult to find the years when US engagement with China turned into a combination of engagement and containment – congagement being a popular term at the time – and then into a classic containment policy, but it is certain that the years of the Trump administration were the ones when the change in tone and policy became more than obvious even to superficial observers. The dilemma of what to do with China was explicitly addressed in the literature decades before the Trump years. This academic dilemma was not recognized widely until China's economic and political power grew and reached the threshold of foreign-policy attention that we can place around the turn of the millennium. The term BRIC, coined in the early 2000s, and the debate over the rise of China (Moldicz, 2021) show that China began to be viewed as a new emerging superpower that could challenge US leadership in the long term.

Regardless of how we feel about the rise of China, the country's sheer size in terms of population, purchasing power, technological development, and so on, is bound to cause problems. Schweller and Pu view China as the game changer of the system that will overthrow the rules-based liberal world order (Schweller & Pu, 2011). Others point out that China adheres to the rules of the system – see China's WTO membership. McNally uses the term Sino-capitalism to describe why China poses a challenge to the existing system. He believes that China's resurgence is producing Sino-capitalism, a capitalist system with global reach but different in important ways from Anglo-American capitalism.

We believe that the dilemma posed by China is better understood by drawing on the concept of the developmental state. Originally coined in the 1980s, the concept described the way in which the Japanese economy systematically differed from Anglo-American capitalism. Later, the concept was also applied to South Korea, Taiwan and Singapore. Among other elements,[8] all of these economies were export-oriented economies in the early stages of their development, with a strong emphasis on manufacturing, followed later in each case by a move up the value chain. China is a latecomer to this story and operates in a different – more globalized and interconnected – economic environment, but can be characterized as a developmental state with Chinese characteristics. The differences between China and the three original models

---

[8] Strong economic planning tools; cheap labour; export-orientation, land reform as the starting point of economic reform and take-off, relatively autonomous bureaucracy and the rule of law in the economic domain.

of the developmental state, Japan, South Korea and Taiwan, lie in the size of the economy, which allows for a great deal of room to manoeuvre in economic policy and creates headaches for the United States.

The competition between China and the United States is often portrayed as a struggle between two giant states, while the interstate rivalry at the level of politics is complemented by the capitalist competition at the level of economics. The two competitions are not fought separately, but are closely intertwined. This kind of competition has a precondition: 'The existence of some centralized political power which can counteract the economic power of the existing centers and the centralizing tendency of market forces' (Gilpin, 1976: 52). It should be emphasized that there were attempts to counter the economic power of the United States. The most notable example was France in the 1960s, which lacked the economic power to do so, while Germany and Japan had the economic power but not the political will. China has both elements and, after the Global Financial Crisis (2008–9), was able to pool financial resources through its state-directed economy to expand globally. This was the moment it launched the Belt and Road Initiative and 16+1 cooperation. (Read more about the cooperation between China and CEE in Chapter 3!)

There are analysts who question whether China can act as an integrating force in the global economy. They argue that China will inevitably be part of global capitalism shaped by US supremacy because Chinese economic development would in many ways be driven by foreign capital. Panitch and Gindin are sceptical about China's ability to assume a leadership role: 'China's entry into the circuits of the international economy, many commentators now predicted, marked a fundamental "realignment" of the global capitalist order. Far from displacing the American empire, however, China appears to be taking over Japan's complementary role by providing the steady inflow of financial resources necessary to maintain the U.S.'s primary role in global capitalism' (Panitch & Gindin, 2013: 146).

After the Global Financial Crisis, this argument was less tenable than ever. In addition to the infrastructure programmes mentioned earlier (BRI, 16+1 cooperation), the launch of the Made in China 2025 programme clearly showed that China was not satisfied with its previous inferior position in the global division of labour.[9]

---

[9] The 'Strategic Emerging Industries' was the fifteen-year plan adopted in 2006. The plan included innovation, whereas 'Made in China 2015' focused on all areas of production, therefore 'Made in

2.2.2. Locked in a triangle? China, the CEE region and the United States

When it comes to the final assessment of China's role in Central Europe and its intentions at the global level, we can see the following logic behind the development of relations between China and CEE:

- China's global and European initiatives are designed to aid in the 'rejuvenation of the nation', and help the Chinese economy catch up. Because of the sheer size of the economy, the catch-up process has global and geopolitical consequences.
- In this context, the United States is the country that most wants to stop this rise, because it threatens American global leadership.
- In the Central European region, China has no relevant geopolitical interests, and even its economic development interests are more related to the Western European region, which has benefited far more from cooperation with China than the Central European countries.
- It is logical that China would not pursue a geopolitically motivated foreign policy in the region, but is more interested in doing business rather than in engaging in long-term commitments. At the same time, the US global strategy puts the United States on a collision course with China, whose rise is global, and the US response to it must logically be global as well.
- This is why certain elements of cooperation between China and CEE are viewed with suspicion. One area worth highlighting is the transfer of technology from China to these countries. Trade between China and Central European countries appears to be a smaller problem for the United States.

Technological cooperation appears to be a particularly sensitive issue, as the new Biden administration sees certain areas such as 5G networks, gears and artificial intelligence (AI) as strategically important to the geopolitical contest with China and discourages its regional allies from using critical Chinese technology. The irony of the situation is that, if there is one area where the Visegrad countries could benefit significantly from relations with China, it is 5G and AI.

China 2015' targeted traditional industries and modern services, and the other difference is the latter strategy allowed more room for market forces (Kennedy, 2015).

In support of the so-called Prague proposals,[10] Poland signed a joint declaration with the United States on cybersecurity in September 2019 (Trump, 5 September 2019). Czechia was among the early sceptics of 5G cooperation with China, but the joint declaration on 5G was not signed until May 2020 (Reuters, 6 May 2020). Slovakia also signed this declaration with the United States in October 2020, but this does not mean that Huawei would be completely ousted from the region. Hungary is the only country in the group that has not signed this declaration, which rules out cooperation with China in this area.[11]

Another issue that is more symbolic of US strategy is the search for an alliance with Central European countries on the situation of human rights and minority rights in China. The reason why Central European countries respond differently to this challenge is to be found in their foreign policies. More pragmatic foreign-policy strategies[12] are less likely to address these arguments against China because they realistically assess that they have no leverage over China and do not want to bear the financial burden of a foreign policy that would be sanctioned by China.

Lithuania, Czechia and Slovakia are good examples of foreign policies that are more responsive to US human rights arguments. Political relations between China and CEE cooled significantly during 2020, and political relations sank to a low point during Czech Senate president Milos Vystrcil's visit to Taiwan in 2020 (Blanchard & Tian, 2020, 31 August). Since then, the country has shown solidarity, so to speak, with the Baltic countries and pursued a clearly pro-American foreign policy. The visit of a Taiwanese delegation to Czechia and Slovakia added to the already simmering tensions between the regions.

The other trigger was the opening of a Taiwan Representative Office in Lithuania. The office used 'Taiwan' instead of 'Taipei', a name China prefers as it is

---

[10] The Prague Proposals are basically a collection of recommendations announced at the Prague 5G Security Conference in 2019. The thirty-two countries participating included the Visegrad countries, too.
[11] Moreover, Huawei is one of the main Chinese investors in Hungary, and the company established its European logistics and production centre in Hungary in 2005. Over a period of more than fifteen years, the company has invested around US$ 1.2 billion in Hungary, employs 2,000 people and cooperates with around 600 Hungarian companies. The company estimates that the economic impact of Huawei's investment in Hungary is 0.39 per cent of GDP.
[12] Hungary's foreign policy is an excellent example of a pragmatic approach, which is less influenced by values, or to put it more precisely, does not get involved in 'democracy export'. The futility of the American democracy approach is vividly explained by Gregory Gause using Middle East examples. He argues: 'It is foolish to think that the choice in the Middle East's weak and failed states is between good governance and bad governance, or between democracy and authoritarianism. In reality, the choice now is between harsh governance and no governance' (Gause, 2022: 10).

more in line with the One China principle. In retaliation, imports of Lithuanian goods into China were halted, after which the European Commission initiated a case against China at the World Trade Organization, as the Commission put it, 'over (China's) discriminatory trade practices against Lithuania, which are also hitting other exports from the EU's Single Market' (European Commission, 2022).

The problem for China in responding to the foreign policies of EU members using trade policy tools comes from its economic interdependence in the EU. If China wants to act effectively, it must act against the entire region (the European Union). However, the question remains how much China itself would suffer from such a move. In other words, it is extremely complicated to impose economic sanctions on EU countries. If China nevertheless decides to take this route, it would face the reaction of the entire EU. We should not forget that, given the fact that the twenty-seven countries operate a common market, trade policy is one of the common policies in the EU. A common trade policy is the only thing that makes economic sense in a customs union.

We see that the Baltic countries, Poland and Czechia take a different stance on China for the simple reason that they are more easily swayed by US arguments because of security guarantees against Russia. The difference between Hungary and other CEE countries was clear in the perception of Russia before the Ukraine war. However, even in this case, Hungary respected the obligations arising from its NATO membership and its membership in the European Union. It also imposed economic sanctions on Russia after the annexation of Crimea in 2014 and tried to maintain economic relations within the framework set by those sanctions, although economic pragmatism would push the country to diversify its trade and investment relations, and an expansion of economic relations with Russia would have contributed to this process.

The question is how these countries' relations with Russia have evolved over time and how the Ukraine war came about.

2.3. US Confrontation with Russia: Consequences for CE region

2.3.1. Rosy beginnings and overt hostilities: From the 1990s to the annexation of Crimea

At the end of 1991, the disintegration of the Soviet Union was officially initiated by the leaders of Russia, Belarus and Ukraine, soon followed by other republics of the Soviet Union. After realizing that the Soviet Union de facto no longer existed, Gorbachev resigned from office, and the parliament (the Soviet of Nationalities) formally decided to dissolve. During this honeymoon between the United States and Russia (Soviet Union), the next important changes to take place were the following:

- The negotiation and ratification of the START II treaty to reduce nuclear weapons, which took place in 1992, wherein the treaty was signed in 1993, ratified by the United States in 1996 and then by Russia in 2000. (The treaty was declared null and void by Russia two years later.)
- Russia also contributed to the terms of German reunification and agreed to its membership in NATO.
- Russia and the United States cooperated on the liberation of Kuwait after Iraq invaded that country (Rumer & Sokolsky, 2019: 5).

Although the optimistic tone prevailed for several years, phrases such as Clinton's remark about US–Russian relations in 1993 became rare. He said to Boris Yeltsin, the first president of the new Russia: '[the negotiations] laid the foundation for a new democratic partnership between the United States and Russia' (Clinton, cited by Nelson, 1993). Russian economic development in the 1990s did not achieve the hoped-for results before the economic transition, however. The Russian economy was in a state of limbo during that decade; the mechanisms of the planned economy could no longer function properly, while the forces of capitalism were constrained by the oligopolies, which also contributed to the rise of the so-called oligarchs, a thin, ultra-rich stratum of society that grew rich through the special rights that corporations enjoyed due to exploitation of natural resources. The Russian economy is an excellent example of the so-called Dutch disease: a term used to describe resource-rich countries where the exploitation of natural resources (in this case, primarily oil and gas) and the extra profit from exploitation directs all capital to that sector. During this process, the domestic currency becomes stronger, making the production of other goods less competitive. At the end of the process, the economy is lopsided, specializing only in oil and gas production, and even public budget revenues come from this source (Reisinezhad, 2020: 3). This manner of economic development has two direct effects on politics: (1) the oligarchs have an outsize influence on the state, and (2) other sources of revenue lose importance and therefore the opinion of voters, since they do not have to be taxed as much.

The Asian crisis easily spread to Russia, not because of particularly close ties to the Southeast-Asian region, but because the fundamentals of the economy were weak. Russia devalued the currency in August 1998. After a political crisis, Boris Yeltsin resigned in 1999, and Putin became the Russian president.

After the first Chechen war in 1994–6, the real conflict between the United States and Russia erupted the summer that the United States bombed Kosovo despite the absence of a Security Council resolution from the UN. This act was perceived by Russia as an American tendency to act unilaterally, and as the United States contributing to the dismantling of the world order, which was supposed to have been based on international law. Maynes offers several other examples of unilateralism from 1999:

> the charge of unilateralism goes deeper. Others, including some of America's closest friends, were dismayed by the American decision to stand alone, through the use of its veto, in denying Boutros-Boutros Ghali a second term as Secretary General of the United Nations. They are increasingly troubled by the American unwillingness to fund its fair share of the budget of the International Monetary Fund, the World Bank and the United Nations family. They also question whether one member of an alliance should be able to impose its views on the others regarding such an important issue for European security as the expansion of NATO. (Maynes, 1999: 515)

At the same time, Russia offered support in Afghanistan after the terrorist attacks in New York in 2001. The reasons for this support are explained by Baev: 'It wasn't pure good will [sic] that underpinned that element of short-lived "reset" in Russia-U.S. relations during the early Obama administration and Medvedev interregnum but rather the undeclared understanding in Moscow that the sustained U.S.-led operation actually answered Russia's security interests by containing a potentially explosive conflict to the south of its borders' (Baev, 2021).

The spirit of the Joint Declaration of the two countries quickly evaporated, although the United States and Russia reaffirmed in the statement that they do not see each other as enemies or strategic threats (Joint US–Russian Declaration, 2002). When the United States invaded Iraq for the second time a year later, it was met with Russian opposition and the United States began to criticize Russia's record on human rights and democracy. During these years, the so-called colour revolutions in neighbouring countries (Georgia in 2003, Ukraine in 2004, Kyrgyzstan in 2005), which Russia perceives as its 'near abroad', were interpreted in Moscow as an encirclement strategy. Similarly, the expansion of NATO in 2004 with Russia's neighbours (the Baltic countries) and Romania, Bulgaria, Slovakia and Croatia confirmed the view that Russia was being encircled by the United States.[13] Part of this slow-motion spiral between the two countries was the Bush administration's plans in 2007 to deploy missile systems in Poland and Czechia, to which Russia responded by violating arms control agreements. Putin's speech at the Munich Security Conference in 2007 added a new layer to Russia's interpretation of US unilateralism. In this speech, he emphasized the non-democratic nature of unilateralism, describing it as a world ruled by one master, one sovereign, which has nothing to do with democracy, in which the interests and opinions of the minority are also taken into account (Putin, 2007). The situation culminated in Russian opposition to Georgian and Ukrainian NATO membership – see the pledge at the NATO Bucharest summit – and led to war in Georgia (2008).

The Obama-initiated reset of US–Russian relations offered a brief respite and relaxation, but it did not last long. New tensions emerged with the Arab Spring and the civil war in Syria. Based on the quick and successful annexation of the Crimean Peninsula (2014) and the successful intervention in the Syrian civil war, Russian thinkers jumped to conclusions about Russia's regained military strength. Pukhov concluded, 'The availability of these experienced commanders, a record of a successful and victorious military campaign, and the lessons learned from using air power, modern technology and special operations forces will provide a major boost to the Russian military machine for years to come' (Pukhov, 2017).

The annexation of Crimea triggered the first wave of economic sanctions against Russia. The subsequent economic downturn was relatively mild and short, and the Russian economy adapted relatively quickly to the new conditions, while at the same time the concept of 'Greater Europe' was replaced by the concept of 'Eurasia' in foreign policy. The process began earlier, however, when several steps were taken to accelerate Russia's turn towards Asia:

- Russia joined the Asia-Pacific Economic Cooperation in 1998;
- The country became one of the founders of the Shanghai Cooperation Organization in 2001;
- In 2015, it founded the Eurasian Economic Union;

---

[13] Poland, Hungary and the Czech Republic joined NATO in 1999.

- It became China's largest oil importer, replacing Saudi Arabia; and
- 60 per cent of Russian arms exports go to South Asia (India, Laos, Vietnam, Myanmar, Philippines and Indonesia).

In many ways, Russia's pivot to Asia is about deepening relations with China, and dedollarization seems to be the most important project the two countries have in common. For China, too, dedollarization is a logical step in response to the US trade war and decoupling strategy. Also of importance is the International North-South Transport Corridor (INSTC), which would allow faster and cheaper connections between Russia and India. Vinokurov estimates that delivery times between Mumbai and St. Petersburg could be cut in half, from thirty to forty-five days to fifteen to twenty-four days.

Even before the Ukraine war and the imposed sanctions, Russian trade relations have shifted towards China. While the EU accounted for 43 per cent of Russia's foreign trade, that share dropped to 36 per cent in 2021. China has been Russia's largest trading partner since 2019, and more interestingly, Russia is among the few countries in the world that have a trade surplus with China.

After the Crimean conflict, the scope for the development of the Russian economy became smaller, and the response to the economic sanctions were classic import-substitution policy steps. Self-sufficiency was prioritized and previously neglected sectors became more prominent and began to flourish due to growing demand, but shortages of labour and capital, and limited access to new technologies, limited this type of economic development. It was also easy to make a case for Russia turning to Asia because most Asian countries did not impose sanctions on Russia after the annexation of Crimea, or the impact of those sanctions was negligible.

2.3.2. Locked in a triangle? Russia, the CEE region and the United States

As we saw in the previous sub-chapter, the spiral between the United States and Russia has been in slow motion since the end of the Cold War. At the same time, the Russian invasion of Ukraine has accelerated this spiral and brought the world to a point where there was even talk of the threat of nuclear war.

Russian forces launched an offensive against Ukraine on 24 February, 2022. This was the first time since the end of the Second World War that the world witnessed a shooting war between two sovereign states in Europe. (The Yugoslav war is considered a military conflict that started as a civil war and led to the disintegration of the country.) Under international law, war is not one of the permissible means countries may use to settle their differences. This may sound trivial, but before 1945, war was considered a legal means of settling international disputes between states. In other words, the military invasion by Russia may be explicable, but it is neither legally nor morally acceptable.

Russia may achieve some strategic goals with the war, but its long-term strategy of expanding its spheres of influence will fail, as these spheres are based not only on military power, but also on economic influence and soft power.

When it comes to the final assessment of Russia's role in Central Europe and its intentions at the global level, we can see the following logic behind the development of relations between Russia and CEE. In addition to the long-term strategic failure of Russia's invasion of Ukraine, which has created distrust of Russian intentions, Russia is a weak and declining economic power.

Even in the event that Russia manages to avert a sovereign default and a collapse of its currency thanks to its economic cooperation with China, it can either survive only as an economic satellite of China or experience a rapid decline, as economic sanctions affect not only trade but also technology transfer and capital. In essence, Russia has very little to offer to Central European countries, either technologically or economically, other than threatening them militarily or cutting off their access to energy. Had Russia continued its peaceful cooperation, it could have offered some degree of trade diversification. But that is no longer the case.

In contrast, the United States can offer Central European countries capital, technology, access to the institutions of the current world order and security guarantees. When it comes to the energy supply of Central Europe, it is almost impossible to replace Russia, but it can be done within a period of five to ten years if significant investments are made in the region to improve the energy infrastructure and develop energy production. It is obvious that all these steps are possible, but they will slow down economic growth in the region. The price of cutting off Russia will be high. And we doubt that either the United States or the EU will pay the price that small Central European countries will have to pay for geopolitical superpower competition in the region.

3

The newcomer in the region

China

The history of the People's Republic of China's (PRC) relations with Central Europe could not be more different than China's relations with the West. After the end of the Chinese Civil War in 1949, Mao's Chinese Communist Party (CCP) took power and proclaimed the People's Republic of China. After the proclamation of the People's Republic of China, the former socialist countries rushed to recognize Mao's China diplomatically, while Western European countries and the United States did not recognize the PRC diplomatically until the 1970s. At the same time, relations between China and the CEE countries were far from rosy between 1949 and 1991, as relations deteriorated from the mid- to late 1960s, when simmering tensions between the Soviet Union and China escalated into open hostilities between the two major socialist countries. The Soviet Union's satellite countries did not have much leeway in their foreign policy decisions and implicitly followed the Soviet Union's foreign policy, so relations with China cooled significantly.

As the former socialist political regimes in Central and Eastern Europe collapsed in the late 1980s and early 1990, both China and the CEE region focused on themselves for the next decade: The CEE countries rebuilt their trade and investment ties with Western Europe and the United States and integrated their economies into the existing economic and political institutional framework, while China – after the Tiananmen Square interlude in 1989 – resumed economic reforms when the CCP endorsed the Chinese model as a 'socialist market economy' in 1994. To solve the ideological dilemma of the market economy under socialism, Deng gave the next definition of 'socialist market economy': 'Whether the emphasis is on planning or on the market mechanism is not the essential distinction between socialism and capitalism. A planned economy is not socialism; there is planning under capitalism too. A market economy is not capitalism; there is market regulation under socialism, too' (Deng Xiaoping quoted by Myers, 1992).

With this ideological turn and the collapse of the Central European socialist bloc, the earlier attention to the socialist reforms of the Central European countries waned. Chinese policymakers paid particular attention to the Hungarian reforms of 1968, which attempted to combine a socialist economy with limited market mechanisms. Kornai wrote in 1986:

> The Hungarian Economy has undergone major systematic changes in the last 30 years. The impact of the reform is felt by every Hungarian citizen. The influence of the Hungarian experience, however, does not stop at the borders of this small Eastern European country. At least, the temptation to follow a similar road appears in other socialist countries. The leaders of the Chinese economy are studying the Hungarian situation carefully in an effort to learn from its successes and failures (Kornai, 1986: 1687).

It basically took more than two decades after the political and economic transition of the Central European countries to turn back to East Asia and rebuild relations with China. This period of improving relations can be explained by at least three factors:

- China's accelerated growth and the export orientation of its economy required ever greater internationalization (i.e. new markets) for their companies – see the 'go out strategy' later in this chapter!
- Central European countries have reached a certain point in their economic strategy where their development cannot continue without further diversification of trade, investment relations and technology transfer, since their 'dependent economic model' depends only on Western capital and technology. Myant defined the typical elements of the 'dependent model' of Central European countries as follows: 'Most obviously, the level of development of financial systems required for a liberal market economy is absent, as are the cooperative relationships between firms and with trade unions that are at the heart of the notion of a coordinated market economy' (Myant, 2018: 294). Further development without a change in economic relations would only have increased their

dependence in a division of labour, using them as cheap assembly bases for multinational corporations.
- In the wake of the Global Financial Crisis, further impetus for growth could not come from the West, but from the East. In 2009–10, the global economy was kept alive by China's demand and stimulus package, so the pivot to Asia – essentially, to China – was obvious to the leaders of Central European countries. What seemed to be a relief for Central European countries could also be interpreted as a sign of a global power shift. As Grant and Wilson put it, 'But if the crisis has generated problems for the Chinese leadership, they are problems that other world leaders might well prefer to their own challenges. And to say that China's response was not cost-free does not mean that it was unsuccessful – far from it. Indeed, as it began to appear that China's response to the crisis seemed to be working, there was an upsurge in interest within China to the idea of a "China model" that might act as an alternative to Western modes of development' (Grant & Wilson, 2012: 13).
- The Obama and Trump administrations' refocused foreign policy approach – the Pivot to Asia – not only neglected Central European countries, but devalued Europe as a whole in the grand strategy. While the Obama administration paid some lip service to European allies, President Trump was exclusively hostile to traditional European allies and to the European Union in particular, supporting Brexit and attacking NATO allies for not spending enough on their militaries. At the same time, he explicitly supported Brexit and established good relations with some European leaders who are viewed as populist politicians by the liberal mainstream media and intellectuals. This shift in foreign policy has also been called the 'Jacksonian revolt', in reference to the first populist American president. Mead highlights the foreign relations implications of this policy as follows: 'The role of the U.S. government, Jacksonians believe, is to fulfill the destiny of the country by attending to the physical security and economic well-being of the American people in their national home – and to do so while interfering as little as possible with the individual liberty that makes the country unique. Jacksonian populism is only sporadically concerned with foreign policy, and indeed with politics in general' (Mead, 2017: 3–4).

As of 2016 or so, the Trump administration's withdrawal policy no longer supported economic globalization in the world. In addition, the trade war with

China, the deliberate decoupling from the Chinese economy, efforts to bring manufacturing home and Brexit all reinforced de-globalization. This is when China had the chance to successfully launch new institutions and initiatives (Belt and Road Initiative, 16+1 cooperation, etc.), partly reordering the global order, and partly showing that initiatives could come not only from the West but also from the East.

The sanctions against Russia in 2014 and 2022 added to the trend of de-globalization that was already present in the system. But what is the connection between de-globalization and China's economic development? What we need to understand is that China's intentions are best understood by looking at the country as a particular version of the Asian developmental model. (See Chapter 2!) One of the main features of the developmental state model is export-led growth. The basic idea behind the Belt and Road Initiative (BRI) is to open markets to Chinese goods by building the necessary infrastructure to get the products to the target markets. As the EU is China's most important trade and investment partner on the Eurasian continent, the EU is the most important region of the BRI. The need for such infrastructure is evident in the vast Central Asian and Eastern European regions that link China and Western Europe, the two hubs of global trade. If there is one country in the world economy that needs more globalization and can benefit from globalization, it is China. The problem, however, is that since the 2010s, there have been several factors that have, by design or not, supported de-globalization: (1) China's economic success; (2) populist movements; (3) the 2020–1 global pandemic; (4) economic sanctions against Russia; and (5) the establishment of parallel international institutions.

1. *China's economic success* challenges the existing world order. The success and size of its economy has meant that its very existence challenges current global multilateral trade and investment institutions. To protect the global order, Western countries restricted China's access to this institutional framework and impeded China's economic integration. (At the same time, we must add that China's reforms also stalled after it joined the WTO in 2001.)
2. Since the 2010s, *populist movements* in power have actively helped create barriers to international trade and capital flows. The withdrawal of the United States from several international commitments (in 2017 from

the Trans-Pacific Partnership and the Paris Agreement, in 2020 from the World Health Organization), the introduction of a screening mechanism for foreign direct investment in EU member states has exacerbated these problems. Although the Biden administration reversed these withdrawals, the genie was out of the bottle, and the institutions of the global order were challenged, beginning the process of redesign.

3. De-globalization received a new impetus from the *global pandemic* that broke out in early 2020. Not only did the lockdowns restrict economic activity and cause a collapse in global trade and a decline in GDP, but they also prompted countries to focus on supply chain security and to revise these policies to rely less on economic cooperation and to prioritize (at least regional) self-sufficiency, although it remains to be seen whether that is a reasonable and feasible policy. Although the restrictions were relaxed in 2021 and 2022, the fear remained and changed the economic policy decisions. We should add that China's continuation of the zero-Covid policy has the same effect, whether it is intended or not.

4. The Biden administration's *economic sanctions* during the Ukraine war also did not support globalization. Intentional and forced decoupling from Russia (and Russian energy and raw materials) may be an effective foreign policy, but it will create trading blocs in the global economy unless the policy is reversed after the war.

5. The decoupling of Russia and China drives these two countries together, whether they want to deepen economic integration or not, and it also encourages *the establishment of parallel international institutions*. And there is another aspect: the economic sanctions against Russia have shown the world how vulnerable it can be when it relies on the financial and economic infrastructure built and managed by the United States after the Second World War. The temptation to create and participate in parallel international institutions is growing, ultimately leading to a breakdown of the world order in terms of trade, investment, technology and financial infrastructure.

All these factors have led to a slowdown and possibly a reversal of globalization. Between 2008 and 2022, this situation created a power vacuum in Central European countries that was not filled by any country.

The war with Ukraine showed that Russia wanted to fill this vacuum but did not have the power to do so, while the United States had the political, economic and military power but did not want to fill this vacuum – at least not until the war in Ukraine. Later we will see if it is capable in the long run to stand by the European Union, which was apparently not prepared for any kind of geopolitical, let alone military, conflict in the region. (Even before 2022, the reluctance to enlarge the EU to include the Balkans showed that the EU was not prepared to act as a political and economic superpower.) Although there are more positive voices on this issue, we do not believe that the EU's assertive response to the war would show Europe's awakening to its superpower potential. Lopez elaborates on this idea and summarizes the possible consequences of this awakening as follows, 'One way this could play out is through Europe more aggressively protecting itself. That could help free up American resources now devoted to European security, which would in turn allow the US to embark on a long-promised refocus on Asia to help counter China' (Lopez, 2022, 15 March). Another possible consequence of the war is that the militarily threatened and economically weakened EU – as an unintended consequence of sanctions against Russia – will be more likely to pursue a foreign policy that serves US interests in the region and globally. Indeed, one of the consequences of the war could be a Europe that is more hostile to China.

Ironically, what China wants from the region is trade – the flow of investment and technology in both directions. China has neither the need, nor the will, nor the power (political or military) to act as a major power in the Central European region. Rather, what China needs is to open up new markets and internationalize its economy.

3.1. From 'open door policies' to 'dual circulation'

Before discussing the 'open door policy' of the 1970s and 1980s, it should be noted that opening up to the world has always been seen as a must by Chinese reformers, while also being associated with bad experiences. The so-called treaty port industrialization of China – enclaves of the Chinese economy under foreign rule – was economically successful, but severely limited economic sovereignty and led to a one-sided development that created an asymmetrical dependence of the Chinese economy (Naughton, 2007: 43).[1] The overreaction came in the form of Mao's heavy industry and state-directed industrialization, which finds its precursor in Manchurian industrialization. This second type of industrialization was originally initiated by the Japanese state to exploit China's resources, focusing on heavy industry. The model was adopted by the Kuomingtang government and basically created the foundation on which Mao's Big Push industrialization was based. Treaty port industrialization could not solve the dilemma of modern China's economic development, namely how to accelerate technological development without creating asymmetric dependence and increasing reliance on Western technologies and capital investment. The other problem of Mao's Big Push strategy[2] was the unsuccessful modernization of agriculture, which was unable to provide sufficient food for the Chinese population.

The 'Open Door' policy is associated with China's leader Deng Xiaoping, who initiated the opening of the economy in 1978, initially in the form of special economic zones (Kobayashi, Baobo & Sano, 1999). The model successfully combined the positive elements of the two earlier types of industrialization:

- The 'Open Door' policy avoided excessive reliance on external capital and technology, thus reducing the leverage of foreign capital;
- The 'Open Door' policy was able to attract foreign capital without creating a 'dual economy' typical of emerging and developing economies where the newly created modern sector has almost no links to the traditional sector of the economy. The traditional sector provides cheap labour to the modern sectors, but this does not significantly increase domestic incomes and produces for the international market rather than the domestic market. China could avoid this trap, although there are large differences in levels of development within the country.

---

[1] It is worth noting that the imbalance is also characteristic of the Central European region, but the room to manoeuvre is more limited than in the case of China, which can take advantage of the huge market and protect selected Chinese companies from international competition for a while, allowing them to grow until they can successfully enter other markets.
[2] The 'big push' strategy was developed by P. N. Rosenstein-Rodan in the 1940s. According to him, 'there is a minimum level of resources that must be devoted to . . . a development program if it is to have any chance of success. Launching a country into self-sustaining growth is a little like getting an airplane off the ground. There is a critical ground speed which must be passed before the craft can become airborne' (Rosenstein-Rodan, 1961: 57–81). Taiwan and South Korea can be seen as successful implementations of this idea, while African countries failed to achieve significant progress with this approach.

The internationalization of the economy usually occurs in two phases. In the first phase, inward internationalization means that foreign companies increasingly invest in the domestic economy, mainly in the form of greenfield investments. In the case of China, this phase coincided with the 'Open Door Policy'. In the second phase, domestic companies go abroad and engage in international activities. This phase is referred to as 'outward internationalization'. It is clear that the 'go out' strategy initiated by the Chinese government in 1999 fits into the second phase of internationalization of the economy.

In addition to these major concepts, the Chinese government also anchored the Chinese economy in the global economy by creating numerous institutional linkages.[3] When looking at recent initiatives to make the Chinese economy more international,

- the internationalization efforts of the Chinese currency since 2009,
- the launch of the 16+1 cooperation with Central and Eastern European countries (2012),
- the Belt and Road Initiative (2013),
- the establishment of BRIC bank, the New Development Bank in 2015, and
- the setup of the Asian Infrastructure Investment Bank in 2016

can be mentioned as key pillars of this process. The economic reasons for internationalization are problems with the old growth model, the need for

---

[3] (1) China joined the Asia-Pacific Economic Cooperation (APEC) in 1991; (2) The ASEAN-China dialogue began in Kuala Lumpur in 1991; (3) Greater Mekong Subregion Economic Cooperation Program (GMS-ECP) was established in 1992, whose members are China, Vietnam, Laos, Myanmar and Thailand. (4) In 1996, the Shanghai 5 group was established, a security agreement between China, Kazakhstan, Kyrgyzstan, Russia and Tajikistan. The group serves as a predecessor to the Shanghai Cooperation Organization. (5) Since its establishment in 1996, China has participated in the ASEM partnership, which brings together European and Asian countries to discuss political issues and strengthen economic cooperation. (6) China joined the World Trade Organization in 2001. (7) FOCAC, the Forum for China–Africa Cooperation, began with a ministerial meeting in 2000, and since then five ministerial conferences and three summits have been held between China and the fifty-three African member countries. (8) Since 2002, China has also participated in the so-called Asian Cooperation Dialog. The thirty-five members of the dialogue cooperate in twenty areas, including energy, agriculture, biotechnology, tourism, poverty alleviation, IT development, e-education and financial cooperation. (9) Between 2014 and 2018, China signed fourteen strategic partnerships with countries in the Middle East and North Africa. (10) The 'China Plus Central Asia' meeting was first organized in July 2020 between China and Kazakhstan, Turkmenistan, Uzbekistan, Kyrgyzstan and Tajikistan to discuss economic cooperation issues. China became the founder of RCEP, the Regional Comprehensive Economic Partnership, in 2020. RCEP, whose members include Australia, Brunei, Cambodia, China, Indonesia, Japan, South Korea, Laos, Malaysia, Myanmar, New Zealand, the Philippines, Singapore, Thailand and Vietnam, accounts for about 30 per cent of global GDP and 30 per cent of the world's population. (11) China has also diversified its trade relations by signing numerous free trade agreements (FTAs) around the world, and as of 2015, China has greater FTA coverage of global GDP covered by FTAs than the United States (Pe'er, Graham & Bhusari, 2022).

markets and more natural resources, while the specifics of China's going out programmes can be traced to 'the ties between China's foreign aid and exports, resource-backed financing of many investment projects and the low level of attention paid to corporate social responsibility by Chinese companies operating abroad' (Wang, 2016), and to domestic political and economic institutions. In the next sub-chapter, we discuss the elements of recent initiatives and the opportunities or threats they pose to Central European countries.

The last stage in the history of the opening policy seems to be the implementation of the so-called 'dual circulation' strategy, which has become one of the main priorities in the government's fourteenth Five-Year Plan (2021–5). There are two main interpretations of this concept. It is a rebalancing strategy, which is a logical step in the catching-up process of China's economy, involving a shift towards higher value chains and GDP growth based more on services. At this stage of development, the emphasis is on technological development and indigenous innovation. The second explanation, which does not preclude the first, is that this is a response to the American decoupling from the Chinese economy – triggered by Trump's trade war and continued under the Biden administration amid growing great power rivalry between the United States and China. The disruption of global supply chains by the global pandemic and war in Ukraine was just the last straw.

3.2. China policy in the EU and its nuances

After the establishment of diplomatic relations between the People's Republic of China (PRC) and the European Economic Community in 1975, diplomatic and economic relations initially developed rather slowly (the United Kingdom established diplomatic relations with the PRC in 1950, France in 1964, and the four remaining countries in 1974). It took nine years for the first ministerial-level meetings to take place, and thirteen years for the Beijing Delegation of the European Commission to open in 1988. But contractual ties existed between China and the European Economic Communities before 1988, and in 1985 they signed a Trade and Economic Cooperation Agreement. This agreement established a joint commission to oversee the development of all aspects of economic cooperation (Djordjevic, 2016: 52–3).

After the setback caused by the Tiananmen Square protests, a new round of bilateral dialogue was initiated in 1992. It is difficult to track and sort out the relevance of the documents. The agreements were signed by the two partners, but the changing attributes attached to China–EU relations are more revealing: long-term relationship in 1995, comprehensive partnership in 1998, maturing partnership in 2003, strategic and enduring relationship in 2005 and systemic rivalry in 2019. Since 1998, the EU–China summits have laid the foundation for the European Union–China relationship.

The twenty-second EU–China summit was conducted in 2020, but was held by video conference due to the coronavirus (European Council, 2020). After the meeting, president of the European Council Charles Michael said, 'But, at the same time, we have to recognise that we do not share the same values, political systems, or approach to multilateralism. We will engage in a clear-eyed and confident way, robustly defending EU interests and standing firm on our values.'

Emphasis on values, reciprocity and a level playing field based on rules are the recurring slogans of European institutions and politicians. The twenty-third EU–China summit was also held online, and the negative elements predominated in the discussions. The following points were discussed in detail:

- Russia's military aggression against Ukraine and China's role in evading sanctions.
- In the case of the Single Market, China's decisions against MEPs and countries were criticized.
- In addition to the fight against COVID-19 and global warming, European Union concerns about market access for European companies were also mentioned.
- The most contentious issue remains that of human rights and foreign policy. While reaffirming its commitment to the one China principle, the EU also named four individuals and one entity responsible for human rights abuses in the Xinjiang region on 22 March 2021, and criticized Hong Kong's new national security law.
- Cybersecurity is a hotly debated issue in bilateral relations, as the EU claims it has been subjected to repeated cyber-attacks, and has therefore imposed cybersecurity sanctions on two individuals and two entities (European Council, 2022).

Although MEPs called for more unity in foreign policy, the EU does not enjoy uniformity on foreign policy issues. The war in Ukraine demonstrated the importance of speaking with one voice. Duclos and Wright contextualized this problem as follows: 'While France has welcomed the US' outreach to European partners throughout its talks with Russia, it regrets that European divisions and disunity prevent it from being around the negotiating table. Macron knows the EU will only be taken seriously on security and defense if it can speak with one voice and has the means to exercise power' (Duclos & Wright, 2022, 25 January). These sentences were written a few weeks before the outbreak of the Ukraine war, but the claim that only the EU is considered a significant power has held true since then, although EU members often pursue their own very different strategies. What is true of EU–Russia relations is also true of EU–China relations.

It may sound trivial, but an often overlooked aspect is that EU members do not share the same views on issues related to China, and these views often clash with the China approach advocated by the European Commission and the European Parliament. European countries' opinions on China policy differ due to their different stages of development. While the trade relations of Western European countries are much broader than those of Central European countries, Central European countries are asymmetrically dependent on Western Europe. This is the main reason why Central European countries consider China as a potential source of diversification.

Not only the different levels of economic development, but also the different corporate structures in Western and Central Europe mean that decision-makers come up with very different answers.[4] This can be illustrated by a simple example: regional supply chains in Europe are organized by German, French and Italian firms, not by Central European firms. When Chinese firms enter the domestic market through foreign direct investment, Western European firms have more to lose than Central European firms.

To make matters worse, the Single Market and EU-level policies provide a common framework for the policies of individual countries in the European

---

[4] Central European economies were transformed in the early 1990s, and the transformation was based mainly on capital and technology from the West, and to this day these Western European companies dominate these markets. See more on this transformation in Salamon (1995). This also means that Western European companies with significant interests in the Central and Eastern European region would lose out to China's growing economic presence in that region.

Union. Moreover, members of the European Parliament have been eager to publish documents condemning China, while the President of the European Commission and the High Representative for Foreign Affairs and Security Policy have been more restrained in their interviews and discussions.

We should add that in addition to the different levels of economic development, the history of these countries is also very different, leading to different economic structures, including business structures. The Central European economies were transformed in the early 1990s, and the countries relied on Western capital and technology for that transformation. Today, Western European companies continue to dominate these markets, all value-added, and exports from these countries. (See more on transformation in Salamon, 1995.) The concrete implication for relations with China is that Western European companies have an interest in maintaining their dominance in the region. They would definitely lose from the increasing Chinese presence in the economies of the region, while Central European countries could benefit – in terms of jobs, capital and increased competition – from this process.

When it comes to Chinese investment in Western Europe, the fears of Western European countries seem to be more well founded, because here investing Chinese companies can gain access to new technologies, while in Central Europe, where Chinese companies mostly operate with greenfield investments, this is not a realistic threat. When Chinese companies enter the Single Market, the common legal framework applies to these companies, while the interests of these countries are different. Common rules, different interests: this is an explosive combination. It is not easier to align Chinese policies when non-EU European countries are involved, because EU member states that have access to EU transfers (i.e. grants) have more leeway in choosing appropriate financing instruments, while non-EU members are more restricted in their choice, and for this reason need more Chinese loans than EU members. In summary, we can distinguish four elements that make a united front against China difficult:

1. The EU still does not have a jointly exercised foreign policy.
2. There are differences between the EU institutions in their attitude towards China – compare the European Commission and the European Parliament!
3. Western and Central European countries have different needs in terms of economic cooperation with China.

4. Multinational companies with headquarters in Western Europe are not interested in Chinese companies entering the markets of Central European countries.

3.3. China policy in Central Europe

3.3.1. The Belt and Road Initiative and the 16 + 1 cooperation

In addition to traditional diplomatic relations, there are two Chinese initiatives that are worth analysing if we want to understand Sino–European relations: the Belt and Road Initiative and 16+1 cooperation. The Belt and Road Initiative (BRI) is an economic development strategy, or the last piece of globalization strategy adopted by the Chinese government in 2013. It is difficult to give concrete contours to the BRI because it partly reflects the Chinese approach, which ranges from overarching structures (principles) to small details. The Western approach is just the opposite – take the example of European integration. The European integration project started with an agreement in the coal and steel sector (1951) between the six founding countries, which was extended to other areas of cooperation after the first clear successes, while the BRI started with a comprehensive approach, in which the details, and smaller projects, will make themselves evident later. Many arguments can be found in the literature as to why the BRI was launched by the Chinese. They can be divided into two groups: geopolitical and economic arguments.

A few of the geopolitical arguments can be found in this list:

- The BRI was initiated *because the new isolationism of the United States offered an opportunity to the Chinese.* Trump's policy of focusing on core US interests did not make the US commitment to global leadership credible. As Silverstein puts it, 'The United States, meanwhile, is withdrawing from the Paris climate agreement, allowing China the room to play a more integral role' (Silverstein, 2019).
- The *BRI is the answer to an aggressive American foreign policy*, the 'Pivot to Asia', or AUKUS. Asif et al. emphasize that the BRI is driven by external goals: 'First and foremost it intends to guard state security (China). China plans to form a web of commercial interdependence that will tie her regional control which will allow her to fence in opposition to United

States' coalition building in the region and will support its neighbors if they give favor in return' (Asif, Adnan & Ullah, 2019: 245).
- The BRI will not succeed if the Chinese do not solve the problems in their 'backyard'. Mobley emphasizes that the *BRI is strategically important to solving China's dilemma in the Strait of Malacca*, which makes the country's trade dependent on American influence. He says, 'China's increased presence and influence in the region, access to and creation of new ports, and strategic moves to overcome its Malacca Dilemma are all important steps toward achievement of this objective' (Mobley, 2019: 66).
- Another argument states that the *Chinese want to divide the European Union* and this is the reason for the 16+1 cooperation and the BRI. Among many other researchers, Chirathivat and Langhammer point out, 'China pursues divide and rule practices (in the following called DRP) by marketing its Belt and Road Initiative (BRI) in East and Southeast Europe while Northern and Western European countries have refrained from formally joining this initiative (called 17 plus 1)' (Chirathivat & Langhammer, 2020).

And a few economic arguments are as follows:

- China wants to find *new markets for its products*. Chinese industrial overcapacity is often cited as the main reason for the BRI (Council of Foreign Relations, 2021: 3).
- The *abundance of capital* in China originally boosted BRI projects, but two years and more into the COVID era, Chinese foreign lending seems to be drying up, Wilson says. He quotes Yunnan Chen, an expert at ODI, a London-based think tank, who said, 'Addressing the pandemic and economic slowdown at home means the abundance of capital that fueled the BRI isn't there anymore' (Wilson, 2022).
- *Lack of access to raw materials and energy resources* also motivates Chinese decision-makers. This argument can be easily applied to BRI projects in resource-rich African countries and the Middle East. Richardson argues that unlike the United States, China cannot be independent of oil and gas and therefore must continue to make investments to secure energy and raw materials for China (Richardson, 2020).
- Chinese loans for the projects also *strengthen the role of Chinese currency in financial transactions*. It is also often argued that there are malicious

Chinese intentions behind easy lending and that China is burdening poor countries with unsustainable debt (debt traps). Apart from the fact that it is difficult to prove malicious intentions behind overseas lending, we should emphasize that lending is a risky business not only for the lender but also for the borrower. As Liao puts it, 'What is distinct about the BRI is that it is a state-led lending initiative aimed at exporting not only China's excess capacity and capital, but also the Chinese economic growth model centered on infrastructure investment. However, expanding this model internationally entails a high degree of financial risk, particularly in the Global South where many countries have a record of debt defaults' (Liao, 2021).

- The Eurozone crisis also exposed *the financial vacuum in the Central and Eastern European region*, a time when it became clear that Central European countries could also turn to China for external financing. Brattberg argues that China took advantage of the situation of the crisis-ridden countries. He writes, 'In the European countries hardest hit by the euro crisis, China struck advantageous deals with cash-strapped governments that needed to privatize national assets, including critical infrastructure' (Brattberg & Soula, 2018). The question is, rather, where Germany, the Netherlands, Austria and the northern countries were when the PIGS countries – an acronym for Portugal, Italy, Greece and Spain, which were affected by the euro crisis – needed fresh money and, more importantly, demand from these countries after the eurozone crisis.

When it comes to a general evaluation of the BRI, it would be difficult to draw conclusions from its achievements, as they are sporadic and unclear. Schulhof et al. provide us with a thorough literature review of the BRI. They emphasize that the BRI promises investments of more than US$ 8,000 billion, affecting half the world's population and one-third of global GDP (Shulhof et al., 2022: 1). At the same time, they outline four scenarios for the future of BRI. The scenarios are (1) the Asian BRI, (2) the Irrelevant BRI, (3) the Living Vibrant BRI, and (4) the International BRI.

1. At the end of the paper, they conclude that the Asian BRI seems to be the most plausible scenario. In this version, they point out that the global trend of reshoring manufacturing capacities, the resurgence of nation states, and de-globalization tendencies are causing China to focus

on Asia and reduce investments in other parts of the world, including Central Europe – not only because these investments are less relevant to China, but also because they appear to be riskier because of the geopolitical risks involved (Shulhof et al., 2022: 6–7).
2. *Irrelevant BRI* is basically the same concept, but it assumes multilateral frameworks rather than the revival of nation states. Therefore, BRI will be less relevant among the many multilateral frameworks that may also have better institutional embedding and a longer history (Shulhof et al., 2022: 7).
3. *The Vibrant BRI* concept assumes that the global economy will recover quickly from the COVID-19 pandemic and that China's leadership will be critical in this process. This version is the most optimistic, but also the least likely in light of the Ukraine war (Shulhof et al., 2022: 7–8).
4. At the same time, *the International BRI* future scenario similarly assumes a rapid economic recovery, but without China's leadership. In this version of the future, globalization trends prevail and gain new momentum (Shulhof et al., 2022: 8–9).

If we were forced to choose from the above scenarios, our choice would be the Asian BRI scenario. Of course, when Schulhof et al. wrote this article, they could not have foreseen the war in Ukraine, but the war strengthens the opportunity of the Asian BRI concept because (a) while the West and Russia are fighting a proxy war in Ukraine, there is no longer a chance for BRI in Europe, (b) at the same time, Asian countries can benefit from BRI, and the newly launched RCEP (Regional Comprehensive Economic Partnership) and (c) the recent (de facto) enlargement of the Shanghai Cooperation Organization with Iran and Türkiye striving to increase membership strengthens the likelihood of the Asian BRI scenario dominating.

Richardson presents a less complex but compelling future scenario for the BRI. He contends that the full success of the BRI would mean that China can pull Africa, the Asia-Pacific region and the former Soviet Union into its geopolitical and economic zone (scenario 1). In this scenario, the China-led zone would account for 68 per cent of global demand. In scenario 2, the United States is more successful and it 'attracts into its zone Europe, South and central America and North America, richer countries in Africa and developed economies in Asia-Pacific such as India, South Korea, Japan and Taiwan. This would leave the US with 1.61bn of global consumption, a 51% share of the global total' (Richardson, 2020).

Neither Schulhof's Asian BRI concept nor Richardson's world with two completely different trade- and geopolitical zones is attractive to Central Europe. This is bad news for Central European countries and the special cooperation framework, the 16+1 cooperation.

The other institutional framework, the 16+1 cooperation, is also showing signs of fatigue on both sides. The cooperation was launched on 26 April 2012, as a cross-regional cooperation platform with the keywords: win-win situation and traditional friendship between the participants. The cooperation was formulated negatively in certain aspects:

- From the beginning, cooperation was accused of being used as a Trojan horse by the Chinese. The famous quote by Halford Mackinder has often been cited in this context to illustrate the importance of this region for world politics: 'Who rules East Europe commands the Heartland; who rules the Heartland commands the World-Island; who rules the World-Island commands the world', Mackinder wrote at the beginning of the twentieth century (Mackinder, 1919: 150). In today's world, it is no longer enough to focus only on geography, because there are other, equally important aspects. Of course, technology is the most important, as it can override the importance of time and distance, though not entirely, of course.
- A fairer argument for criticizing the collaboration is that it was never clear to external observers whether it was just a platform for jointly launched projects or the beginning of a more institutionalized collaboration. The fact that the cooperation established secretariats caused some headaches in Western Europe, while the secretariats served only as channels of communication and coordination.
- Because of the confusion about the form, the contents were also not clear, or at least they were not clearly communicated. This is because economic cooperation projects are managed on a bilateral basis, not at the 16+1 level.

The honeymoon between the CEE countries and China lasted until about 2019, when the problems of 16+1 cooperation became increasingly clear. Regional cooperation began in 2011, when the Chinese prime minister attended an economic conference between China and CEE in Budapest. At the end of the conference, Wen put forward his five-point proposal, which called for greater cooperation in areas such as (1) trade, (2) investment, (3) infrastructure building, (4) financial cooperation and (5) people-to-people and cultural exchanges (Turcsanyi, 2016: 15.16).

These five pillars later served as the main points of the 16+1 cooperation. Ironically, six years earlier, in 2005, the then Chinese prime minister had made a similar five-point proposal to the EU, but it was never properly responded to. In 2011, the 16+1 format was formally announced. The main platform for cooperation is the annual summits, which are held regularly, with the exception of 2022. In 2012 Warsaw hosted the summit, in 2013 Bucharest, in 2014 Belgrade, in 2015 Suzhou, in 2016 Riga, in 2017 Budapest, in 2018 Sofia and in 2019 Dubrovnik. The 2020 summit was postponed, then never held due to the pandemic situation, and even the 2021 summit was held online.

Zuokui claims that cooperation between China and CEE has gone through four phases since the first summit in Warsaw:

1. In the first phase, the focus was on regional cooperation as partners rediscovered each other. During the eurozone crisis, Central European countries looked to the East, which was perceived as an opportunity by Chinese decision-makers.
2. In the second phase, the focus shifted to connectivity between China and Europe, as suggested by Chinese proposals at the 2013 Bucharest summit.
3. The third phase was about building the Belt and Road Initiative in Europe. The Belgrade summit proposals reflect this new approach.
4. The fourth phase focused on synergies between the development strategy of China and those of European countries (Zuokui, 2016: 4–5).

Zuokui made this classification in 2016. Since then, the cooperation has faced several challenges. (1) China was often reproached by Western politicians and observers who claimed that China was trying to divide the European Union. (2) Central European countries are different from each other, so the 'one-size-fits-all' approach probably does not work in the region. (3) This is also the reason why China is waiting in vain for an integrated response from the region. China would need it, because that is the main reason why the platform was created. Central European countries are too small and too numerous to negotiate effectively with each other bilaterally.

In addition to Zukoui's classification, we can add at least two new phases:

5. In the fifth phase, the problems of 'one-size-fits-all' planning became more apparent, exacerbated by the increasing American influence on the foreign policy decisions of certain Central European countries.
6. The COVID-19 pandemic and the war in Ukraine necessitated a recalibration and reassessment of cooperation, in which the chances of continuing the previous China strategies decreased significantly.

3.3.2. The yuan's digitalization

When we talk about China's economic influence in the Central European region, we usually focus on trade, investment and technology. However, the global power shift is also leading to an overhaul of the global financial infrastructure, a process that seems to have been accelerated by the war in Ukraine. The war in Ukraine has focused countries' attention on the potentially devastating effects of US economic sanctions against each country. This deliberate display of US power may discipline reluctant countries in the short term, but it also prompts them to seek alternative solutions in the long term. And that's where China comes in, with its own financial solutions and, of course, its digitized currency, which could help escape the US- and dollar-dominated financial world.

The consequences of the internationalization of the yuan have already been discussed in Chapter 1 (5.2), where the importance of a more internally used yuan was analysed. Now we focus on the digitization of the currency. In 2020, the PBoC published what it called the Draft Banking Law, giving legal status to its digital currency. According to Article 19 of the law, the RMB includes both physical and digital forms, and the law also prohibits the production or sale of digital yuan (Article 22).

To clean up the market, Chinese authorities imposed a ban on all crypto transactions and mining in 2021. This measure hit Bitcoin and other major coins and put pressure on crypto and blockchain stocks (John, Shen & Wilson, 2021). This was not the first measure to control and restrict this market. In 2013 and 2017, there were similar legal actions, but due to the complexity of cryptocurrencies, it was not easy for the government to find and close every potential loophole in the market. China has made headlines with this action, but China is not alone: Egypt, Iraq, Qatar, Oman, Morocco, Algeria, Tunisia and Bangladesh have also explicitly banned cryptocurrencies. According to Quiroz-Gutierrez, forty-two countries have tacitly banned digital currencies (Quiroz-Gutierrez, 2022).

The ban, aimed at facilitating the adoption of the digital yuan, has been misinterpreted by several analysts and policymakers. The best example is Republican US Senator Pat Toomey's tweet, 'Beijing is so hostile to economic freedom they cannot even tolerate their people participating in what is arguably the most exciting innovation in finance in decades' (Toomey quoted by John, Shen & Wilson, 2021). Economic freedom is not synonymous with deregulation, the absence of rules. In other economic models, government intervention and regulation play a greater role than in the American version of neoliberal economic governance.

There are other voices as well. Quiroz-Gutierrez emphasizes: 'Although not all governments are moving to ban crypto, many are looking into how to regulate digital currency, including Gary Gensler, the U.S. chairman of the Securities and Exchange Commission, who has called crypto "the Wild West" and said he wants to impose more regulation on digital currencies. Gensler hired a senior adviser specializing in cryptocurrency last week' (Quiroz-Gutierrez, 2022). What we need to understand is that behind these differences there are also different views on how the economy should be developed.

The PBoC has also defined its goals with the issuance of the digital yuan:

- Diversify forms of cash,
- Support fair competition, efficiency, and security in retail payments,
- Improve cross-border payments.

Obviously, the third objective is more important for the Central European countries. It is at this point that the PBoC paper starts cautiously: 'Therefore, though technically ready for cross-border use, e-CNY is still designed mainly for domestic retail payments at present. Looking ahead, the PBoC will actively respond to initiatives of G20 and other international organizations on improving cross-border payments and explore the applicability of CBDC in cross-border scenarios' (PBoC, 2021).

The European countries of the 16+1 cooperation are in a very different position as far as the currencies they use are concerned. Indeed, while several countries (Slovenia, Slovakia and the Baltic countries) have already joined the eurozone, others do not seem to have the intention to join (Poland, Hungary and the Czech Republic), and several countries use currency board solutions, that is, they peg their currencies to the euro (Bulgaria). In addition, there are several countries in the 16+1 formation that are not EU members. The different groups of countries could be affected to varying degrees by the internationalization of the digital yuan. As mentioned earlier, there are three main channels through which the weakening of the dollar's international position could be felt: central bank reserves, foreign exchange and international trade transactions.

We expect the impact to be felt primarily through international trade transactions. However, further liberalization of Chinese yuan transactions could increase the attractiveness of the Chinese yuan as a foreign exchange reserve. This is not yet the case; the process is slow, while China's progress in international trade appears to be much faster. In 2002, 80 per cent of countries traded more with the United States than with China, but this pattern has changed: 70 per cent now trade more with China than with the United States. Of the sixteen countries, only the Baltic nations still trade more with the United States than with China (National Bank of Canada, 2021). This means that a successful internationalization of the digital yuan could have a significant impact on them.

3.4. Disillusionment over China

The path that led to disillusionment with China most likely began with political scandals that drew the attention of the Central European public to political issues related to China. However, as we have already seen, political scandals were easily triggered when cooperation with China–CEE did not bring significant economic success in certain countries and did not provide these countries with real diversification opportunities in terms of trade, investment and technology. Certain countries (Slovenia and Hungary) were more successful, so political scandals did not take place there the way that they did in other, less successful countries such as Czechia, the Baltic countries and Poland.

The visit to Taiwan by Milos Vystrcil, the president of the Czech Senate, which lasted from 30 August to 5 September 2020, greatly angered Beijing. One interpretation is that the visit was staged as a 'boyish provocation', as Czech president Milos Zeman characterized it (Zeman was quoted by Xinhuanet, 2020). The Chinese response was short and clear: 'The Chinese government and Chinese people won't take a laissez-faire attitude or sit idly by, and will make him (Vystrcil) pay a heavy price for his short-sighted behaviour and political opportunism,' said Chinese Foreign Minister Wang Yi (Blanchard & Tian, 2020, 31 August).

The other interpretation is that the visit of eighty-nine Czech politicians was 'historic' (Schultz, 2020: 12). The incident was preceded by the scandal that Prague terminated its partnership agreement with Beijing when the mayor of Prague did not accept the 'one-China' clause of the agreement in October 2019. Instead of Beijing, Prague entered into an agreement with Taipei.

The scandals also reflect how divided local elites are over China policy and foreign policy in general. It is sad, but Central European countries often do not have long-term foreign policy strategies, or even if they have developed one, China policy often becomes a victim of domestic politics. We could observe similar stories of over-politicization, such as the case of Fudan College, which wants to open a branch campus in Budapest, or the Budapest–Belgrade railroad plan, which was attacked by local elites regardless of economic necessity.

At the same time, the expectations of local elites regarding the volume of FDI from China have not been met. As we could see in Table 3.1 (Chapter 1), only Slovenia and Hungary can boast significant Chinese FDI, but even in these cases the amounts fall short of initial expectations.[5] Why? We need to

---

[5] A recent example is the investment of the Chinese CATL (Contemporary Amperex Technology Co.), one of the largest battery producers in the world, which has decided to invest in Eastern Hungary. According to the company's plans, a battery factory worth 7.3 billion euros is to be built in Hungary, the largest in Europe to date. After obtaining the necessary permits, the construction of the 100 GWh plant is expected to take no longer than sixty-four months. Once built, the factory will be able to supply batteries to Mercedes, BMW and Volkswagen (Reuters, 2022a 12 August). Mercedes has already confirmed the collaboration between the two companies, saying, 'With CATL we have a technology-leader as our partner to provide us – as the first and biggest customer of the new plant's initial capacity – with top-notch CO2 neutral battery cells for our next generation EVs in Europe,' a management board member said (Reuters, 2022b, 12 August). The investment was interpreted very differently in China, Hungary and the West. While the majority of the Hungarian press was positive about the investment, an article in Portfolió criticized the Hungarian government's support (Komócsin, 2022, 18 August). The article claimed that the investment was a mistake by the government because there are plans in Europe to get rid of 'Chinese raw materials and products'. The article is not only biased, but also insufficiently informed. China has never been a major importer of raw materials into the EU. The article's second argument is also flawed, as the author claims that the investment will not result in technology transfer from China. Obviously, neither Suzuki nor Mercedes nor Audi is spreading its technology, because it is precisely this technology that forms the

Table 3.1 Chinese Direct Investment in the EU and the United Kingdom 2000–21 (billion euros)

United Kingdom	79.6	Poland	2.4
Germany	30.1	Malta	1.5
Italy	16.0	Romania	1.4
France	15.7	Czechia	1.3
Netherlands	13.5	Slovenia	1.3
Finland	13.0	Austria	1.2
Sweden	8.3	Denmark	1.2
Ireland	8.0	Croatia	0.3
Portugal	6.8	Bulgaria	0.3
Spain	5.5	Cyprus	0.3
Greece	4.5	Slovakia	0.3
Hungary	2.9	Estonia	0.3
Belgium	2.7	Latvia	0.1
Luxembourg	2.5	Lithuania	0.1

Source: Kratz et al. (2022: 7)

clarify that the motivation for Chinese investment only partially coincides with the conditions that Central European countries can offer. If we use Dunning's classic framework to understand the motivation of Chinese direct investment, we need to look at four factors. Dunning divides the motivation for foreign direct investment into four categories (Dunning, 2000: 163–90):

basis of its competitive advantage over other market players. But there are spillover effects in any case, and the 9,000 jobs will also be an important contribution of the CATL investment.

The Chinese Global Times argues in its editorial that the investment decision was not the result of excellent political relations between the two countries, but the result of a simple business decision: 'Why did Hungary attract investment from CATL? Anyone with discerning eyes can tell that this is a perfectly normal business decision. The geographical location in the heart of Europe, with a good industrial support base, allows Chinese companies in Hungary to be closer to their European customers and be able to respond to their needs in a timely manner. More critically, Hungary offers Chinese companies predictability in terms of policy and business environment. Hungary, the first country in Europe to sign Memorandum of Understanding with China on jointly building the "Belt and Road" Initiative, has offered Chinese companies a lot of preferential policies for their investments' (Global Times, 2022, 15 August). The argument can be supported by the fact that SK Innovation, a Korean auto parts manufacturer, also chose Hungary last year as the location for its European electric battery plant. Moreover, Hungary seems to be the preferred location for Asian investors in this sector. Currently, Asian companies in the electric battery sector have invested nearly 7 billion euros in seventeen locations. On the other hand, the sector seems to be of strategic interest for the Hungarian economy in the long term. At the inauguration of the Korean investment, the Hungarian foreign minister said, 'Whoever wins the electric car investments will win the future, and can lay the foundations for future economic growth' (Szijjártó quoted by Hungary Today, 2022, 17 June). The interpretation of the Hungarian government is obviously positive, seeing the link between the investment and the policy of opening to the East. State Secretary Levente Magyar said, 'The Chinese investment is in the field of electric vehicle manufacturing. This also confirms that the government made the right decision when it announced its strategy of opening up to China and identified the electric vehicle industry as one of the main axes of Hungarian economic development' (Magyar quoted by Deme, 2022, 22 August).

1. Resource-seeking direct investments;
2. Market-seeking direct investments;
3. Efficiency-seeking direct investments;
4. Strategic asset-seeking direct investments.

1. Central European countries are poor when it comes to *natural resources*. Poland is perhaps the only country where raw materials (copper) play an important role in the export structure. Slovakia, Slovenia and the Baltic countries export wood and wood products to China in a rather insignificant volume. Hungary is the least resource-rich country in the region and offers no natural resources to China. The only resource these countries can practically offer is relatively cheap labour, which is no less abundant in China than in these countries, meaning that the two regions compete rather than complement each other.

2. The *markets* of the countries are small – only Poland can offer a larger market – but even in this case we should add that the main attraction for China is the Single Market with about 448 million customers. In other words, it is highly unlikely that Chinese companies would target any Central European country, but the entire Single Market.

3. *Efficiency-seeking investments* are typical when the division of labour between subsidiaries can contribute to better and more efficient production at the group level. Exploiting local advantages and combining local strengths or compensating for weaknesses is one reason why multinational companies invest in other countries. Usually, this investment phase prevails when previous investments (market- and resource-oriented investments) can be reorganized, and in this way higher efficiency can be achieved. We have argued earlier that neither resource-oriented nor market-oriented investments are prevalent in China–CEE relations, so efficiency-oriented investments are not typical either.

4. Among strategic assets, technology, brands and land are worth mentioning. Regarding technology and brands, Western and Scandinavian countries are more attractive to Chinese companies than Central Europe. Although Italy does not score well in innovation, its classic luxury brands are very attractive to Chinese companies, something Central Europe can rarely offer China. Investments aimed at acquiring strategic locations (land, ports, etc.) are typical of Chinese investments in the world, but they are also not typical of the Central European region.

Table 3.2 Chinese FDI in the EU and the United Kingdom between 2000 and 2021 (as of GDP, %)

Malta	10.32	Germany	0.84
Finland	5.14	France	0.63
Luxembourg	3.41	Romania	0.58
Portugal	3.22	Czechia	0.54
UK	3.15	Belgium	0.53
Slovenia	2.50	Croatia	0.52
Greece	2.46	Spain	0.46
Ireland	1.90	Bulgaria	0.44
Hungary	1.88	Poland	0.42
The Netherlands	1.57	Denmark	0.36
Sweden	1.56	Slovakia	0.31
Cyprus	1.28	Latvia	0.30
Estonia	0.98	Austria	0.30
Italy	0.90	Lithuania	0.18

Source: Own Compilation Based on World Bank Database and Kratz et al. Data

Looking at these four motivations, we can understand why the main targets of Chinese direct investment in Europe are not Central European countries, but Western Europe. Only Hungary performs better than its stage of development and location in Central Europe would suggest. However, the first three major Western European countries (the United Kingdom, Germany and Italy) account for 39 per cent of Chinese direct investment in the region. The figures show that the main destinations of Chinese direct investment are large, mature economies, and smaller Western European economies also do well, such as the Netherlands and Finland. Both alone have attracted more Chinese direct investment than the entire Central and Eastern European region (Table 3.2).

Looking at Chinese direct investment in terms of GDP, it is still not clear why Chinese companies invest relatively more in one EU member state and less in another. The only thing that is clear is that Chinese companies do not invest relatively more in Central Europe – if one wants to divide the European Union in this way. Since about 2017, several articles have been published with the message that China wants to divide Europe through investment. Research papers and articles with titles such as 'China's Offensive in Europe. Is There a Master Plan in Beijing?' (Wall Street Journal, 2016), or 'China as a Dividing Force in Europe' (2019, Evert), or 'A Divided Europe's China Challenge' (Corre, 2019) were not uncommon; however, they contained only conjecture, and assertions that were not supported by facts and figures.

4

Russia

Behind the new Iron Curtain?

Unlike the United States and China, there are two great powers that have determined the economic and political development of Central Europe for centuries and whose presence and influence in the region are not the result of the history of the 20th and 21st centuries. These two countries are Russia and Germany. Their geographical proximity ensures that these countries cannot "pay no attention" to the region, while China can easily abandon Central Europe if its interests so dictate, and the United States' main interest in exerting political and economic influence in the region is primarily related to its never-ending competition with Russia. This chapter looks at the evolution of Russian foreign policy from 1991 to the present. Germany is covered in the chapter with a focus on the European Union, as it is difficult to make a distinction between what is and is not in Germany's interest in the name of the European Union.

4.1. From the collapse to a more assertive foreign policy: Russia's foreign policy

Mandelbaum argues that Russian foreign policy is dramatically different from Soviet foreign policy because Russia is also very different from its predecessor state, the Soviet Union. He argues that not only were the borders of the Soviet Union drawn differently, but Russia also differed from the Soviet Union in its lack of ideological fervor. After the collapse of the Soviet empire, it was uncertain what foreign policy Russia could pursue. In

1998, Mandelbaum sketched two scenarios for how Russian foreign policy might develop in the future, based on historical parallels with the collapse of other empires. He noted that the collapse of the Ottoman Empire and its subsequent development is the closest parallel to the Russian experience that we can use and predicted the next two possible scenarios in this regard (Mandelbaum, 1998):

- The final borders of modern Turkey were established in a bloody war with Greece in 1921-1922, which included ethnic cleansing. He argued that Russian elites were not satisfied with the sovereign independence of regions that had been Russian/Soviet provinces in the past. Adding to this unabated dissatisfaction is the fact that large groups of ethnic Russians now live in other countries without having chosen this situation. Mandelbaum's sober and sad conclusion was that the worst part of the collapse of the Soviet Union was yet to come. The idea that Russia is pursuing a revisionist foreign policy is not new. This idea has been voiced since 2014, with Moscow's annexation of Crimea. (See Krastev [2014], Stent [2022: 1], or the National Defense Strategy of the United States of America [2018:2]!) The war in Ukraine obviously only fuels fears of a revisionist Russian foreign policy.
- In the context of the collapse of the Ottoman Empire, Mandelbaum argued that Turkey was able to launch a partially successful state modernization project. This future scenario envisions a Russian state that is successful in political and economic reforms and is content with the fact that world politics can proceed without inviting Russia to the table where key decisions are made. Andrei Gromiko, the former Soviet foreign minister, said that no international dispute can be settled 'without the Soviet Union or in opposition to it'. (Gromiko, quoted in Bialer, 1980: 327) It is quite clear that Russia has achieved only partial success in modernizing its political system and its economy has been in relative decline from 1991 to the present, although its nuclear arsenal, control of significant energy resources and raw materials, and successful military campaigns (Syria, Crimea, Georgia) still make Russia a significant power in world politics, less so in the world economy. And one thing is clear: Russia is not satisfied with the possibility that major political decisions could be made without Russia's involvement.

Obviously, then, the first scenario is the one that seems closest to reality at present. The annexation of Crimea and the invasion of Ukraine have shown that Russian foreign policy leaders have never been satisfied with the geopolitical landscape that took shape after 1991. In this part, we briefly show how Russia's cooperative foreign policy morphed relatively soon after the political and economic turnaround of the early 1990s into a policy that can be interpreted as revisionist (see above) or as an attempt to transform the unipolar world order into a multipolar world in which not only the United States but at least Russia, China, and India are at the table when decisions are made.

Most analysts believe that Russian foreign policy after 1991 can be divided into two phases. The first phase is characterized by Yeltsin's foreign policy, which was more pro-Western and aware of the democratic deficits of the Russian political system, while the second phase is the Putin era, which is anti-Western and confrontational. Gorenburg takes up this simplification again, arguing, 'The main driver of Russian foreign policy both under Yeltsin and under Putin has been the effort to restore respect for Russia as a major power in world affairs. From the Russian point of view, this respect was lost as a result of Russia's political and economic weakness after the collapse of the Soviet Union.' (Gorenburg, 2019) He also mentions the disregard of Russia's opposition to the constant expansions of NATO and military interventions in Kosovo and Bosnia. The fact that relations were not free of tensions even in their best days is easily demonstrated. When Russia was still trying to integrate into existing Western institutions in the 1990s, the supposedly pro-Western Yeltsin also scolded Clinton when the U.S. failed to show Russia respect. When he visited China, Yeltsin told the press, 'Yesterday, Clinton permitted himself to put pressure on Russia, . . . It seems he has for a minute, for a second, for half a minute, forgotten that Russia has a full arsenal of nuclear weapons. He has forgotten about that.' (Yeltsin quoted from Laris, 1999: 35) Whether or not we are satisfied with the term 'revisionist', we can say that Russia has always wanted to change the balance of power, and Central Europe became part of this game when the region also became part of NATO.

The foundation for EU–Russia relations was laid in 1990 with the Partnership and Cooperation Agreement, which was ratified in 1997. At the time, it was considered self-evident that after the collapse of the socialist bloc, the new world would be built on the values and norms of the Western European region that had been developed and refined from the 1950s to the 1990s. It is easy to recall the zeitgeist of this period when thinking of the famous phrase 'The End of History' by F. Fukuyama, who wrote about 'the total exhaustion of viable alternatives to Western liberalism'. (Fukuyama, 1989: 3). Although many countries of the old Eastern Europe were admitted to the European Union, Russia's membership was never really sought by either side. At the same time, a deep and well-functioning partnership was adopted by the partners. Until 2014, the two sides were involved in so-called high-level political dialog, with two summits held annually.

Lukyanov claims that the attempt to transform Europe into a politically consolidated subject while projecting a normative framework is based on the assumption that the EU is superior to its neighbors. (Lukyanov: 2021) The attempt to achieve an institutional partnership in the 1990s provided an opportunity for pro-Western idealists and pragmatists to transform Russia's relations with the West. At the same time, they failed to convince people of the benefits of giving up certain elements of sovereignty in favor of the European model. This raises another question: how would the EU and its richer member states have reacted if Russia had pursued a different foreign policy and had been willing to integrate more fully into the EU, adopt its rules, and join its institutions? The question is not hypothetical, as Russian EU membership would have opened large markets for Western European companies. However, the cost of Russia's inclusion in the EU's agricultural and cohesion policies would have been enormous or unmanageable (i.e. financially impossible) unless the existing EU rules and the logic of allocating EU transfers are not substantially changed, resulting in a different European Union.

The cause of the pro-Westerners seemed lost as Anti-Westerners gained the upper hand in Russian foreign policy since the early 2010s. McFaul characterizes the four main political schools or currents of Russian political philosophy as follows:

1. *The pro-Western idealists* who mainly contributed to the collapse of the Soviet Union believed in the market economy, democracy and self-determination, and therefore integration with the West seemed inevitable to them and was an integral part of their philosophy. Yeltsin and his government are perhaps the best example of this approach.
2. While representatives of the former group did not benefit financially from integration with the West, a powerful economic interest group

also emerged, the *pro-Western pragmatists*, with a vested interest in maintaining relatively good relations with the West. McFaul illustrates the why with the same examples, 'A billion dollars in transfers from the International Monetary Fund is a billion dollars that Gazprom does not have to pay in taxes. A multi-million dollar World Bank investment in restructuring the Russian coal industry also represents costs avoided by domestic capitalists. Even the smaller investments in institutional reforms provided by such international actors as the Agency for International Development or the European Bank for Reconstruction and Development represent projects that benefit local capitalists paid for by foreign governments.' (McFaul, 1999)

The emergence of the group of pro-Western idealists and pragmatists affected the position of Central European countries only slightly, as they seemed to be moving in the same direction. As we know, Central Europe was successful in integrating with the West, the only direct consequence being that both Russia and these countries competed for Western capital and technology.

One of the main arguments why this group could be influential was that the majority of the population in the 1990s found that good relations with the West were important. However, unilateral actions by the United States such as the NATO bombing campaign in the former Yugoslavia and the second Iraq war alienated Russians from this course after 1999, and as public support behind the pro-Western current in Russian politics disappeared, it became increasingly difficult to maintain influence over Russian foreign policy. Another element that must have aided in the fall of the anti-Western idealist and later pragmatist was Europe's waning economic superiority, combined with the rise of China. (Since early 1980, the EU's share of the world economy has halved. While it was nearly 30 percent in 1980, it shrank to less than 15 percent by 2020).

3. *The anti-Western pragmatists* similar to the first group try to maintain their influence on the values and norms that determine Russian politics and, consequently, foreign policy. The thinking of this group is based more on the old approach of 'realpolitik' in foreign policy, which generally does not believe in win-win situations, but in zero-sum games.

In this world, the constant expansions of NATO could have been perceived as a clear threat to Russian interests. Over the past two decades, this group of thinkers could easily find evidence to support the claim that U.S. influence in the world is weakening and that the unilateral world may soon be replaced by a multipolar world in which Russian influence will grow and Russia will eventually be one of the defining powers of world politics.

To achieve the transformation of the unilateral world, anti-Western idealists believe that three main steps should be taken: (1) strengthening one's own economic and military position, (2) weakening the Western alliance by fomenting divisions, and (3) balancing through greater cooperation with China, Iran, and other countries.

Looking back over the last decade, foreign policy makers in Russia have basically taken a page from this playbook. The main consequence for Central European countries was a growing interest in influencing political and economic trends in the region. One of the main figures was Yevgeny Primakov (foreign minister between 1996 and 1998 and prime minister between 1998 and 1999). He was a clear supporter of multilateralism. The so-called Primakov Doctrine led to increased cooperation with China, India, and Brazil and eventually triggered the formation of the BRIC countries.

The doctrine is based on the idea that a unipolar world organized by the United States cannot be accepted by Russia and that its foreign policy should aim at change and push the world toward multilateralism. This approach is also pragmatic, as it assumes that Russia cannot compete with the U.S. alone, but needs alliances or close cooperation with other actors. And at the end of this global transformation, Russia should reach a position where it has a voice and a veto as an indispensable actor. (Rummer, 2019)

The anti-Western pragmatists are also aware of Russia's weakness on many levels and therefore believe that Russia needs the West's financial support (capital, technology, etc.) to improve its relative position in the global economy and politics. Obviously, short- and long-term strategies are different, and it is a challenge for this group to separate long-term and short-term goals. McFaul concluded in 1999, 'This view of world politics is most prevalent among Russia's foreign policy elite. The chief proponent of this perspective is prime minister Yevgeny Primakov. Moderate members of the Communist Party of the Russian Federation also adhere to these foreign policy goals as do some important nationalist organizations such as Spiritual Heritage. Directors of military enterprises, Ministry of Defense officials, and the Russian intelligence communities also understand foreign policy through this lens.' (McFaul, 1999). This sentence is no longer true, as anti-Western ideologues seem to have taken the lead and are determining current Russian foreign policy.

4. *Anti-Western ideologues* agree with the former group in their 'balance of power' approach, but are not motivated by economic gain; rather, they believe that ethnic, civilizational, and religious aspects must also be part of the calculus. In the 1990s, this current of political thought was attributable to Vladimir Zhirinovsky and his Liberal Democratic Party of Russia and was labeled an extreme political movement, but today anti-NATO, anti-Islamic, or even anti-Semitic tones are no longer uncommon in the mainstream of Russian foreign policy discourse. Although Russian President Putin apologized for the anti-Semitic remarks of Russian Foreign Minister Sergei Lavrov, who said in a May 2022 conversation with an Italian journalist, 'the biggest antisemites are the Jews themselves.' (Lavrov quoted by VOA News, 2022, May 5), the remark indicates the mindset of decision-makers in Russian foreign policy.

Another source of influence came from Alexander Dugin, who stated, 'When there is only one power which decides who is right and who is wrong and who should be punished and who not, we have a form of global dictatorship. This is not acceptable. Therefore, we should fight against it. If someone deprives us of our freedom, we have to react. And we will react. The American Empire should be destroyed. And at one point, it will be . . .' (Dugin, 2012:193) Despite the mass media coverage of Dugin, we cannot take his direct influence on Russian foreign policy for granted. He argues that China poses a threat to Russia, which should seek the support of South Korea, Japan, Vietnam, and India to counterbalance this rising power (Radin & Reach, 2017), while the 'Russian pivot' to Asia can be understood as a pivot to China. Thus, it can be argued that Dugin's view of Russian foreign policy may have been inspirational, but not the only one, as it is often portrayed in the mass media.

Today, Russian foreign policy is basically determined by anti-Western ideologues, whose ideology was implemented with one significant change. In the original version of the ideology, China was often featured as a civilization whose rise threatens Russia, while the current Russian foreign policy is built upon the assumption that the West cannot be defeated without a deep cooperation with China. The next sub-chapter in the light of the Russian and Ukrainian war discusses the question of whether a coalition of Russia and China can emerge and what consequences it might have on the Central European countries.

4.2. Russia and China standing together, and its consequence for Central Europe

On March 7, 2022, the Chinese foreign minister told the international press, 'No matter how perilous the international landscape, we will maintain our strategic focus and promote the development of a comprehensive China-Russia partnership in the new era, . . .' (Wang, quoted by Moitsugu, 2022). On the opening day of the Winter Olympics, the two countries issued a joint statement in which they questioned the wisdom of the unipolar world order that had emerged after economic and political transformation, advocating instead for a multipolar world. The detailed document began by noting that trends pointing to a shift in the global balance of power have intensified in recent years. The Sino-Russian statement also included elements that were new to the two countries' bilateral relations:

- China adopted a position on NATO enlargement the first time, taking a stand against it. It was a crucial element of the joint declaration as Russia – based on the declaration – could be sure that China would not oppose the Russian invasion of Ukraine.
- Also for the first time, Russia made clear that the American Indo-Pacific Strategy and the AUKUS–the security pact of Australia, the United Kingdom and the United States – would negatively impact world peace.
- In the document, Russia reaffirmed its stance on the Taiwan question and its adherence to the 'One-China' principle, and rejected attempts that aim at Taiwan's independence in any form. Some analysts argue that this part of the document is implicit proof that China aims to take back Taiwan with military force. (We cannot know how the question is approached by

Chinese leaders, however, it is sure that the assessment of the impact of Western economic sanctions on Russia will be taken into consideration by the Chinese leadership.)
- The partners confirmed that the nature of Sino-Russian relations is different from the alliances in the Cold War and there are 'no limits' regarding the fields for cooperation between the two countries.

In addition to these main principles of cooperation, the joint statement addressed a shared concern about the continuation of U.S. high-precision satellite programs in the world, as well as problems with international regulation of the Internet that violate national sovereignty, plans to reduce the role of the U.S. dollar in trade, and increase the role of the yuan and ruble in international trade. The partners also agreed on oil and gas deals worth about US$117 billion.

Although the term 'alliance' does not appear in the joint statement, it is clear that the statement encompasses deeper cooperation than a simple affirmation of good bilateral relations. How analysts perceive this cooperation varies widely. According to Scott Kennedy, a China analyst at the Washington Center for Strategic and International Studies, this cooperation, despite the rhetoric, has its limits. He says,: 'China is willing to stand with Russia through thin but not thick, . . . If a war breaks out over Ukraine or Taiwan, we can expect this partnership to fracture.' (Kennedy, 2022, quoted by Munrou, Osborn & Pamuk) According to Yan Xuetong, the dean of the school of international relations at Tsinghua University: 'China believes that its rise to great-power status entitles it to a new role in world affairs – one that cannot be reconciled with unquestioned US dominance.' (Xuetong, 2021: 40) At the same time, Li Daokui, former advisor to the People's Bank of China, the country's central bank, argued that the 'no limits' cooperation was situational and should be taken with a grain of salt (Daokui, quoted by Huang, 2022, March 22).

In February 2022, it was not yet possible to foresee what meaning the phrase 'no limits' might have in the future, but we can say that certain harbingers of major changes were already appearing on the horizon at that time. Not only does the Ukraine war signal global geopolitical changes, but there are other signs pointing in this direction. Recently, several regions in the world have emerged where the U.S. commitment to global leadership has been put to the test:

- One of these regions is Eastern Europe, where the war in Ukraine is challenging U.S. global leadership. The question has arisen, and has not yet been answered, as to how far the United States is willing to go to ensure American superiority in this region. The final frontier that the United States cannot cross is direct military conflict with Russia, but that does not preclude arms deliveries and other assistance to the Ukrainian government. U.S. arguments fall short, however, when aid is portrayed as a struggle between democratic forces and authoritarian or totalitarian forces in the world. As Duss points out, 'The democracy versus autocracy framing also glosses over how the United States continues to treat many autocratic regimes as key partners for stabilizing global energy markets, especially amid efforts to cut off Russian gas.' (Duss, 2022, May 4). Aside from this moral problem, we cannot see how the Russian economy could collapse or the Russian military could be defeated if this type of deterrence policy is pursued.
- In Western Europe, the United States has taken steps to strengthen NATO and show its allies that it has a presence and influence in the region. One of the most obvious signs of these efforts is that the United States is pulling strings in the Middle East and South America to secure energy resources for Western Europe. At the same time, it is hard to reject arguments that sanctions against the Russian economy also serve the interests of U.S. oil and gas companies, which increased their LNG shipments to Europe after the outbreak of war in Ukraine.
- It is also certain that China will not take the Taiwan issue off the table, as challenges to the U.S. could arise in this region as well. China will certainly wait for the final outcome of the war in Ukraine and weigh how the Chinese economy might react to similar sanctions.
- The Chinese foreign minister's visit to India on March 25, 2022, also tests the U.S. commitment to global leadership, as the visit was surprisingly friendly and the international media described India's foreign policy as balancing the two powers. A CNBC article aptly describes the situation, 'Russia and the West are battling to get China and India to take their sides in the Ukraine war' (CNBC, 2022). Not only do Russia and China pose a challenge to the United States, but India and Brazil from the BRIC group could also cause headaches for the United States. Look at the example of India, which is clearly pursuing a balancing strategy between China,

Russia, and the United States. Despite U.S. warnings, India is now clearly benefiting from cheap Russian oil and is unwilling to support the United States sanctions strategy.
- The conflict with Iran and Venezuela has not been resolved, but the United States may be forced to give in on certain issues, as stabilizing the global oil market may be more important to the United States than any action, sanction, or intention to discipline these two countries.
- In 2022, U.S. troops in Iraq and Syria were attacked several times by local military groups without triggering a serious counterattack by the United States, which also calls into question U.S. leadership.

Following the withdrawal from Afghanistan, the United States faces the challenge of having its commitments in every region and every way tested as to how many more casualties and human losses it can accept while maintaining its previous foreign policy course. What are the direct consequences of this new geopolitical situation for the foreign policy strategies of Russia, its competitors, and the indirect consequences for Central Europe:

1. The United States will most likely have to change its 'all fronts strategy'. The term 'all fronts strategy' means that since 1990, the country has been able to conduct foreign policy in the belief that it has sufficient financial and military resources to intervene and act in virtually any conflict in which its interests were affected. That is no longer the case. The question is in what cases and conflicts does the United States need to engage other countries – and do so with a multilateral approach – and what issues are still so important that the country seeks to influence events unilaterally.

   Is the Middle East, China, or Eastern Europe a priority for U.S. foreign policy? The results of the virtual summit between the U.S. and Chinese presidents on March 18, 2022, have been heavily interpreted. The Chinese side highlighted that 'Biden reiterated the commitments he made during his virtual meeting with Xi last November: the U.S. does not seek a new Cold War with China; it does not aim to change China's system; the revitalization of its alliances is not targeted at China; the US does not support 'Taiwan independence'; and it has no intention to seek conflict with China. This, to a certain degree, reflects the strategic sobriety and rationality of the Biden administration." (GT, 2022, March 19). At the same time, the European interpretation has been that the United States has warned China not to provide material support to Russia. By the term 'material support', the U.S. president may have had in mind military equipment and arms shipments. When we look at the actions and measures taken by Beijing, China's foreign policy can best be described as balancing rather than supporting Russia, whereas when we look at the Chinese government's communications and press releases, we might have the impression that China is more supportive of Russia than it is. With this balancing strategy, China is in an advantageous position, but this position can be reversed if Russia is defeated in a war. The term 'defeated' refers to the collapse of the Russian economy, which seemed unlikely until today (June 10, 2022). The indirect consequence for the Central European countries is a stronger American influence in the region, because it seems very unlikely that the United States would abandon the Central European region and make Russia the dominant power. Not only does NATO dictate commitments in this way, but abandoning Central Europe would also mean that the European Union will be more vulnerable than ever, and dangerously close to the sphere of Russian influence.

2. When it comes to China, the country needs a thorough cost-benefit analysis, because the Chinese economy can benefit from the isolation of the Russian economy, but the Russian market is not enough for China; economic relations with the United States and the European Union are much more important. For example, China exports ten times more to the United States than to Russia. China is also much less dependent on Russia for resources than Europe. 16 percent of its imported oil, 15 percent of its coal, and 10 percent of its natural gas comes from Russia. In other words, the main supplier is not Russia. (Downs, 2022, March 16) The only scenario in which China would commit to Russia in the long term would be if China were also subject to Western sanctions and the West tried to make China a pariah of international relations and the world economy.

In our view, the West lacks not only this power but also the political will, given the still very close economic ties between the United States and China. The indirect consequence for Central European countries is that China's economic presence will increase in the long term, while the short- and medium-term consequence will be a realignment of political and economic relations between China and Central European countries. We cannot predict how China will develop its relations with the region and how the Central European countries will respond. However, we can be sure that the new Chinese approach will be more focused and country-specific. The 16+1 formation may not disappear, but it will lose its importance for the region.

3. While we concluded above that Russian foreign strategy is consistent in its opposition to the expansion of NATO and its commitment to building a multilateral global order, the steps of Russian foreign policy are less predictable because Russia may also reach a certain point where it must or can end the war. Either because the Russian economy has suffered enough, the political regime is undergoing internal change, or Russia has achieved its foreign policy goals. In any case, the Central European countries are facing a new world in which Russian influence in the region will be weakened. The region will not be able to return to pre-war conditions.

4.3. Central Europe in the world of emerging economic blocs

In this chapter, we address a future scenario that envisions the rise of economic blocs, one in the West with the United States and the European Union as the main players in this bloc, and another in Eurasia with China and Russia as pillars of this bloc. The chapter focuses on the possible consequences of such a scenario for Central Europe. This hypothesis may seem extreme and overstretched, but it can predict the contours of the future geopolitical landscape. The following factors signal this change:

- A war with no end in sight and permanent economic sanctions against Russia may accelerate the formation of new economic blocs.
- Economic blocs should be interpreted in the broad sense of the word and would include not only trade but also technology and capital transfers.
- Independent (or less dependent) technological and financial ecosystems may be the key features of this new world order.

- The economic sanctions imposed on the Russian financial system may accelerate the development of parallel financial systems in other countries as well.
- American and Western companies leaving the Russian market are accelerating the building of substitutes for Russian brands and companies, a process that has always been part of Chinese economic development policy and is far less typical in Russia. This provides great business opportunities for Chinese companies that can replace Western companies in certain segments and provide Russia with products and services that embody key technologies.
- Russian companies have been integral to European supply chains, but far less so than Central European companies. Chinese companies could take advantage of this situation and benefit from Russia's decoupling from the West, but they are less likely to also transfer technology in the form of foreign direct investment.

In the next points, we briefly look at what would happen if this change were to take place, in the following order: a) trading blocks, b) independent technological ecosystems, c) parallel financial world, and d) supply chains with substitute brands.

4.3.1. Trading blocks

Central European countries are at the top of the list of countries whose economies are relatively open to the world. Usually, we use the export ratio in relation to GDP to illustrate the openness of economies. A look at Table 4.1 shows that all Central European countries are extremely dependent on foreign trade, with the exception of Croatia, whose competitive strength lies in tourism and not so much in manufacturing. Therefore, any restriction that might result from the newly emerging trade blocs would hurt these countries more than other regions.

If these countries had to choose between two trade blocs, let us call them: the Western trade bloc and the Sino-Russian trade bloc, they would naturally choose the former for geographical and political reasons, but it is important to avoid this situation. The share of China and Russia in the trade of Central European countries is small, but the structure of goods is also important. Before the war in Ukraine, we could argue that neither imports nor exports to Russia are important, but these countries depend on Russian energy and other

Table 4.1 Export in terms of GDP (%, 2020)

Countries	Export of GDP	Ranking
Slovakia	88.44	8
Hungary	79.48	10
Slovenia	77.88	11
Lithuania	73.50	15
Estonia	71.68	16
Czechia	70.99	17
Latvia	60.33	23
Poland	56.18	27
Croatia	40.02	49

Source: World Bank database

raw materials. What the European Union wants to achieve with economic sanctions is to minimize dependence on oil and natural gas from Russia. At the same time, it is clear that Central Europe is not a uniform region in this respect, and the difficulty of replacing Russian energy imports varies in these countries.

The political debate leading up to the EU's sixth round of economic sanctions against Russia clearly demonstrated these differences. The European Commission announced its sixth package of economic sanctions against Russia in April 2022, but imposing restrictions proved to be a difficult task and agreement was not reached until May 2022. The reason for this delay is that one-size-fits-all solutions have always had their problems because they cannot truly reflect the different conditions and needs of EU member states. In this case, the originally planned decision only reflected the interests and conditions of countries with access to the sea, which can more easily change their supply routes. The interests of landlocked countries that rely on pipelines were not considered in this proposal. (Transporting oil by truck is not a reasonable or cheap choice for any country, not to mention the environmental damage it would cause.)

The core of the plan was to hit the Russian oil industry by banning oil imports from Russia. Originally, EU countries were to ban oil imports from Russia by the end of this year, and landlocked countries (i.e. Slovakia and Hungary) would have received an additional year. The Hungarian side rejected this proposal and made it clear that not only is the transition period too short for Hungary, but also the adjustment costs are extremely high.[1] The European

---

[1] Hungarian refineries are adapted to process Russian oil, so the refineries will have to be significantly modernized to cope with other types of oil.

Union's next proposal was to extend the oil ban deadline for Russian oil until the end of 2024. This proposal was also rejected because the adjustment would require not only time but also significant financial resources. The immediate ban on Russian oil would mean a price increase of 50-60 percent in Hungary, which would basically lead to galloping inflation and most likely the end of economic growth in Hungary.

The Hungarian foreign minister told the press that the modernization of the energy sector would cost between 15 and 18 billion euros. In response to Hungary's stance on the planned sixth package, the European Commission earmarked 2 billion euros for investment in the energy infrastructure of countries severely affected by the EU ban on Russian oil. Budapest responded with its original proposal, which excludes oil transport by pipeline and applies only to oil transport by ship.

The final agreement on the sixth package did not include the ban on Russian oil through the pipeline and showed how much influence Russia still has on the economic development of these countries, the replacement of Russian oil and natural gas is almost impossible. (There is another reason why it is difficult to achieve change in Russian foreign policy. Sanctions are not an effective policy tool because other countries can also buy Russian oil, and besides, the increase in oil prices can compensate Russia. Energy Intelligence concluded: 'The Russia government take from crude and products export duties and taxes was US$71.8 billion during the first five months of 2022 – or an average of US$14.4 billion per month – compared to US$41.8 billion over the same period last year.' [Energy Intelligence, 2022]).

When it comes to replacing Chinese goods, it seems much easier because Chinese imports into the region are mainly ITC products, which are important products, but disrupting the flow of these products into the region is less of a threat to the region's daily activities.

4.3.2. Technological sovereignty

In relation to Russia, there are fewer projects involving technology transfer from Russia in Central Europe than in relation to China. The Hungarian nuclear power plant modernization project is a good example of technological cooperation with Russia. The case of the Paks Nuclear Power Plant shows why Russia can still be important in this field. Russia's share in this world market was 60 percent before the Ukraine war because Russian nuclear exports are very cheap. (Liu-Pappa, 2022) At the same time, Russian involvement is not dominant. Russia had another project in Finland, which was canceled by Helsinki, and limited cooperation in Czechia, Slovakia, and Bulgaria (Rossatom, 2022).

Chinese technology transfer involves much smaller projects, is broader in scope, and offers greater long-term potential for the development of Central European countries as it relates to advanced communications technology. The nature of Russian and Chinese technology transfer is also different because it would be easier to substitute or not use Chinese technology, as Chinese companies offer existing technologies from other sources. If two economic blocs with more or less independent technological ecosystems were to emerge, with few transitions between the two systems, it could be strategically important to maintain compatibility with both blocs. Therefore, Chinese technology transfer may be critical to increase diversification that can provide business opportunities for these countries.

This may be less clear when it comes to technological sovereignty, but it is more obvious when it comes to the formation of a parallel global financial infrastructure.

4.3.3. Parallel financial infrastructures

Prior to 2022, there were clear trends that threatened the U.S.-dominated global financial order, see some examples below:

- Expressing concern about the dominance of the dollar in international trade, Russian Deputy Foreign Minister Sergei Ryabkov said in 2017, 'We will of course intensify work related to import substitution, reduction of dependence on U.S. payment systems, on the dollar as a settling currency and so on. It is becoming a vital need, . . .' (Ryabkov quoted by Radio Free Liberty, 2017).
- After the annexation of the Crimean Peninsula, Russia began to implement the System for Transfer of Financial Messages, which can replace the globally accepted SWIFT. The system has been in operation since 2017 and includes 399 banks to date.
- Since 2019, the Russian Central Bank has significantly reduced its U.S. dollar reserves and its holdings of U.S. bonds. Prior to the invasion of

Ukraine (January 2022), 11 percent of Russia's foreign reserves were held in U.S. dollars, down from 21 percent in January 2021 (Minami & Anujima, 2022).

- Meanwhile, Russia increased its yuan reserves from 4 percent to 17 percent. Gold accounts for 22 percent of reserves and the euro accounts for 34 percent of Russia's foreign exchange reserves. (Minami & Anujima, 2022)
- The growing cooperation between Russia and China is also reflected in the distribution of Russian reserves. China is the largest custodian of Russian foreign exchange reserves, at 17 percent. (Germany: 16 percent, France: 10 percent, U.S.: 6 percent.) The largest portion of this, 22 percent, is apparently gold stored in physical form in Russia. (Minami & Anujima, 2022)
- In May 2022, Russia set the price of 5,000 rubles for a gram of gold, making the ruble a gold-backed currency. The former president of Commerce Bank in Chicago responded as follows: 'It forces people to go to the Russian central bank and pay gold to get rubles to make the transactions. . . . . Now the ruble basically recovered, trading 80 rubles to the dollar. And it's because of the way they pegged the ruble to gold.' (Jack Bouroudjian quoted by Sherman Forbes, 2022, May 2).
- In the summer of 2021, Russia announced that it would completely remove U.S. dollar assets from the National Wealth Fund. (Shead, 2021 June, 3).
- While 97.1 percent of Russian exports to China were denominated in USD in 2014, this share declined to 22.7 percent by 2020, while the share of the euro (0.8 percent in 2014, 65.3 percent in 2020) and the yuan (0.7 percent in 2014 and 6.3 percent in 2020) increased sharply. (Bhusari & Nikoladze, 2022)

The question is how other countries might respond to the emergence of blocs in terms of trade, technology, and financial infrastructure. Wu Xinbo, the dean of the Institute of International Studies at Fudan University concludes that, 'The global game around the Russia-Ukraine conflict has sent the following signal: international relations, which used to be dominated by the ideas of cooperation and seeking consensus, are increasingly splitting the world into two confrontational camps and a neutral one. Countries in the neutral camp don't want to take sides. They instead prefer to adopt a pragmatic attitude to decide their positions according to specific matters.' (Xinbo, 2022)

Xinbo's conclusion may be satisfactory when it comes to African and Latin American countries that can form a neutral bloc. However, the conclusion may be flawed when it comes to Central European countries, as geographic proximity to Russia pushes these countries into a Western orbit. At the same time, cooperation with China in financing would be more attractive if the yuan's role as an international currency reserve were stronger. A look at the U.S. dollar shows what the yuan lacks at the moment. In addition to convertibility, China must have a negative current account balance, which means that more money (yuan) is leaving the country than is coming in. And why? This is the only way foreign central banks can accumulate yuan on a significant scale. While the U.S. has run a current account deficit since the mid-1970s, China's balance has been positive since China began its reforms in the late 1970s. This is the point where cooperation between China and the CE region can develop, but we definitely do not see this potential in cooperation between Russia and Central European countries. And we should add that the international role of the Chinese yuan cannot be strengthened without full convertibility of the currency. IMF Chief Economist Gita Gopinath summarized the requirements this way, 'If a country is aspiring to be a global currency, then in that case, you would need to have, you know, basically fully and freely mobile capital, full capital account liberalization, full convertibility of exchange rate, which is not the case right now in China, right now . . .' (Gopinath, quoted by Lawder, April 11, 2019).

4.3.4. Parallel brands, and supply chains

At this point it is worth looking at a historical analogy. In interwar periods (1918 and 1938), the internationalization of companies has historically slowed down due to the newly created borders and customs systems. At the same time, the internationalization of companies has continued, and thus international companies with parallel structures emerged. This basically means that companies established subsidiaries in other countries and set up a 'mirror company' that manufactured the same products in the target country. This way, they did not have to pay the additional high tariffs. In the case of China, this parallel development of companies existed even before the Ukraine war.

Obviously, this development was not due to high tariffs, but to the planned economic development, while this kind of development gained momentum in Russia after the imposition of economic sanctions against Russia.

The above-mentioned historical analogy has strong limitations:

- In the recent case, the parallel company is not established by the parent company, but Russian and Chinese companies establish companies with similar product lines to meet domestic demand and reduce dependence on foreign capital and technology.
- In our case, the development is also driven from two sides, as the U.S. and Western European sanctions or 'voluntary' withdrawal from Russia also create free space for Russian and Chinese companies.
- Another limitation is that clustered production makes it difficult to copy product lines. The difficulty lies in the complex vertical integration of today's companies.
- The rise of parallel brands and supply chains could also be limited by the lack of necessary technology. China is much better in the technological realm, while in the case of Russia, this could be the most important factor limiting Russia's room to maneuver.

Looking at the above factors and the role of Russia, the trends point to the formation of economic blocs. In principle, it would make sense to maintain compatibility of Central European countries with both blocs, but when it comes to trade blocs, parallel brands and supply chains, this seems to be a difficult task, as the European Union's single market is the decisive factor (e.g. Central European countries cannot import Chinese cars if they do not comply with EU regulations).

When it comes to technological cooperation or parallel financial infrastructures, the potential seems great, but in any case, cooperation with China rather than Russia has greater potential for the Central European region. Russia's importance to the region is in energy and raw materials imports. The EU is trying to cut off supply routes from Russia and replace Russia with other countries (Israel, Turkey and Azerbaijan) and boost renewable energy production. Adjusting to this new reality is painful, as it not only requires time and financial resources, but it is coming at a time when it is clear that the world is starving for energy. The situation of the Central European countries, especially the landlocked ones, is extremely bad, as they are torn between geopolitical fears and economic rationality.

Does the emergence of the two economic blocs mean the end of globalization? We too can ask ourselves this question. The sanctions against Russia are an important element in this story, but they have only accelerated already existing trends. (1) Populist movements since 2010 have contributed to growing barriers to international trade. U.S. disengagement policies, Brexit, scrutiny of foreign direct investment in the EU due to geopolitical fears, the migration crisis in 2015 are all pieces of the puzzle that reinforce de-globalization. (2) China's economic rise and size soon led to a situation where existing multilateral institutional frameworks for trade and investment were easily challenged. The West began to build obstacles to stop China and prop up the multilateral institutions created and dominated by the United States. (3) Sanctions against Russia increased countries' fears about what would happen to them if they were sanctioned by the United States, making them seem to want to join the slowly emerging parallel world as well. (4) Countries in Central and Eastern Europe are being driven by the Ukraine war to strengthen self-sufficiency in areas where it is possible or to reduce dependencies where self-sufficiency is not an option. (Posen, 2022, March 17)

The consequences of de-globalization trends for the Central European region are many, but when it comes to Russian influence in the region, Russia's political and economic influence is bound to decline. The systematic downgrading of Russian economic relations will most likely be an integral part of the long-term strategy for foreign trade and relations in the region, even though this is contrary to the economic interests of these countries. The foreign policy response of these countries remains varied and depends on factors determined by historical experience with Russia, geographic proximity to Russia, relations with Ukraine, economic dependencies on Russia in terms of trade and technology transfer, etc.

Table 4.2 shows eight aspects that factor into the Russian policy of the Central European countries. If we simply create another table (Table 4.3) showing in how many areas the country in question has a factor for or against strong Russian relations, we can understand that these countries very much have interest-based foreign policies, and they are much less influenced in their relations with Russia by the United States or Germany and France than observers seem to assume. Hungary and Slovakia appear to be the countries that benefit most from solid and stable economic relations with Russia and yet

Table 4.2 Factors of Russia–CEE region relations

Factors for stronger Russian relations	Factors against strong Russian relations
Stronger dependence on oil supplies from Russia (Slovakia, 78.4%, Lithuania 68.8%, and Poland 67.5% in 2020 based on Statista data)	Weaker dependence on oil supplies from Russia (Slovenia 8.9%, Czechia 29.8% and Estonia 32% in 2020 based Statista data)
Stronger dependence on gas supplies from Russia (Latvia 93%, Estonia 79.0% based on Statista data)	Weaker dependence on gas supplies from Russia (Romania 10%, Hungary 40%, Slovenia 40% in 2020 based on Statista data)
Being landlocked (Hungary, Slovakia, Czechia)	Access to sea routes (Baltic countries, Poland, Croatia, Slovenia)
No borders with Russia (Hungary, Slovakia, Czechia)	Borders with Russia (Poland, and the Baltic countries
Did not belong to the Soviet Union* (Poland, Czechia, Slovakia, Hungary, Slovenia, Croatia)	The country was part of the former Soviet Union. (the Baltic countries)
Dependent on Russian nuclear fuel (Czechia, Hungary, and Slovakia)	Not dependent on Russian nuclear fuel (the Baltic countries, Poland, Slovenia, Croatia)
Russia building or modernizing nuclear power plant (Hungary)	No other nuclear cooperation (the Baltic countries, Poland, Czechia, Slovakia, Slovenia, Croatia)
Conflict or political debate with Ukraine (Hungary)	Strong relations with Ukraine (the Baltic countries, Poland, Czechia, Slovakia, Slovenia, Croatia)

Source: own compilation
Note: */ the fact that the country was formerly part of the Soviet Union, strengthen fears of Russia and lessens the willingness to cooperate with Moscow.

Table 4.3 Relations of pro and con arguments in Russia relations

	How many factors for strong Russian relations?	How many factors against strong Russian relations?
Hungary	6	2
Slovakia	5	3
Czechia	4	4
Poland	2	6
Latvia	1	7
Lithuania	1	7
Estonia	1	7

Source: own compilation

have the most to fear from Russia, while the economic relations of the Baltic countries are less dominant in pursuing their Russia relations. All these policies are clearly reflected in their foreign policy actions. And for this reason, one should not be surprised that tensions arose when the Russian-Ukrainian war broke out. While Hungary did not send arms shipments to Ukraine or allow arms shipments to pass through the country, Poland, Czechia, and Slovakia actively participated in the West's efforts to supply Ukraine with weapons, and as mentioned earlier, the country did not agree to a total ban on Russian oil and said it was not ready to discuss a ban on Russian natural gas. The different attitude toward Russia led to tensions in the Visegrad countries, especially growing tensions between Poland and Hungary. Ponczek also notes that these tensions can be exploited by the United States and the European Commission to create a rift between the two governments. As she puts it, 'It is not yet clear how this will develop – the two populist leaderships have covered each other's backs in disputes and may do so again. But Poland is enthusiastically pro-NATO in a way that Hungary very clearly is not. Poland constantly lobbies for more NATO, including deployments on its soil, while Hungary is cautious, if not suspicious. It is not hard to discern what EU and U.S. diplomats will make of the current split between the governments in Warsaw and Budapest. Given its NATOphilia and critical geostrategic position, there is a clear opportunity to improve relations with Poland.' (Ponczek, 2022, April 20)

The lesson from this history is that while Central European countries pursue a Russia policy that best suits their interests, they are less influenced by external powers than we might assume. At the same time, when tensions or fault-lines arise in the region, major powers seek to exploit them to increase their influence in the region. Not only does the United States use this strategy, but so does Germany, whose foreign and trade policies are the subject of the next chapter.

5

Germany and its European Union

Central European aspects

5.1. EU on collision course with Central Europe?

5.1.1. The controversial idea of an 'ever closer Union'

The so-called unity of the European Union has been challenged and tested many times in the past few decades – the war in Yugoslavia, the reaction to the Iraq war or the eurozone crisis, the migration wave in 2015 – but the war in Ukraine is the most recent and perhaps the strongest test of this purported unity. Based on the previous crises, we cannot be naive or idealistic about what the outcome will be when we look at the diversity of EU member states. The real question is whether it is reasonable or sensible to expect more unity from the European Union than it has shown so far.

In this context, it is worth exploring the question of why the gap between Western and Central Europe is so wide with regard to the future of the EU. National identity and nation states are two concepts that seem to be more important for Central Europe than for Western European countries. This division of the continent can be explained by the late state formation and slower, dependent economic development in the Central European region, while the Western European countries were at the forefront of modernization and democratization, and many were the countries that exploited the resources of other continents by force for centuries.

Despite the different economic and social development of these regions, a division of labour united them, but cultural and ethnic diversity prevailed with a growing number of small states. If one wants to find a truly European feature, the coexistence of unity and fragmentation on the continent is perhaps the most characteristic. While there has always been constant competition between countries, a certain degree of integration has also been maintained. If we go back to the Middle Ages, the flow of information, people, ideas and even capital was a constant feature of the region. At the same time, Europe was never centralized or governed from a centre, although there were attempts to centralize Europe, all of which failed. This means that despite the continent being highly fragmented, a degree of integration was maintained between these countries that left room for competition.

In this division of labour, the Central and Eastern European countries have lagged behind the West in recent centuries, despite various attempts to close the developmental gap between Western and Central Europe. The most extraordinary of the concepts used to explain this European puzzle is that of the 'two Europes', which goes back to Leopold von Ranke, who emphasized the importance of the delayed development of this region, which he believed led to late processes of state and nation formation (Berendt, 2011: 3–9).

Certainly, the process of state and nation formation began much later in Central Europe than in Western Europe. For this reason, Central European countries seem to have shied away from greater integration and from easily abandoning certain elements of their sovereignty (their own currency, foreign policy, border control policies, etc.).

The desire to coordinate more and more with the policies of EU members is aptly expressed in the phrase 'ever closer Union' which can be found in Article 1 of the Treaty on European Union: 'This Treaty marks a new stage in the process of creating an ever closer union among the peoples of Europe, in which decisions are taken as openly as possible and as closely as possible to the citizen' (Treaty on European Union, Article 1). The vagueness of the wording led to a heated debate between those who advocate a more supranational ('above the nations') Union pointing to the 'ever closer' part, and those who advocate a Europe in which the nations are more important than the supranational elements, pointing to the 'among the peoples' part of the wording.

In 2017, Morillas argued: 'The logic behind "ever closer union" was gone well before the Brexit referendum' (Morillas, 2017: 1). He added that the Lisbon Treaty was the last attempt to achieve deeper integration of the European Union. He categorized the different approaches to a future EU:

1. *The 'More Europe, better Europe'* approach obviously expects the 'better' from the 'more' and the idea of centralized decision-making is promoted

by them. In recent months, the idea of abolishing the right of veto in foreign policy issues has been supported by those adhering to this school of thought as a reaction to the slow decision-making process of the EU. The idea of mandatory energy sharing in the event of an EU-wide alert also emerged in the wake of the 2022 energy crisis (Council of the EU, 2022, 26 July).

2. *The 'practical Union'* approach refers to an ideology-free management of issues, but the proposal is based on strengthening the political centre, especially Germany, being at the core of the EU. The problems associated with this approach are that political priorities differ among EU member states. While migration is important for Germany, employment issues are of greater interest for Mediterranean countries. These differences are difficult to reconcile, especially if policy and reform agendas are set only by Germany and France. The main problem is that Germany has had a credibility problem since the eurozone crisis, when it hesitated to show solidarity with Greece.

3. The *'intergovernmental approach'*. This school of thought starts from a paradox, often called the integration paradox. It reveals the contradiction between the successes of integration and the fact that the results so far have been achieved mainly through the cooperation of governments. Since the Maastricht Treaty, most of the results have been achieved in this way, and the eurozone crisis has also increased the power of states in the EU decision-making process. Poland and Hungary clearly prefer this method. The best example of this is the decision of the Polish Constitutional Court on 7 October 2021, when the court declared various articles of the Treaty on European Union unconstitutional (Schliephake & Beaven, 2022, 17 February). Another example is the Hungarian prime minister's speech at the 'Thirty Years of Freedom' conference in Budapest in 2021, in which he outlined his vision of the future of Europe. He emphasized that the EU was founded in the hope that European nations will be able to determine their own destiny. In describing the challenges ahead for the EU, the prime minister cited a number of sobering facts that highlight the EU's relative decline. He argued that reforming the European Union requires a proactive stance, as the EU will not return to the right path, and strongly advocated an active role for Central Europe in this reform. After discussing the

challenges facing the EU, he also presented proposals in the form of seven theses: (1) The EU is heading towards an empire-like polity; (2) The EU is a tool, not the goal; (3) Decision-making in the EU is being outsourced to NGOs and other political forces; (4) The EU is built on economic success; (5) We live in the age of migration and pandemics; (6) The European Parliament must be reformed; (7) Serbia must become a member of the EU (Orban, 2021, 19 June). Of course, the Hungarian prime minister is not the only representative of the intergovernmental approach, but his stance on the future of the EU illustrates the differences between those who advocate for more and better Europe.

4. *'Differentiated integration'*. This approach was very popular for many years and was hailed as the solution that can resolve the contradiction between 'more Europe, better Europe' and the 'intergovernmental approach'. The approach has many names: 'multi-speed Europe', 'enhanced cooperation', a 'Europe à la carte', 'variable geometries', 'first-class/second-class EU', and 'concentric circles'. They all point to the fact that even after many years of integration, these countries are still different and will remain so in the future. As a result of this differentiation, the integration process cannot continue without compromising on the issues and timing of integration. However, the approach was useful until countries had a shared vision of the EU's ultimate goal. The Brexit, the eurozone crisis, the migration wave of 2015 and the spreading disputes are all milestones in this disillusionment process that started after the Global Financial Crisis in 2008 and 2009 (Morillas, 2017: 2–5). Some analysts argue that there is a West–East divide in the European Union that has blocked further integration and proper functioning of the European Union in recent years. The next section looks at the question of where the dividing lines between the West and East lie, and whether or not these lines are real.

5.1.2. Cultural, social gap between the West and East?

There being a regional divide of opinions and views is not a novelty in the history of the European Union, as the West–South divide has made headlines before. At the same time, the difference is that during the eurozone crisis, the West–South divide focused on finance, while the West–East divide seems to encompass not one but several debates: migration policy, the rule-of-law debate and policy towards Russia. Lehne disagrees with this view, saying the divide is constructed rather than real. He highlights five points to support his claim (Lehne, 2019):

1. *The myth of the two opposing factions.* He points out that the Central European region is as diverse as the entire European Union (Lehne, 2019). Zielonka vividly describes this diversity: 'Newspapers often use the term "Eastern Bloc" even though most countries allegedly belonging to this Bloc are at odds with each other over history, commerce, borders and political aims. How Hungary can belong to the same bloc as Romania and Slovakia is a mystery to me. What does Bulgaria have in common with Latvia in terms of economic and political culture?' (Zielonka, 2019).

   In the given geopolitical situation, the main dividing line in Central Europe seems to be the relationship with Russia, as we could see in the previous chapter of this book. Apart from this point, there are other differences: some countries are members of the eurozone, others are not; some countries have joined the Shengen zone, others have not been able to do so yet and so on. So, we can say that the region is at least as diverse as the European Union itself. However, in our opinion, the diversity of Central Europe does not mean that it is indistinguishable from Western Europe, because common features can be found.

2. *The myth of opposing views on migration.* Lehne argues that the initial seemingly wide gap on this issue can be easily explained by historical factors, as the Central European region is ethnically homogeneous as a result of border changes, mass murder and expulsion in the twentieth century, so the price these countries had to pay for the original ethnic diversity was high. And having learned this lesson of the twentieth century, they are much less willing to pursue liberal immigration than the Western European countries that had this experience and received migrants in large numbers in the course of decolonization and, in later periods, due to labour market shortages. At the same time, Lehne argues that the wide gap on this issue, especially on mandatory migration quotas, is slowly disappearing. Not only does the European Commission's proposal violate the sovereignty of member states, but

the ideas also cannot be properly implemented because of the Schengen area. Why should migrants settle for much lower wages and government subsidies when they can choose richer countries (with work permits)? Lehne adds that even some Western European countries reject the system of mandatory migration quotas (Lehne, 2019).

He explains the changes that have taken place since then as follows: 'In the last three years, the situation has changed. As Western European states have also adopted much more restrictive policies and the number of new arrivals has diminished, the difference between East and West is now much smaller than it used to be. The reluctance to give up national sovereignty to develop stronger EU structures and policies is widely shared' (Lehne, 2019).

Anti-migrant policies are often explained by the rise of illiberal regimes in Central Europe. The narrative about the rise of illiberal regimes with authoritarian features is flawed. Rather, it is a culture war imported from the United States to Europe. Fukuyama traces the struggle between the ultra-liberal left, popularly termed 'wokism', and right-wing populist movements with their identity politics. In the twentieth century, political fault lines formed around economic issues, and political parties responded to these challenges. However, the collapse of the Soviet empire and the disappearance of the working class, whose rights had been protected by the social democratic parties, made it impossible for classical left-wing politics to continue. The so-called 'Third Way' reflected this ideological uncertainty. The movement, represented by Tony Blair, the British prime minister between 1997 and 2007, and the social democratic theorist Anthony Giddens, attempted to reconcile centre–left ideas with those of the centre–right, but was essentially a reaction to the end of classical social democratic politics. Giddens's 'Third Way' was never really successful, and the solution came from American left-wing movements that recognized that promoting the interests of marginalized groups such as women, ethnic minorities, LGBT people, immigrants and so on, was not a good idea. As these policies have proven successful, the American right has redefined its mission. While it protects traditional national identity, the policies it pursues are often linked to race, ethnicity and religion. The wrong conclusion drawn by many political analysts – including Fukuyama – is to equate the American right with Hungarian or Polish conservatism. He says, 'Some countries that seemed to be successful liberal democracies in the 1990s – including Hungary, Poland, Thailand and Turkey – have slid toward authoritarianism' (Fukuyama, 2018: 91). On the one hand, it is an extreme generalization to lump Hungary and Poland together with Thailand or Turkey, but on the other hand, Hungarian and Polish economic policies are about the majority of the population, and the popularity of these governments, contrary to the opinion of liberal analysts, is not based on identity politics, but on comprehensive economic welfare measures that have improved the quality of life of citizens in these countries, aimed at improving the competitiveness of Hungarian and Polish businesses and increasing national ownership shares in banking, insurance, retail and other sectors. Identity politics cannot work in these countries the way it does in the United States, which is ethnically and culturally diverse, while Poland and Hungary are much more culturally and even ethnically homogeneous and have deeply rooted historical religions.

3. *The myth of rule-of-law deficiencies.* Lehne points to the deficient rule of law as the third focal point of the West–East divide. He defines this problem and highlights that none of the EU member states is free of rule-of-law challenges. The historical legacy of these countries – the Ottoman Empire in the south of the region, but especially the decades of communism – makes it difficult for these countries to address weaknesses in governance. He adds that there are tendencies in these countries for ruling parties to try to consolidate their rule by dismantling constitutional checks (Lehne, 2019). In our view, these attempts are much more about strengthening these states, which in the 1990s and early 2000s were simply following policies dictated or recommended by Western multilateral organizations (IMF, EBRD, EU etc.). In our view, the Global Financial Crisis in 2008–9 was the great dividing line for two reasons:

   a. First, these countries cannot rely on Western structures in crisis situations. Greece, which has suffered for years from the eurozone crisis, is the cautionary example that makes Central European countries hesitate when it comes to adopting the Euro and other federalist structures and solutions.

b. Second, Germany's unwillingness to help Greece also called into question Germany's commitment to the European project. Until that point, the dominance of German companies in the region could be seen as an integral part of economic integration in the Single Market, but the absence of German aid exposes German economic policy and makes it look like an economic colonization of the region.

Against this backdrop, German criticism of Poland and Hungary, with their alleged rule-of-law deficits, seems to be less about genuine concerns about the state of the rule of law than about the relatively worse position of German economic actors in the region. In this environment, it should come as no surprise that conservative Central European governments are easily attacked by left-liberal political forces – a version of American identity politics – that also have very different ideas and concepts regarding family, identity, nation, homeland and so on. Combine these factors – the social and cultural divide between the two regions of Europe and Germany's (relatively) deteriorating positions in the region – and it is easy to understand why the European Commission initiated an Article 7 procedure in December 2017 in response to the risks to the rule of law and EU values in Poland. And in September 2018, it initiated the Article 7 procedure for Hungary as well. Both countries would need more fresh capital from countries other than Germany and more trade with countries other than Germany. In addition, more culturally homogeneous societies might be less tolerant of identity politics ideas. Although the mechanism does not involve EU transfers, EU funds can be withheld by the European Commission until a solution is found to the European Commission's 'rule-of-law' concerns. The logic of this mechanism is based on financial resources or, more precisely, their being withheld. While Lehne argues that more understanding and support for these countries would help improve government efficiency, we can add that less direct financial blackmail and pressure could help convince us that these countries are not discriminated against in the EU. (See more in point 5!)

4. *The myth of opposing stances on integration.* Lehne emphasizes that the narrative that Central European countries are reluctant to integrate economically is false. If we look at the number of infringement cases in the Single Market, we find that only Poland has a number of infringement cases significantly above the EU average, while Czechia

Table 5.1 Number of Infringement Cases in the European Union

Country	Number of infringement cases	Country	Number of infringement cases
Spain	58	EU average	*31*
Italy	50	Slovenia	28
Greece	49	Slovakia	27
Germany	48	Croatia	26
Bulgaria	42	Malta	24
France	39	Netherlands	24
Poland	39	Sweden	24
Belgium	38	Cyprus	23
Portugal	37	Ireland	23
Romania	37	Latvia	22
Austria	35	Denmark	19
Hungary	32	Luxembourg	19
Czechia	31	Lithuania	17

Source: European Commission: Single Market Scoreboard. Retrieved from: https://single-market-scoreboard.ec.europa.eu/governance-tools/infringements_en#more-information

and Hungary are only slightly above average and all other Central European countries perform better than the EU average. (See Table 5.1!)

We must add that, during the Soviet era, the Central European countries had the experience of forced integration by Moscow. The elites of these countries are less motivated by common solutions. These countries have just regained their sovereignty and freedom, so their motivation for seeking EU membership was not about giving up sovereignty, but strengthening it.

5. *Discrimination against the newcomers?* Lehne argues that there is no such discrimination against countries of the former Eastern Bloc in the European Union, but he also mentions two occasions when such discrimination can be confirmed. The first occasion was when the United Kingdom left the EU and major EU agencies had to be reallocated to the EU, and none of them were (re)established in Central Europe, but in Paris and Amsterdam. The other occasion was the Versailles Summit in 2017, when Germany, France, Spain and Italy adopted the concept of two-speed Europe (Lehne, 2019). The discrimination we are talking about is light and elegant, and it is hard to put into numbers. The tone with which the Western European media treat and refer to Central European countries and their leaders is telling. More importantly, we can see the systematic restriction of the rights of EU members, especially when we look at the ideas of the European Commission, German leaders and politicians.

The President of the European Commission, van der Leyen, introduced the idea of majority voting in foreign policy issues in 2022, where unanimity has applied until now. She referred to the need to move faster on geopolitical changes. The same demand was repeated a month later, in July 2022, by German Chancellor Olaf Scholz. Burchard summarized the logic of the proposal and the reactions: 'Over the past weeks, Scholz has repeatedly urged countries to move from unanimity to qualified majority voting on foreign policy matters. Crucially, he said that the EU first had to reform itself before admitting new member countries such as Ukraine or Western Balkan countries. However, some bigger countries like France but also smaller nations like the Baltic states have expressed hesitancy about giving up their veto right on crucial foreign and security policy decisions' (Burchard, 2022, 18 July).

Contrary to Lehne's interpretation, we believe that there are fundamental differences between the West and the East of the European Union, and these differences are long term and will not disappear soon:

(1) Europe's hierarchical dependencies have always been an integral part of the region's development. The West is the core in the division of labour, and the East is the periphery of the continent, whose role is to serve as relatively cheap labour for Western European capital investment. Immanuel Wallerstein's theory of core and periphery abandons nations or countries as analytical units and does not use any other concept of political and power structures, relying, instead, on the economy or, more precisely, the 'world economic system', which, according to him, is divided into core, semi-periphery and periphery. Core countries are capital-intensive; workers here have high wages, and economies can be characterized by high-tech patterns. The Western European countries are core countries, while the Central European region belongs to the semi-periphery, which is less developed than the core and more advanced than the periphery. Periphery and semi-periphery countries are characterized by their dependence on core countries for capital and technology, and the fact that these countries provide labour and materials (Wallerstein, 2013: 12–18).

Of course, critics have often pointed out that the theory, which focuses on economics and ignores cultural and social factors, simplifies historical events, but we can use it as a basic framework to understand why the centralization of power and the strengthening of states in Central European countries inevitably lead to tensions with Western Europe, and why these moves run counter to the interests of Western European capital owners.

(2) *The delayed development of the region* and the very different historical experiences of the region also lead to a different concept of nation and nation state. For this reason, it is not natural for these countries to abandon sovereignty or the concept of the nation state so shortly after regaining sovereignty in the 1990s. As mentioned earlier, these countries are much more culturally and even ethnically more homogeneous than Western European countries, and for this reason identity politics does not work the way it can in the United States or Western Europe. It is a complete misreading of political events in Central Europe that right-wing conservative governments would engage in identity politics in the way that the American right has done in recent years; on the contrary, economic policies that affect entire societies are much more typical.

Therefore, we argue that the role of the European Union is less significant than one would assume based on the headlines about how and why Central European countries, especially Poland and Hungary, are being pressured by the European Commission or how debates with the EU are developing. The main player in shaping CEE–EU relations is Germany. For this reason, the next section looks at the historical development of German diplomacy with the region and how Germany has built a strong economic hinterland for its economy and the development of the region's relations with Germany. Special attention is paid to German–Polish and German–Hungarian relations.

5.2. Germany in Central Europe: Drive to the East?

With the reunification of Germany and the subsequent enlargements of the European Union, the borders of the EU shifted eastwards and Germany suddenly became the centre of the European Union rather than its border in the east. Of course, West Germany has always been the economic engine of European integration, but the eastwards expansion of the EU opened up new business opportunities for Germany, and German companies took full advantage of them. We must understand that the dynamic expansion of the European Union was driven only in part by the collapse of the former Soviet bloc and people's desire to live in democratic countries – in other words, by politics.

The unfolding wave of globalization in the late 1980s was another important driver of the EU's transformation. Growing international competition and new technologies allowed companies to manage their economic activities in faraway locations from the company's headquarters while producing in countries with cheap labour. Central European countries were an ideal place for German companies to relocate assembly and production while keeping the high value-added areas of production (innovation, research and development, sales and customer service) in Germany. In addition to low costs and traditionally strong ties to these countries, it was knowledge of local cultures that led German companies, whose strengths lie in manufacturing, to reorganize their production in Central Europe. (This process was aided by the fact that German was the first foreign language in the Central European region at the time.)

Why it was so obvious and effortless for Germany to take advantage of the transformation period in the 1990s can be understood if we consider Germany to be a country whose foreign policy attention was always more focused on the East, as we can see in the four periods of post-war German foreign policy:

1. The first period (1949–55) was characterized by the debate over whether Germany should integrate into the Western institutional framework.
2. The second period (1969–72) saw the signing of the so-called 'Eastern Treaties', in which the Federal Republic of Germany concluded an agreement with Poland and the Soviet Union on Germany's eastern borders (the Oder-Neisse line). In 1972, relations between the two German states were regulated by the Basic Treaty. These steps – also called 'Ostpolitik'– were a clear break with the 'Hallstein Doctrine' of the previous conservative government, which did not recognize the existence of the socialist countries.
3. The third period (1977–83) was characterized by a growing domestic debate about the modernization of the military and the stationing of NATO nuclear weapons in West Germany.
4. The fourth period is more or less a consistent foreign policy, still adhering to a practice that developed after the Second World War. This practice involved restraint in raising Germany's military profile and participation in military missions. The mismatch between economic strength and military weakness is mirrored with Japan's position in international politics. Other principles of foreign policy are:

- European integration and the European Union;
- The transatlantic partnership;
- Commitment to peace and security;
- Democracy, the rule of law and human rights; and
- Commitment to a multilateral international order.

The abovementioned pillars of foreign policy are defined by the current German government, but previous German governments from the 1990s onwards also had the same guiding principles. At the same time, foreign policy practice towards the United States, Russia and China has changed over the past decade:

1. Although the *United States* remains Germany's most important partner, the Trump administration and its foreign policy have raised doubts about the US commitment to serve as a guarantor of security in Europe, about the solidity of the common value base and about differences in trade and climate policy (Mair, 2021: 117).
2. Mair argued for *compartmentalization of relations* with China and Russia into cooperation, competition and confrontation. There seems to be general agreement on this approach, but Germany and other Western countries seem to take these approaches in the same area of relations. The problem with this approach to China is that China does not accept the division of relations but takes a 'one basket' approach. In other words, you can trade with me if we have good political relations.
3. The failure of this approach is very clear on this point. Prior to the war in Ukraine, Mair claimed, 'One example of semi-successful compartmentalisation is Western policy towards Russia. Sanctions have been imposed to penalise Moscow for human rights violations, the annexation of the Crimean peninsula, and military intervention in eastern Ukraine. These punitive measures have indeed affected mutual economic relations and Russia's willingness to cooperate in international disarmament policy. But they have not led to a complete breakdown of exchanges in either area, let alone to Russia's withdrawal from the Paris Agreement' (Mair, 2021: 118).

    The approach is flawed for three reasons: (a) It is questionable whether Russian foreign policy can in any way be changed by imposing economic sanctions on the country's economy. When sanctions were imposed on oil exports, Asian and African countries did not hesitate to buy relatively cheap energy resources. (b) This approach also excludes the revision of its own foreign policy mistakes, especially the constant expansion of NATO and disregard for Russian security interests. (c) EU and German foreign policy will be guided by US foreign policy interests as long as Europe is unable to defend itself. This statement is especially true for Germany, which – plagued by post-war guilt – acquired the image of a pacifist economic power.

The war in Ukraine was a wake-up call, and the German Chancellor, Mr Scholz, spoke of a new era – 'Zeitwende' – in foreign policy (Hasselbach, 2022, 11 April). Immediately after the outbreak of war, Germany lifted its ban on arms exports to conflict zones. It also announced the reconstruction of the German army and supported German military investments worth 100 billion euros. The failure of this policy is reminiscent of the US approach towards China, which was pursued in the belief that economic progress would lead to positive social and political change there. The German version of this policy was 'Wandel durch Handel' (change through trade). Obviously, this policy has failed in relations with Russia, but the question is, rather, whether it ever had a chance to succeed.

After the annexation of the Crimean Peninsula, Mischke and Umland predicted the total revision of Germany's foreign policy towards Russia, which they formulated thus: 'The German government's reaction to the Ukraine crisis has calmed most of the initial fears. Merkel has offered a tougher than expected response, threatening broad-based sanctions that would do "massive" damage to the Russian economy. But it's Steinmeier's response, which has largely matched Merkel's in forcefulness, that gives an indication that Germany's strategy toward Russia may be undergoing more than just a temporary shift' (Mishke & Umland, 2014, 19 April).

They were definitely right about that. The question remains how Germany will react if Central Europe is threatened, because unlike China, Germany has deep geopolitical interests in Central Europe. Ukraine is not part of this region, but what is happening there is a serious threat to the (invisible) economic empire that Germany has built in Central Europe. The next section deals with the rise of this invisible economic empire.

5.2.1. Germany in Central Europe: The rise of an economic hinterland

Since 1989, Germany has become the most important trade and investment partner for the region. The region has been attractive to Germany for several reasons; German companies have been able to:

- reduce production costs;
- increase the pressure on German workers;
- acquire the skilled workforce of the region;
- take advantage of geographical proximities;
- benefit from EU regulations now that countries in the region have joined the EU;
- enjoy high standards of legal protection, which are certainly higher here than in competing FDI destinations (see Southeast Asia, Africa);
- cope with the shortage of engineers in Germany;
- benefit from economic cooperation supported by EU funds, with Germany being the largest contributor, while the country also benefited from the funds through its companies in the region;
- secure regional supply chains, which was the case at least until the war in Ukraine.

The last argument for production in the region was formulated by Poplawski as follows: 'The current period of global political and economic instability has increased the importance of Central Europe for Germany. Firstly, the region's geographical proximity ensures that this economic cooperation will not be disturbed by geopolitical problems, and there is no risk that the continuity of supply will be interrupted' (Poplavski, 2016: 6). We should add that not only could the growing geopolitical risks change German foreign policy and trigger more active German responses, but the possibility of losing Central Europe as a good location for assembly also makes Ukraine more valuable for German industry.

A look at Table 5.2 shows that the Central European region is Germany's most important export and import partner if we add up the size of these economies. Table 5.2 also shows that the East Asia and Pacific region is the most important partner, but this is a group of thirty-seven countries that also includes China, Japan and South Korea. The importance of the region for the

Table 5.2 Germany's Export and Import by Country and Region (2019, %)

	Import		Export
East Asia and Pacific	13.53	East Asia and Pacific	17.49
Central Europe	12.53	Central Europe	14.47
United States	8.94	China	10.03
France	7.99	Netherlands	7.86
China	7.55	United States	6.57
The Central European region by countries			
Poland	4.93	Poland	5.20
Czech Republic	3.31	Czech Republic	4.30
Hungary	2.02	Hungary	2.58
Slovakia	1.05	Slovakia	1.59
Slovenia	0.41	Slovenia	0.57
Croatia	0.28	Lithuania	0.19
Lithuania	0.26	Croatia	0.16
Estonia	0.14	Latvia	0.08
Latvia	0.13	Estonia	0.07

Source: World Bank, Word Integrated Trade Solution Database, Own Compilation

German economy is an often neglected fact, even for German economists who have focused more on East Asia and the opportunities the region can offer the German economy in recent years.

5.2.2. Resilience from Central Europe

Another neglected element is the nature of cooperation between Germany and the CEE region. In the 1990s, Germany saw opportunities in the so-called emerging economies for two reasons. These countries were able to absorb Germany's overproduction and become promising markets for German products and services, while also offering skilled and relatively cheap labour.

The degree of economic colonialism is very much determined by the behaviour of local elites. While China opened its economy to defend its national interests, Central European elites served foreign interests in the 1990s. The real change took three decades, coming only after 2010 when conservative political forces in some Central European countries (especially Poland and Hungary) acted against these economic policies, which were based on adapting local economies to the needs of Western European (mostly German) companies.

Germany supports cohesion funds, the largest beneficiaries of which are found in the CEE region. It is often argued that the grants from the funds are the reason why Central European countries gain more from this cooperation than they lose by serving German economic interests. Again, three aspects have been neglected:

- the money comes mainly from West German taxpayers;
- CEE are also contributors;
- Germany and other Western European countries earn more profits from the region (return on private investment from the West) than European transfers in the other direction.

We can conclude that Western European taxpayers, together with Eastern European taxpayers, finance the profits of German and other Western European capital owners, while Eastern European labour contributes significantly to this process with its low wages resulting from its weak wage-bargaining power.

This picture is admittedly negative, and we can agree with Cassel, who summarizes it thus: 'The economic reality is clear: the 100 million European citizens of the CEECs are cash cows for the German economy, the guarantee of its continental predominance and its global reach. Central Europe does not yet have the weight or the strength to tackle the great question of the increase of wages and standard of living' (Gibelin, 2018, 13 March), still we think that Central Europe showed resilience in its dealings with Germany.

- Hungary was the pilot project for the country's economic rejuvenation after the conservative Fidesz-KDNP won the 2010 elections and has since renewed its mandate several times with a two-thirds majority.
- Poland's national conservative PiS party came to power in 2015 and confirmed its leadership in 2019.
- The 2011 Czech ANO party, led by Andrej Babis, ruled the country with a minority government between 2017 and 2019. The party has been described by Babis as a right-wing party with social empathy.

These governments are the best examples of a new approach to Western and German capitalism. While accelerating economic development, these countries seek to weaken asymmetric dependence, with the following steps being typical:

1. concentration of national capital in the hands of (Hungarian, Polish, Czech, etc.) national capitalists,
2. strengthening of business associations and institutions representing national interests (trade unions, chambers of commerce),

3. strengthening national banks, partly by nationalizing them and partly by giving preference to national owners,
4. keeping infrastructure in public ownership and modernizing it on the basis of long-term national interests and not those of multinational companies,
5. diversifying trade and investment relations (even if this is done at the expense of German companies),
6. reducing dependence on external financing by relying more on domestic bond buyers and reducing public debt.

In Sections 5.3 and 5.4, we focus on how Poland's and Hungary's foreign policies shape their political and economic relations with Germany and the EU.

5.3. Poland's foreign policy and German reactions

The Polish–German reconciliation, which started in the 1970s under Willy Brandt and Egon Bahr, was a slow, process; however, it took final form in the 'Treaty of Good Neighborliness'. Germany supported Poland's membership in NATO and the European Union, and by and large relations developed favourably insomuch that Gebert and Guérot raised the question: 'Germany and Poland have become close political allies. The future of the European Union may be decided in Berlin and Warsaw. But has Poland replaced France as Germany's most trusted European partner' (Gebert & Guérot, 2012)? They argued that the turning point was the tragic event of Smolensk, when the Polish president's plane crashed in 2010 and Germany and Poland decided to bury their conflicts and embark on a course of rapprochement, while relations between Poland and Russia deteriorated because of the investigation into the plane crash.

At the same time, Skóra claims that the turbulent history of Polish–German relations is used as a weapon by Poland's conservative ruling party (PiS) and is often used in domestic politics. What she seems to forget is that the Second World War has always burdened – and, we may add, will always burden – German and Central European relations.[1]

---

[1] When Merkel responded to problems with Hungary in 2013, and said that 'we won't send the cavalry right away', the Hungarian reaction was fast and revealed painful memories: 'The Germans have

We have already seen that relations between Germany and the Central European countries are overshadowed by long-term economic conflicts, which can be explained by Germany's economic dominance in the region. In addition to these problems, we must also mention a cultural gap between Germany (Western Europe) and Central Europe. In 2021, Jaroslaw Kaczinsky summarized the conflicts at the Warsaw summit of European conservative leaders, saying that the EU is moving towards federalization because of German actions and that Germany is trying to eliminate the historical memory of the twentieth century; moreover, it rejects all kinds of identities, even gender identities (Tilles, 2021).

The agenda of Polish–German relations includes bilateral[2] and EU issues, with the latter seemingly gaining in importance.

Bachrynowski points out a crucial difference between the two countries: Poland and Germany have different points of view on the future of the EU. While Poland supports the idea of a 'Europe of the Fatherlands', and protects the sovereignty of the countries, Germany favours a federalist EU with a strong eurozone. Clearly, Germany sees itself as a pioneer of the federalist EU. He says, 'A strong EU under German leadership, with a common euro monetary system and taking over many of the internal competences of individual states – this is the German concept of the community, which Poland does not fully accept at the moment.'

We must add a point here, too. Germany squandered the opportunity to be a responsible and credible leader of the EU during the eurozone crisis, when its reluctance first to adopt bailout programmes, then to allow debt forgiveness, made Greece suffer for years, while Germany earned a total of 2.9 billion euros on interest rates from the Greek Debt Program between 2010 and 2017 (Stam, 2018, 21 June). No significant political forces in Central Europe believe in German leadership, which would not lead sooner or later to more German influence and less sovereignty of the Central European countries.

---

already sent one wave of cavalry to Hungary, in the form of tanks. Our request is, please don't send them again. It didn't work out' (Orbán quoted by Deutsche Welle, 2013, 20 May).

[2] An agreement between the two countries is necessary to reach a compromise regarding the institutional reform of the European Union. We need institutional reform because of the increasing tensions between the institutional design of the Lisbon Treaty (2009) and today's EU. In today's EU, Central European countries are economically stronger and more assertive in their foreign policy. When it comes to bilateral relations, the problems around (1) the legal status of the Polish minority in Germany must be addressed; (2) joint activities to protect the natural environment are important for both countries; (3) the problems related to post-war reparations are still on the agenda (Bachrynowski, 2021).

Another important issue is the two countries' stance on the Ukrainian war and their policy towards Russia. Looking at the Polish and German responses to the war, a pattern of unity seems to emerge, as both countries without hesitation supported Ukrainian efforts by shipping arms to Ukraine and imposing economic sanctions against Russia. To date (24 July 2022), this unity is unbroken; however small frictions can already be seen. While the strongest anti-Russian position was taken by the United Kingdom, Poland and the Baltic countries, 'Germany, Italy and France are more hesitant. They haven't quite let go of the idea, if not the hope, that Russia can still be a partner for dialogue further down the line,' Adler writes (Adler, 2022, 27 June). Adler criticizes this approach in her article; however, Russia is a still nuclear power, which cannot be defeated in the same way as small- and middle-size countries with limited resources and armed only with conventional weapons, and thus some kind of compromise must be found with Russia. Meanwhile, Poland seems to have entirely adopted the American and British stance on Russia, which does not believe in compromises and wants to weaken Russia militarily.

Defense Secretary Lloyd Austin said in April 2022: 'We want to see Russia weakened to the degree that it can't do the kinds of things that it has done in invading Ukraine' (Austin quoted by Ryan & Timsit, 2022, 25 April). We believe that this tension between the Polish and German approach towards Russia – even after the war – will be a long-term factor in the bilateral relations of the two countries. This might be a common point between Germany and Hungary as Hungary's stance on Russia is less hawkish and less fuelled by bad past experiences with Moscow. We should also add that Hungarian and German dependence on Russian energy and resources puts both countries into similar positions. The next section looks at the development of Hungarian–German foreign policy interactions and investigates the question of enforcement of Hungarian interests in the EU foreign policy framework, the CFSP.[3]

---

[3] The EU's Common Foreign and Security Policy (hereafter CFSP) was born in the early 1990s with the adoption of the Maastricht Treaty. The CFSP was immediately put to the test by the first Iraq war in 1991, when cooperation between France, the United Kingdom and Germany to make the decision of either joining or refusing to participate in the war failed completely. Another test was the disintegration of Yugoslavia between 1990 and 1992, where the CFSP failed because it could not unite the EU members in the case of Yugoslavia and could not provide a political framework that would have allowed common steps and actions.

5.4. Hungary's foreign policy in the EU and German reactions

Despite the rosy beginnings in the 1990s and excellent trade and investment ties, bilateral relations between Germany and Hungary today are fraught with several problems. Rohac points out that German 'strategic patience' has not affected bilateral relations. He points to the long struggle between the German Christian Democrats and Hungary's ruling Fidesz-KDNP party (Rohac, 2022, 17 April). The former tried to expel the Hungarian conservative Fidesz party from the European People's Party, while the latter decided to leave the parliamentary group of European conservative parties. (Since 2010, Fidesz has worked in symbiosis with the Christian Democratic KDNP, which is still a member of the European People's Party and whose members sit in that group in the European Parliament.) But he could also have referred to the rule-of-law debate, and the Article 7 debate that was triggered. (See more on this in Section 5.1.2.!).

In the next part, we do not focus on bilateral relations, as the main problems usually arise in the EU context. We present three cases in which Hungary vetoed decisions of the European Council and opposed Germany's interests. At the end, we present one more case in which Hungary was able to support EU decisions, with differences revealing fundamental and long-term differences in interests between the two countries.

In recent months, Hungary has vetoed the adoption of joint declarations in the EU Council on several occasions, triggering a heated debate among politicians and analysts on whether majority voting should be introduced in foreign policy matters. The main argument of those seeking to change the CFSP is that the EU cannot exert influence if it does not speak with one voice on certain issues. The following case studies were prepared by the author for the China–CEE Institute's external briefings in 2021 and 2022. The studies are published with the permission of the China–CEE Institute.

5.4.1. The case of Hong Kong

The scheduled European Council meeting was held on 25–26 March 2021. Hungary blocked the adoption of an EU Council statement criticizing China over its new security law in Hong Kong. Reuters journalists quoted an unnamed diplomat as saying Hungary argued that the EU already has too many problems with China (Chalmers & Emmott, 2022, 16 April).

The German foreign minister called Hungary's veto 'absolutely incomprehensible'. He added: 'I think everybody can work out for themselves where the reasons are, because there are good relations between China and Hungary' (Maas quoted by Bede, 2021, 12 May).

It must be clear that the case did not start here, but earlier, when both the EU and China imposed sanctions over Western allegations of human rights abuses in Xinjiang. In this case, Hungary did not veto the sanctions. The approach of Hungarian foreign policy is fundamentally different from the strategy of German foreign policy, which aims to impose its political and economic system on other societies – in short, 'democracy export'. Germany is not the most ardent supporter of US democracy export, but it is increasingly embracing the idea, which Germany's then chancellor Merkel was reluctant to openly endorse.

The pragmatic approach of Hungarian foreign policy is very clear in this case; it has primarily Hungarian economic interests in mind when it blocks this declaration. The Hungarian foreign minister said a few days before the EU Council meeting in March that the sanctions were 'pointless' and 'particularly senseless' (Hungary Today, 2021, 22 March), which also suggests that the EU basically lacks the hard power to enforce its interests in a geopolitical conflict of interests between the EU and China. In addition, Germany has geopolitical interests in the Asia-Pacific region, which could explain its tough stance on Hong Kong. At the same time, it is clear that Germany has pursued an ambiguous policy towards China over the years. Condemning China for human rights violations and promoting trade with China have been the two sides of the same coin. Thus, the ambiguous policy has also shaped Hungarian relations. Oertel explains, 'Obviously, Germany has all the tools it needs if it wanted to force Hungary to change positions. But do they really want to do that?' (Oertel quoted by Bermingham, 2021, 21 May). In other words, there might also be hidden cooperation that the two governments did not want revealed at that time.

5.4.2. The case of EU's Africa–Pacific Trade and Development Deal

The EU's Africa–Pacific Trade and Development Deal was blocked by Hungary on 20 May 2021. Since the treaty (also called post-Cotonou) would allow some forms of legal migration from African and Asian countries, Hungary has vehemently opposed these elements of the agreement. The Hungarian foreign minister made the reason for Hungary's rejection very clear when he said in Brussels, 'There is no need for fresh migration waves, especially now' (Szijjártó quoted by Komuves & Emott, 2021, 20 May).

At the core of the rejection, we have a vision of society that is very different from the German models of a more mixed society with multiple cultures. We argue that both choices can be appropriate if they are based on democratic principles, that is, majority support is behind each decision. In Hungary, the majority of society does not seem to support broad-based migration and the transformation of the one-culture society into a multicultural society, so it seems to be a rational decision not to support migration. Germany, on the other hand, has been clear on this issue: it has welcomed immigration for decades and the new Chancellor Scholz will continue to do so in the future. He wrote an article in the *Frankfurter Allgemeine Zeitung* in which he promised new proposals as Germany seeks to strengthen relations in the areas of migration and defence policy, as well as technological sovereignty and democratic resilience (Scholz, 2022, 17 July).

5.4.3. The case of the Israel-Palestine ceasefire

Hungary also blocked an 18 May, 2021, EU Council declaration that would have called for a ceasefire in the conflict that had just erupted between Israel and the Palestinians. Hungarian Foreign Minister Szijjártó told the AFP news agency, 'I have a general problem with the European statements on Israel (. . .) They are not of much help, especially in the current circumstances, when the tensions are so high' (Euronews, 2021). What is the intention behind this statement? Why is it not good for Hungary to issue a statement calling for a ceasefire? The statement simply highlights two features of the EU's CFSP: a foreign policy without hard power is useless and the inability to enforce European interests by military means calls into question all common European declarations and positions. The second feature is that the leverage of the EU's CFSP comes exclusively from the EU's economic power. This kind of leverage is capable of influencing actors, but not capable of maintaining balance in tense situations like this one.

The case led to a high-level debate because Mr Laschet, former CDU/CSU candidate for chancellor, said that this kind of veto is the reason why the

EU should make majority decisions in foreign policy. The Hungarian prime minister responded to this proposal when he said, 'Today, a common foreign policy decision can only be made unanimously, while Laschet prefers the will of the majority to be imposed upon the minority in the future. All of this in the name of Europeanism' (Orban, 2021).

In this case, we can also see a different concept of the European Union. The Hungarian concept envisages a Europe of nation states, and in this concept each member state would retain its right to an independent foreign policy, which is the core element of sovereignty. The concept presented by Laschet is about an EU in which minority voices can be subdued.

5.4.4. The case of Belarus

The last case involves an incident in which Hungary supported the common sanctions and did not veto them, even though observers had suggested before the EU Council meeting that Hungary was likely to veto the decisions. In 2021, a Belarusian fighter jet forced a Ryanair flight to land in order to arrest an anti-government journalist on board. The European Union condemned the action and imposed sanctions on the country. The EU banned Belarusian airlines from entering EU airspace and demanded the journalist's release. Hungary supported the measures and the Hungarian foreign minister declared Minsk's action 'unacceptable, especially since the airliner in question was traveling between two European Union countries' (Vaski, 2021). The case clearly shows that a CFSP decision by the EU that has a leverage effect and can influence the situation can earn Budapest's support, especially if it does not contradict Hungary's interests (see the Hong Kong case) and does not entail long-term commitments (see the Africa–Pacific Trade and Development Deal).

Based on the cases presented earlier, we can understand the logic of Hungarian vetoes in the CFSP of the EU. The principles can be summarized as follows:

- German foreign policy receives Hungarian support if it does not contradict Hungary's economic interests.
- German foreign policy is supported by Hungary if it does not interfere with the way Hungary organizes its society in light of its historical experience.

- German foreign policy is supported by Hungary if it does not impose long-term obligations on the country and does not force it into a relationship of dependence.
- German foreign policy is supported by the Hungarian government if it has a significant leverage effect.

5.5. Summary

We have seen that German interests are in many respects at variance with those of the Central European countries, as we have shown in the case of Poland and Hungary.

- The interests of German companies overlap – to some extent – with the interests of Polish and Hungarian nationals in terms of importing capital and technology, but beyond a certain point, more capital and technology only lead to deeper economic dependence on Germany.
- The strategy of German foreign policy is unclear for two reasons. Mrs Merkel's departure from office has left a void and ambiguity in German foreign policy. During her time as chancellor, Berlin was too cautious to fully embrace US leadership on Russia–China policy, while the new leadership appears to be abandoning the idea of 'European strategic autonomy'. In the context of the Ukraine war, it is clear that the phrase is elusive and has no real content. While Poland's fear of Russia leads the Polish leadership to join the mainstream of the EU and Germany's Russia policy, Hungary sticks to following its own economic interests, and this pragmatic approach seems to make the country an outsider in European politics.
- German–Russia policy will soon change when the negative effects of economic sanctions backfire and it becomes clear that Russia as a nuclear power cannot be defeated in the same way as middle powers with conventional armies. That will be the point at which Germany's Russia policy will converge with Hungary's position on the war, and German foreign policy will be exposed and it will become clear that the EU's common foreign and security policy serves only German interests.

6

The region as a pray of superpowers?

The term 'Central Europe' includes the phrase 'central', but it is an irony of history that the region has never been at the centre of political power or economic development, but, rather, has suffered and been the means of others' power. The influence of Germany, Russia and the United States has always been extremely high in the region. In the last decade, China has joined the 'club' of powers that wield significant clout in the region. While the Soviet Union promised to lift the countries out of poverty after the Second World War (and failed), the European Union assured these countries that they would regain their sovereignty and become economically stronger. However, the performance of these countries after the collapse of the Soviet bloc fell short of their own expectations, and the process of catching up began but was never completed. In theory, the strong relations with China could be used to diversify the trade and investment relations of these countries. However, geopolitical problems in the world have recently intensified, and this opportunity seems to be falling victim to geopolitical competition between superpowers.

The United States is the biggest loser of the change of the world order, because the rules of the world order were dictated by Washington after the collapse of the Soviet Empire in 1991. The current turbulent period, which began with the Global Financial Crisis in 2008–9, and continued with the global pandemic, the war in Ukraine and the geopolitical tensions over the island of Taiwan, is a time when the global leadership role of the United States is being openly challenged by Russia and China. The United States' continued position as the global leader, the hegemon, seems to be at the heart of these debates. At the same time, the United States is also trying to emerge victorious from these disputes, as part of a pre-emptive strategy, so to speak.

The slow but definite shift of economic and technological power to the East could be halted and even reversed if the United States succeeds in winning the current confrontations with Russia and China. Logically, both Central Europe and Taiwan are the focus of this competition, so we argue that Central Europe is contested by superpowers, but – although the region can be characterized by common features, it is not one country – it is a region where countries with slightly different endowments (economic development, historical experience) provide very different responses to the same challenges, and therefore the region can easily be divided by these powers. For this reason, the next sub-chapter deals with the question of what an ideal Europe would look like for the Central European countries. We then focus on how these countries can accelerate the chat-up process and free themselves from the 'dependent model' of economic development. In the last two sub-chapters, we will identify two basic types of responses that these countries give to the challenges.

6.1. The ideal EU for Central Europe

In Chapter 5, we discussed various theories or ideas about European integration. We mentioned the concepts of 'more Europe, better Europe', 'the practical Union', the 'intergovernmental approach' and 'differentiated integration'. The literature on this topic is vast, and the list of these concepts is extremely long, especially if we include the concepts of European integration that described the functioning of the EU in the 1960s or 1970s. All these concepts boil down to one question: What is the role of states in integration? In other words, how member states and EU institutions are organized in a web of interdependencies that we call European integration, what powers member states and the Union have and in what areas these actors share power. One of the main lessons of integration theories is that states that are economically interdependent pursue different policies than states whose economic ties are weak and tend to pursue inward-looking policies. Countries that are more closely interconnected tend to be less confrontational. Therefore, we can expect that increasing integration among these countries will lead to different policies. The main problem to which European integration theories do not provide an answer is the question of where the integration process stops, or whether it stops at all, leading to a federal state.

Since the Global Financial Crisis, Central European countries have tended to say 'no' to further integration, preferring to keep the boundaries between state and union clear, while people in the West seem to be awaiting a federalist EU at the end of the integration process. We believe that the eurozone crisis has been a dividing line for Central Europe, for at least two reasons: (1) The Greek case has clearly shown that European solidarity is sometimes little more than a slogan and should be treated with caution and (2) the ease with which China handled the financial crisis in 2009 showed that all roads do not lead to Washington or Berlin.

Although the dividing line in terms of the finality of EU integration seems to run between the West and the East of the EU, there are other discernible dividing lines:

1. *Large and small countries* also disagree about the finality of EU integration. It is obvious that the smaller countries are aware of the dangers associated with the creation of a supranational, federalist EU, while the larger countries tend to believe that they can benefit more from a United States of Europe or lead the EU. At the same time, only Germany and France are capable of pursuing this strategy, as evidenced by their call for the abolition of unanimity in foreign policy or their demand for 'European solidarity in energy matters'. The idea of the death of the nation is an integral part of Central European thinking. For Western Europeans, the notion of 'destruction of the nation' is a bombastic image, not a Europe (See more on Bibó, 1946: 25). Bibó, arguably the most influential Hungarian political scientist of the twentieth century, pointed to the significance of unresolved historical traumas (the Russo–Prussian–Austrian partition of Poland from 1772; the German–Hungarian partition of Czechoslovakia in 1938-9; the Hungarian defeat in the 1848-9 revolution against Habsburg rule and the partition of Hungary after the 1920 Treaty of Trianon, etc.).
2. *The left and the right* disagree on the finality of EU integration. The political left in the West has never been too concerned with concepts such as nationality and sovereignty, while focusing on equality, social rights and internationalization. Therefore, the abandonment of sovereignty is a decision that is felt less dramatically than in the ranks of right-wing, conservative political parties. Of course, this is a

generalization, and exceptions can readily be found. Nevertheless, left-wing and left-liberal political forces are much more inclined to support a federalist European Union than right-wing or right-liberal political movements or forces.

And, of course, there is also the divide between the West and the East on the finality of EU integration. By and large, this statement can be confirmed, but Brexit has shown that the reluctance to further integration can also be found in the West. The characteristic that Central Europe and the United Kingdom seem to share is their peripheral position in the EU, or the feeling that we do not belong. This attitude is reflected in the famous quote by W. Churchill: 'We are with Europe, but not of it. We are linked but not comprised. We are interested and associated, but not absorbed' (Churchill, 1930, 15 February). The situation in Central Europe is more complicated because countries have to choose Europe; the only question is whether they are ready to choose a federal EU.

Putting all these elements together, we can argue that small Central European countries where conservative parties are in power have a good chance of supporting a European Union built on nation states, while large Western European countries with social democratic governments are most likely to support the creation of a federal European Union.

For conservative governments in Central Europe, the most ideal EU would seem to be a Europe of nations, while leftist or left-liberal governments prefer a more federal EU. The only problem with the latter approach is that it seems to work only in good times. When crisis hits the region, however, unilateral dependence on the West with more integration reveals economic and social problems.

Between 2002 and 2010, Hungary was governed by socialist and liberal parties, and during that time Hungarian foreign policy was ready to accept more integration, including the introduction of the euro. At the same time, the Global Financial Crisis in 2008–9 revealed the shortcomings of unilateral dependence on Western Europe, its capital and technology. And the crisis made clear that the catch-up model, 'the dependent model' of Central Europe, is exhausted and new engines of growth must be found.

The next section explains the main features of the 'dependent model' and why the model of economic development is a 'catch-22' for these countries.

6.2. Central Europe's catch-22? Catching up with the West

So let us first take a brief look at the current state of economic development in the region. In Central Europe, Czechia, Slovenia and the Baltic countries are the countries that are very close to the EU average in terms of GDP per capita. In this case, we use data measured in purchasing power parity. These data also include differences in price levels between countries, making the relative position of the poorer countries more favourable and that of the richer countries less favourable. (See Table 6.1!) The second-best country in the region is Slovenia, but its development progress slowed down considerably after the Global Financial Crisis, as did Slovakia's, which is the worst-performing country in the region. Both countries have adopted the euro, which may partly explain their more painful adjustment to the new economic environment and their poorer economic performance. In contrast, GDP per capita data for other countries have improved significantly, as their relative position to the EU average has improved by more than 10 percentage points. While the double-digit growth was not enough to reach the EU average, it was clear that the spectacular change was explained by rising productivity in these countries.

Productivity can be measured in a number of ways. One of the simplest approaches is GDP per hour worked. This figure excludes the negative effects of population ageing, labour market inactivity and suchlike The seemingly positive trends (see Table 6.2) are overshadowed by the fact that the modernization of these economies has been driven mainly by multinational companies that have invested heavily in the region for various reasons:

Table 6.1 GDP Per Capita (EU = 100%, in Purchasing Power Parity)

	2009	2021	Progress between 2009 and 2021
Czechia	87	91	+4%
Croatia	63	70	+7%
Estonia	65	87	+22%
Hungary	65	76	+11%
Latvia	53	71	+18%
Lithuania	57	88	+31%
Poland	60	77	+17%
Slovenia	86	90	+4%
Slovakia	72	68	-4%

Source: Eurostat data

Table 6.2 GDP Per Hour Worked (EU28 = 100%)

	2000	2020	Progress between 2010 and 2020
Czechia	59	78	+29
Estonia	..	78	..
Hungary	55	72	+17
Latvia	40	71	+31
Lithuania	45	82	+37
Poland	50	75	+25
Slovenia	71	84	+13
Slovakia	54	84	+30
EU27	100	100	..
G7	115	119	+4

Source: Own Compilation Based on Eurostat Database

- Cheap and relatively well-educated labour force,
- Proximity to the main Western European markets were important factors in this process, but also,
- Knowledge of the region after the restoration of social and cultural ties drove the process.

In the 1990s, economic transformation was not preceded by a long social debate. The debate raged between those who argued for a '*gradual transformation*' and those who thought a rapid transformation of these societies and economies was the best approach. This approach was often referred to as the '*big bang transformation*'. Lipton and Sachs argued for a rapid replacement of the socialist system with private rights and market mechanisms because they feared that a slow transition would lead to rent-seeking behaviour and the reversal of reforms (Lipton-Sachs, 1990: 75–133), while the gradualists argued for a slower process because a rapid transformation would lead to high social costs. They also maintained that market institutions must come before liberalization in order to maximize efficiency gains during transformation and subsequent development.

Later, there was little analysis of the success of one strategy or another. Based on a comparison of long-term changes in total factor productivity, technological change, and efficiency changes, Czap and Nur-tegin concluded that 'The results of our analysis suggest that in the long run the gradual reform strategy was superior in terms of growth of productivity and its components. Initially, Big Bang reformers performed stronger, but this is probably due to the more drastic cut of unproductive inputs rather than an increase in the efficiency of the existing inputs' (Czap & Nur-tegin, 2011: 49).

Both the so-called 'big bang transformation' and gradualism were based on the logic of the so-called Washington Consensus. At this point, we can point out that the Chinese economic transition, as a slow and gradual change, was in stark contrast to the rapid adjustment process of the Central European countries, and several proposals of the Washington Consensus (controlled capital movements and free convertibility) were never on the agenda of the reformers in Beijing.

6.2.1. Central Europe depending on others: The 'dependent model'

The model, often referred to as the 'dependent model', was successful on many economic indicators; inflation and unemployment rates slowly declined after the initial shock of economic transition in the 1990s; foreign direct investment flowed into these countries and fundamentally reshaped their economic structure. Prior to 1990, these countries were dominated to varying degrees by heavy industry, which was replaced by manufacturing; the automotive industry in particular became a flagship industry in the Central European region. (The automotive industry accounted for 13 per cent of GDP in Slovakia, 10 per cent in Czechia and 4–6 per cent in Hungary in 2019!) (Than & Hovet, 2020, 3 July). Foreign investment and the resulting exports restored equilibrium in the economy; newly created jobs in these industries generated ripple effects; and higher wages boosted domestic demand and affected demand for domestically produced goods and services. So we can argue that the 'dependent model' was successful up to a point in the development of these countries. However, the Global Financial Crisis revealed the weaknesses of the model, which is not only dependent on external financing, but also on a region whose economic strength is relatively weaker. The EU accounted for 15 per cent of global GDP (PPS)[1] in 2017 (excluding the UK), and that share will fall to 9 per cent by 2050. The United States faces the same decline, with its GDP expected to shrink from 16 per cent in 2016 to 12 per cent in 2050. Meanwhile, China's share will rise to 20 per cent, but not only is China expected to increase its share of global GDP, but the so-called E7 countries[2] have also developed significantly. The

---

[1] PPP: Purchasing power standards.
[2] E7: Seven emerging countries: China, India, Indonesia, Brazil, Russia, Mexico and Türkiye.

total GDP of the E7 countries was half that of the G7 countries[3] in 1995 and reached about the same size as the GDP of the G7 group in 2007. According to PwC, the GDP of the E7 could be twice that of the G7 by 2040 (PwC, 2017: 4).

We see that dependence on an economically declining region is a recipe for failure that must be avoided. For this reason, we first address the problems posed by this model of economic development and then examine various foreign and trade policy choices made by Central European countries to address the challenges.

6.2.2. Overreliance on external sources

In the early 1990s, Central European countries rapidly opened their economies to the world and, due to a lack of capital and weak domestic savings, relied on external financing to catch up. As a result, they suffered from chronic current account deficits. Table 6.3 illustrates the profound changes that occurred in the Central European region after the Global Financial Crisis. Between 1992 and 2009, Central European countries, with the exception of Slovenia, recorded current account deficits between 4 and 8 per cent. It should be added that current account deficits are not bad per se; they can simply show that these countries offer excellent investment opportunities to foreign investors, as was the case with most countries in the region. The main problem is when the investment process is one-sided and there is no significant foreign investment

Table 6.3 Current Account Balance as of GDP in Central Europe (%)

	1992–2009	2010–21
Croatia	-4.7	0.8
Czech Republic*	-3.7	0.0
Estonia**	-7.9	0.8
Hungary	-6.6	1.1
Latvia	-5.1	-0.7
Lithuania***	-8.4	0.6
Poland	-4.0	-1.7
Slovak Republic****	-5.2	-1.7
Slovenia	-0.7	3.8

Source: International Monetary Fund database. Notes: * from 1995; **from 1993; *** from 1995; **** from 1993

---

[3] G7: The group of seven: Canada, France, Germany, Italy, Japan, the United Kingdom and the United States.

from these countries. The lack of capital is one of the main characteristics of the 'dependent model' in these countries.

At this point, it is worth distinguishing between loans through the banking sector, which is heavily dominated by foreign banks, the purchase of government bonds by non-residents and foreign direct investment, which has created jobs. The effects of these three types of 'external financing' are different. In the event of an economic shock, the rapid withdrawal of credit and the sale of government bonds can easily trigger a financial and exchange rate crisis in economies that do not deserve it because of their economic performance and development path. An economic crisis in another part of the world can lead to a collapse in these economies and expose the vulnerability of this development model, as it happened during the Global Financial Crisis when the EIB, the EBRD and the IMF stepped in to bail out Hungary, Latvia and Romania.

6.2.3. Overreliance on foreign companies

The improvement of economic development in the 1990s hid a crucial element of this economic development. Because the development was based on the inflow of capital in the form of foreign direct investment and loans, it led to a growing asymmetric dependence. Take Hungary as an example. The dominance of foreign companies is significant in terms of value-added, employment, investment and revenues, although the Hungarian government has tried to limit the role of foreign companies. The 're-Polonization' of the banking sector (Naczyk, 2014: 17) or Hungarian efforts to increase the share of domestically owned banks and financial institutions are examples of this new approach.

Naczyk summarizes these efforts as follows:

> Both in Hungary and Poland, changes in corporate governance and in property rights were thus made through the business community and politicians working together. While Hungary seemingly pursued a more radical strategy of renationalization of formerly privatized companies, both countries were intent on increasing domestic control of the commanding heights of their economies, and in particular of their banking industries. This did nonetheless not mean that the two countries were now closed to foreign direct investment. (Naczyk, 2014: 18)

A look at Table 6.4, which shows the role of foreign firms in Hungary, makes two things clear. The presence and contribution of foreign firms to the Hungarian

Table 6.4 Foreign Firms in Hungary (%)

	2010	2018
Number of firms	3.3	2.5
Share in total revenues	51.6	48.6
Share in total added value	49.3	47.8
Share in gross investment	49.0	40.1
Share in employment	24.7	26.3

Sources: Hungarian Central Statistical Office: Külföldi Irányítású Vállalkozások Magyarországon, 2018, p. 5

Table 6.5 Share of Value-added in Foreign-controlled Enterprises in EU (%)

Country	Share	Country	Share
Hungary	51.4	Sweden	26.5
Slovakia	48.1	Belgium	25.5
Luxembourg	44.6	EU average	25.0
Romania	44.0	Germany	24.8
Czechia	43.3	Portugal	24.0
Ireland	43.0	Croatia	23.4
Estonia	39.3	Finland	23.2
Poland	36.8	Malta	22.8
Latvia	32.9	Spain	22.2
Bulgaria	32.9	Denmark	21.5
Netherlands	29.1	France	16.4
Lithuania	27.8	Greece	16.3
Austria	27.8	Italy	15.8
Slovenia	27.3	Cyprus	13.4

Source: Eurostat Database

economy is not only significant, but it would also be basically inconceivable without them. What we cannot see from Table 6.5 is that Hungary is not alone in the Central European region with these figures. (See Table 6.5!)

While the EU average is 25 per cent, Central European countries have much higher shares, with only Croatia below the EU average, but the economy here is focused on tourism, where there is room for smaller businesses, and size is not as important as in manufacturing.

We can also see that foreign influence on the economy in Hungary is declining, which is a direct effect of the new economic policy that broke with the neoliberal approach after the 2008–9 crisis.[4] Another element is that not

---

[4] The causes of the crisis in Eastern Europe have recently been interpreted in different ways. In a neoliberal understanding, the crisis of these countries was a simple boom-and-bust cycle, as Aslund

Table 6.6 The Share of Foreign Companies in Revenues (Per Cent, 2018)

Slovakia	51.4%
Hungary	48.5%
Czech Republic	46.2%
Lithuania	43.0%
Estonia	41.8%
Poland	39.9%
Slovenia	33.4%
Latvia	33.2%
EU27	28.0%

Source: Eurostat Database

only the share in total value but also that in revenues (see Table 6.6) is higher in these countries than in the EU average. According to Eurostat, the share of foreign companies in revenues in the EU is 28 per cent, while there is no Central European country where this share is not higher than the EU average.

The importance of these companies for employment is predominantly more pronounced in Central Europe than in the EU, although this share is somewhat lower in the Baltic countries. The EU average here is 24 per cent, and the share of foreign companies in employment is 22 per cent in Latvia and 18.5 per cent in Lithuania. At the same time, every third job in the private sector is created in Hungary and by foreign companies (2018: 30 per cent), and this share is higher in Czechia (2018: 35.2 per cent), Slovakia and Estonia (2017: 38.1 per cent).

In summarizing the main elements of this model, it is worth quoting Myant, who gives a good comprehensive picture of the stage of economic development and the model in Central European countries:

> the kind of capitalism that has been established in CEECs, ..., can reasonably be characterised as dependent. Key domestic actors have proved incapable of providing economic dynamism, leaving that role to incoming MNCs for which CEECs are but a small part of global operations. Without a substantial

---

puts it: 'The East European financial crisis was a standard credit boom-and-bust cycle leading to a current account crisis. There is little to say in defense of the overheating and the policies that bred it. Yet loose monetary policy was a global phenomenon, and it was difficult for these small and very open economies to defend themselves against abundant capital inflows' (Aslund, 2011: 1). This interpretation misses the fact that these countries never wanted to resist the influx of capital. Their development model was built on permanent and massive capital inflows, which is why they have run massive current account deficits for many years. The crisis has only exacerbated this situation and led to bailouts in the region.

change from the established variety of capitalism, economic prospects for the foreseeable future will depend on how these MNCs choose to use their CEEC operations. (Myant, 2018)

Dependence on multinational companies goes hand in hand with heavy dependence on the home countries of these multinational firms, to wit: Western European countries and North America. It is clear that the economic and technological rise of China can be a turning point in the economic development of Central European countries, as China's growing trade and investment muscles provide these countries with diversification opportunities necessary to reduce their dependence on Western Europe and create more room to manoeuvre for their economic policies.

6.2.4. Weak overall and corporate research and development performance

Research and development intensity – measured as research and development spending in relation to GDP – in Central Europe is below the EU average. In 2020, none of the Central European countries could exceed the EU average of 2.3 per cent (Table 6.7).

The 'EU Industrial R&D Investment Scoreboard', published by the European Commission, lists 2,500 companies based on their investment in research and development. The 2021 list includes only three companies from the region – CD Projeck (leisure products) from Poland, Richter Gedeon from Hungary (pharmaceuticals and bio), KRKA from Slovenia (pharmaceuticals and

Table 6.7 Research and Development Expenditures (%, in Terms of GDP)

EU average	2.3
Slovenia	2.2
Czechia	2.0
Estonia	1.8
Hungary	1.6
Poland	1.4
Croatia	1.3
Lithuania	1.2
Slovakia	0.9
Latvia	0.7

Source: Eurostat Database

bio) – while tiny Denmark boasts twenty-nine listed companies. The lack of research-intensive companies is a long-term feature of the 'dependent model'.

6.2.5. Weak labour bargaining power

Although de-unionization is a global phenomenon, the trend was stronger in Central European countries than in the West. (See Table 6.8!) Magda summarizes it this way:

> The decline in union density that occurred in these countries [in Central Europe] between the early 1990s and 2012/2013 was much steeper than the de-unionization that took place in Western Europe and the US during that period . . . . Industrial relations in CEE are largely decentralized and fragmented, with collective bargaining taking place mainly at the local or firm level. Collective agreements cover much smaller shares of employees in CEE than in Western Europe, and these shares have continued to decline since the early 2000s in most CEE countries. (Magda, 2017: 2)

The weak bargaining position of workers makes it easy for multinational companies to make additional profits in these economies, but this constellation is not only favourable for Central European countries.

6.2.6. Development traps expressed in figures: The Hungarian example

In a speech at the annual opening of the Hungarian Chamber of Commerce and Industry in February 2022, the Hungarian prime minister summarized the

Table 6.8 Trade Union Density[i]

	Earliest figures	**Most recent figures**
Czechia	27.2 (2000)	11.4 (2018)
Estonia	14.0 (2000)	6.0 (2019)
Hungary	23.8 (2000)	8.3 (2018)
Lithuania	18.5 (2001)	7.4 (2019)
Latvia	21.0 (2003)	11.6 (2018)
Poland	23.5 (2000)	13.4 (2017)
Slovakia	34.2 (2000)	11.3 (2018)
Slovenia	44.2 (2000)	23.8 (2015)
OECD average	20.9 (2000)	15.8 (2019)

[i] Trade union density is defined 'as the number of net union members (i.e. excluding those who are not in the labour force, unemployed and self-employed) as a proportion of the number of employees' by the OECD:

traps that the Hungarian economy must deal with. These traps are widespread in the region:

- *The trap of foreign ownership.* The share of Hungarian ownership improved dramatically between 2010 and 2020 in the energy (56 per cent), banking (54 per cent) and media (51 per cent) sectors. Although the share of Hungarian companies in these sectors exceeds 50 per cent, there are still business areas where foreign companies dominate. German capital leads in insurance, telecommunications, food retailing and construction.
- *The trap of the excessive role of multinational companies in Hungarian exports*, while the country lacks an adequate number of Hungarian small- and medium-sized enterprises. Export revenues are mostly generated by foreign companies (80 per cent), and only 20 per cent of export revenues are generated by Hungarian-owned companies. Although the number of export-capable companies has increased from 10,000 in 2010 to 12,000 in 2020, the foreign share is still dominant. In this respect, it is important to note that trade with the Balkans and China provides additional growth stimulus for Hungarian small- and medium-sized enterprises.
- *The trap of negative profit transfer balance.* In 2021, foreign-owned companies in Hungary generated profits of EUR 8.2 billion, while Hungarian-owned companies abroad generated only EUR 1.8 billion. The balance was a deficit of EUR 6.4 billion. The same figure was EUR 23.2 billion in Poland, 11.8 billion in Czechia and 8.2 billion in Romania. In other words, these countries must embark on a phase of internationalizing their development externally, otherwise this asymmetry will persist.
- *The trap of duality.* Foreign companies in Hungary are more productive than Hungarian companies. Between 2010 and 2016, this ratio was 2.4, while in 2020 it dropped to 1.9. This still means that foreign firms are almost twice as productive as Hungarian firms. The catch-up process can be accelerated by more digitalization and innovation.
- *The trap of rural underdevelopment.* While GDP per capita in the capital Budapest is 151 per cent of the EU average, the same figure in Hungary's northern plains is 47 per cent. Eliminating or reducing these glaring inequalities is key to the economic development of these countries (Orban, 2022).

If we take a look at these challenges, we can claim that these traps can be found in each Central European country in varying degrees. If we also look at the inventory of possible solutions, we can understand that these steps to strengthen the domestic economy, in turn, harm the interests of German companies to varying degrees, putting these countries (especially those that have taken these steps, Poland and Hungary) on a collision course with Germany and German foreign policy interests.

6.3. Different foreign policy strategies in Central Europe

While we have tried to highlight the common strategies and characteristics of the Central European countries, the region, of course, is not homogeneous. The Baltic countries, for example, pursue different foreign policies and even different strategies of economic development. In this section, we focus on the Baltic countries and Hungary and how they perceive the current competition among the great powers and what strategies they pursue.

6.3.1. Foreign policies based on values? The case of Estonia

If we want to find the roots of Baltic distrust of Russia, we should consider the turbulent history of the region. The unfortunate geographical position between Germany and Russia is the most important explanatory factor of Baltic history, because only Lithuania in the Baltic was able to establish statehood before it was incorporated into the Russian Empire. A brief period of independence between 1918 and 1940 was ended by Soviet occupation, followed by German rule during the Second World War. After the war, the region became part of the Soviet Union.

It is estimated that the Nazis killed 290,000 Jews in the Baltics, and the Soviets deported another 590,000 (Paulaukas, 2016: 7). As a result of the period between 1945 and 1991, the ethnic landscape of these countries changed. In 2020, the percentage of ethnic Russians in Estonia was 24.7 per cent, in Latvia 24.9 per cent and in Lithuania 4.5 per cent (Coolican, 2021: 6). The fear that the Russian minority in these countries is a 'fifth column' is palpable, and forms one of the less obvious motivations for these countries' Russia policies. Coolican disputes this argument, saying, 'Although the Russian diaspora in the

Baltic states have been marginalised, actively discriminated against, and seem a ripe target for propaganda, they remain "autonomy seeking citizens" who do not accept Russian-state news blindly, without question or alternative opinion' (Coolican, 2021: 16).

The fundamental concern of the Baltic countries is that conflicts of interest between the United States and its key European allies (Germany and France) could worsen their position and harm their ability to protect themselves against Russia. The Baltic states are using the forums of the EU and NATO to avoid a split between the United States and Western Europe, because a downgraded Europe in US foreign policy also means less security for the Baltic region (Bergmane, 2021).

For many years, these countries were accused of being too negative towards Russia's foreign policy intentions. However, the worst Baltic fears seem to have been confirmed by Russia's invasion of Ukraine in 2022. Just days before Russia's invasion of Ukraine, Foreign Minister Eva-Maria Liimets gave an overview of Estonian foreign policy in the Estonian Parliament. She began her speech with a famous quote from American diplomat George Kennan: 'The jealous and intolerant eye of the Kremlin can distinguish, in the end, only vassals and enemies, and the neighbors of Russia, if they do not wish to be one, must reconcile themselves to being the other' (Kennan quoted by Liimets, 2022, 15 February). She added that this is as relevant to NATO and its members as it was seventy-eight years ago. In the speech, she called for action, using the phrase 'democratic space of values' as an argument for why Estonia must act. Estonian foreign policy is based on the enforcement of democratic values, and Russia is a clear target for this policy.

Unlike in Germany, the war in Ukraine does not represent a turning point, 'Zeitwende', a radical change in Baltic foreign policy, because well founded or unfounded fears of Russia have always been an ever-present factor driving foreign policy in the region. Moreover, in her analysis, Raik blames Germany for NATO not being prepared for the Russian invasion of Ukraine. She puts it this way:

> In 2014, Russia's aggression against Ukraine gave rise to calls in some NATO countries to abandon the treaty which the Russian side was clearly violating through the annexation of Crimea, war in eastern Ukraine and military exercises next to NATO's borders. However, some allies, especially Germany, insisted on sticking to the normative approach on the NATO side. As a result,

NATO limited its steps to strengthen defense and deterrence on the eastern front and only introduced battalion-sized rotational deployments under the enhanced forward presence initiative in 2016. (Raik, 2022)

She also criticizes the politics of engagement of recent decades, saying that engagement with Russia and China has not led to a convergence of political systems and normative commitments. For this reason, the Estonian foreign minister explicitly advocates a policy of containment, or as she puts it 'a policy of smart containment' (Kallas, 2022, 9 March). She also added that sanctions must be hardwired; in other words, they must be permanent elements of the Baltic countries' Russia policy.

The growing Russian and Chinese cooperation in recent months or years, vividly expressed in the phrase 'no limits' has also had a profound and negative impact on 17+1 cooperation. Lithuania left the format in 2021, then Latvia and Estonia decided to leave the cooperation in early August 2022 (Lau, 2022, 11 August). In the statement, Estonia referred to the importance of a 'rules-based international order and values such as human rights'.

The values-based foreign policy being pursued in the countries coincides very well with what the United States is trying to convey to the world on the issue of Russia and China. At a hearing before the Subcommittee on Europe, Eurasia, and Emerging Threats, held by the US House of Representatives Committee on Foreign Affairs, several experts commented on US foreign policy towards the Baltic states in 2017 (House of Representatives, 2017, 22 March). Five years before the war in Ukraine, experts agreed that Russia most likely wants to start a war. For example, Matthew Rojansky, director of the Kennan Institute, emphasized that Russia poses a real threat to the region based on his analysis of the three factors of motive, capability and opportunity. Other experts who attended the hearing expressed similar views.

The Institute of Economics of the Latvian Academy of Sciences summarized the main priorities of Latvia's foreign policy as follows: 'The overarching goal of Latvia's foreign policy remains unchanged – to ensure the country's independence and territorial integrity, sustainable security, and public welfare, as well as to continuously strengthen the country's position in the international environment. The foreign policy is pursued by deepening integration and cooperation in the European Union (EU) and the North Atlantic Treaty Organisation (NATO) based on common values, strengthening multilateralism, developing and expanding bilateral relations, and actively participating in the regional formats of like-minded countries' (Institute of Economics of the Latvian Academy of Sciences, 2022: 1). This quote shows the common features of Baltic foreign policy, which we can summarize in five points:

1. *Russia as the main threat.* Latvian, Estonian and Lithuanian foreign policymakers, unsurprisingly, see Russia as the main security challenge for their countries. The leaders of the three countries visited Ukraine twice in 2022 to express support and solidarity. The first visit was basically just hours before the invasion began on 24 February, and the second visit was in early May.
2. *The Russian ethnic minority as a security threat.* In these three countries, the Russian minority plays an important role in society to varying degrees. There are different approaches in the literature to the question of whether or not Russians pose a threat in these countries, but regardless of the answer, it is always a card that can be played by Russia.
3. *Proponents of NATO and EU integration.* Baltic countries are very small countries, and small countries have different priorities; their existence depends on cooperation with others. The degree of economic and political integration determines the possible number of countries in the world. The more successful the military alliances and the integration of the world economy, the more likely it is to form a new entity (country), as the cost of 'maintaining' countries and the intensity of security threats becomes lower. We live in an age of de-globalization and more frequent military conflicts, so these countries subordinate any other foreign policy goal to strengthening economic and military security.
4. *China is seen as a threat.* Since this security can only come from NATO and the EU, other aspects of their foreign policy are aligned with US and EU priorities. For this reason, it is not surprising that these countries distance themselves from China, even though China poses no real threat to them.
5. *A foreign policy based on values.* This policy is at odds with their economic interests. However, security challenges are more important to them at the moment, so they subordinate their economic interests to security priorities.

Therefore, we can ask ourselves whether the reference to European values and democracy really reflects the essence of this foreign policy or whether these countries are simply pursuing a rational foreign policy in which security is paramount.

6.3.2. Foreign policies based on interests? The case of Hungary

At first glance, the Hungarian approach differs from Baltic foreign policy in that it explicitly supports the assertion of economic and political interests. Hungarian foreign policy is often described as the foreign policy of an 'illiberal, authoritarian state', but we have already pointed out that this misinterpretation is due to the following factors:

- The weak Central European states underwent a centralization process after 2008–9 to respond to the economic and social challenges posed by the Global Financial Crisis.
- This process is mainly aimed at eliminating or at least weakening the unilateral dependence on the West in the economic sphere.
- The restructuring process logically runs counter to the interests of multinational corporations, mainly from Germany, the United States, the United Kingdom, France, the Netherlands, Belgium and Austria.
- These policies are often contextualized as a 'culture war' that takes the form of identity politics in the West, while the reforms of these countries are often far-reaching social reforms.

The Eastern Opening Policy of the Hungarian government is an instrument to reduce dependence on the West for trade, investment and technology transfer. The strategy roughly defines the regions where greater economic cooperation is needed. Since then, several erroneous interpretations of the strategy have emerged. In the following points, we try to dispel doubts.

1. The goal of the strategy has always been to deepen economic cooperation with Asian countries and never political cooperation (i.e. copying solutions of authoritarian regimes).
2. At the same time, Hungarian foreign policy was never aimed at regime or system changes in these countries (such as China, Russia, etc.).

3. Despite increasing cooperation with the East, the policy of opening up to the East was never about replacing the West with another region, as the Hungarian economy is deeply embedded in European supply chains.
4. The policy of opening up to the East was never about a single country, but about diversifying trade and investment relations. It is also about cooperation with Japan, South Korea, India among other countries.

Hungarian foreign policy is no different from that of the Baltic countries, as these countries pursue their own interests, and the type of interests they can pursue depends on the current circumstances. In this case, Hungary has the freedom to focus on its economic development, while the Baltic countries subordinate everything to security.

7

Summary

Central Europe in the 'Heartland'?

The central sentence of Mackinder's work[1] is often referred to in order to illustrate Central Europe's importance in world politics. However, this concept of 'heartland' reflects the period when it was formed for two reasons:

1. The role of technology in ruling the world and shaping world politics was less obvious in 1914 than it is now. Today we can easily rephrase the sentence this way: 'Who is at the forefront of technology rules the world economy; who rules the world economy rules world politics; and who commands both economy and politics rules the world' (Moldicz, 2021: 1). The development of technology and internationalization of the economy, and the rise of multinational companies, do not make space and geography irrelevant, but the historical fate of countries cannot be explained or justified by the geographical position of the country anymore.

2. The idea that main events in history take place in Europe shows a Europe-centric approach to history, and this perception is difficult to defend using any academic tool. In addition to the Europe-centric perception of history that ignores the growing importance of East Asia and Southeast Asia in the world economy, Central Europeans themselves also tend to overvalue the region's strategic importance to world order. At the same time, being between two dominant powers (Germany and Russia) before the Second World War, then being at the border of two ideological blocs after the world war put the region

---

[1] Already cited in Chapter 2: 'Who Rules East Europe Commands the Heartland; Who Rules the Heartland Commands the World-Island; Who Rules the World-Island Commands the World', which Mackinder wrote at the beginning of the twentieth century (Mackinder, 1919: 150).

into a precarious position and tensions in the region tended to be harbingers of shifts in political and economic power on a global scale.

7.1. A geopolitical report on Central Europe

In this section, we attempted to explain the position of the region using different methodological tools:

1. First of all, we defined the concept of Central Europe as it was used in this book. The main goal was to find a relatively homogeneous region in which similarities in foreign policies, strategies regarding development of the economy and state concepts are clear, and similar historical developmental paths can also be found. As a result, we focused on Baltic and Visegrad countries in the book and we also added Slovenia and Croatia to the list of countries.
2. We also delineated the political and economic development of the region, from the transition in the early 1990s to the present day. We made it clear that the Global Financial Crisis in 2008–9 was a turning point as the development path hitherto was called into question – at least – for two reasons in the Central European region.

- Central European countries did not benefit from neoliberal governance of the economy as it led to a 'dependent model'. The main characteristic of the model is one-side dependence on the West. For this reason, these countries are bound to experience significant downslides in their development if the global economy is hit by a crisis. In a model, where countries depend on external financing, import of capital and technology, the exposure to external factors is huge and unavoidable. We should also add that the dependence on West Europe, whose relative economic power is declining, might not be the best choice for the longer term.
- For this reason, the economic rise of China and other East- and South-East Asian countries is attractive to the Central European countries as the rising economies are able – at least potentially – to provide capital and technology, and they also create a demand for Central European goods and services.

The changes in Central European foreign policies that occurred in the early 2010s is the Central European version of the American 'pivot to Asia', with the significant difference being that Central European countries do not have geopolitical interests to pursue in the East Asian and South-East Asian regions, but, rather, economic interests. The opening to the East – even in an official form launched in Poland, Hungary and Slovakia – coincided with the Chinese Belt and Road Initiative and the China–CEE cooperation, whose name underwent certain changes, from 16+1 to 17+1, and reverting to 14+1 cooperation, depending on the number of participating countries.

After a honeymoon period that lasted between 2010 and 2011 and 2018 and 2019 or so, several Central European countries began to take a harsher stance on China and turned away from Beijing. This change in policy was maybe most obvious in the case of the Baltic countries – Czechia, Slovakia and Poland – while Hungary and Serbia still pursue China policies that accommodate more Chinese foreign policy goals.

Factors changing the foreign policy course towards China and taking a hostile stance towards China were the next ones:

- In Poland, the Baltic countries, Czechia and Slovakia, the economic cooperation brought meagre results, and the expectations of these countries were not fulfilled. We must add that these expectations were exaggerated and were not well founded economically.
- The pressure to change course on foreign policy came mainly from the United States, which is fighting a long-lasting geopolitical contest with China on all levels. One of them is Central Europe, where these countries serve American foreign policy interests in exchange for security guarantees against Russia.

But there were factors that led to keeping the foreign policy course towards China, and taking a friendly stance towards China. These factors dominated in the case of Hungary, Slovenia and Serbia:

- In the case of Hungary (and even Slovenia), Chinese investments were much more significant than in other Central European countries.
- The trade deficit with China increased in all Central European countries, but Hungary is the only one where this increase was moderate, and at the same time China could grow into a more important trade partner.[2]

---

[2] The increase in the trade deficit was moderate in Latvia; however, China's share is still very low.

- China's economic development policy is more intertwined with its foreign policy than America's. It simply means that you need very good political relations with China, and this is the only way Chinese companies get the 'green light' from politics and dare to invest in the country in question, while this link between politics and the business sector is much weaker in the American case. *This recognition was reflected in Hungarian and Serbian foreign policies.*

The last pull factor is that nationalism and sovereignty are more reflected in the foreign policies of China and Central European countries than in those of Western Europe.

- *In addition to the shift of global power – reflected in the Central European 'pivot' to Asia –* fewer and fewer countries support the current world order. In the period from 1991 to 2009, the United States maintained order and behaved as a global leader, referring to the system as 'open, rules-based, and liberal', and putting democracy and free markets at the centre of attention. Strikingly, this self-justification could be sold among experts and scholars of international theory for many years, but world order – and this one is no exception – relied on American military, economic and political power. Contrary to those who argue for a change in the word order, we do not find the current way of maintaining power reprehensible; rather, it reflects the true nature of power.
- None of the major powers is truly satisfied with the current world order: the United States has turned away from the UN and the WTO; Russia's invasion of Ukraine and Russian arguments made in justification of this war are obviously clear signs of dissatisfaction; China's initiatives (the Belt and Road Initiative, the launch of 16+1 cooperation, the Asian Infrastructure Investment Bank, etc.) are steps designed to return China to the centre of the world order, and also to show that Beijing is not satisfied with its current role in the world. The growing importance of multilateral forms of cooperation such as the Quadrilateral Security Dialog, the Shanghai Cooperation and the BRICS also provide clues to the new institutional framework on which the new multilateral world order will be based.

The logical response of the Central European countries to the growing anarchy and uncertainty in the world order is to seek a balance with the great powers – to straddle divides. This is not a regional but a global phenomenon. The resistance of many African, Asian and South American countries against joining the economic sanctions regime against Russia is part of these emerging balancing and hedging strategies.

7.2. From reluctant to assertive player? US foreign policy in Central Europe policy

This section focuses on the EU's and Central Europe's role in US foreign policy. The pendulum – priorities of American foreign policy – has swung several times from the 1950s until now. While the United States clearly welcomed and supported the idea of a unified Europe in the 1950s and 1960s, it became more uneasy about the European Union from the early 2000s. The relationship of Western Europe and the United States is best described when using the phrase, a cultivated 'asymmetry of power', which means that asymmetry was not only accepted by partners but also cultivated. In exchange for security guarantees and military protection, the region acquiesced in the acceptance of American foreign policy goals. US foreign policy has always revolved around Russia (the Soviet Union), and American relations to the EU and/or Central Europe are a reflection of American goals relating to Russia.

The European desire for 'strategic autonomy' is a logical, and it could be part of a long-term foreign policy' strategy – the best way to get rid of American tutelage. At the same time, the EU seems to lack cohesion, and will take the necessary steps for several reasons.

1. The Ukraine war (too) showed that there is *no 'strategic autonomy' without 'military autonomy'*, thus the region is reliant on American military power.
2. The economic development goals of Central European countries differ from those of Western Europe, and these differences are permanent, from which one can conclude that foreign policy goals will also differ in the long run.
3. The interpretation of sovereignty in these countries also differs from that in Western Europe, and this discrepancy will not disappear soon.
4. The United States seems to have no interest in fostering the development of a more sovereign Europe.

The game changer is China for at least two reasons in this situation:

- The global shift of economic power to the East made the East Asia region much more important for American foreign policy goals. The 'pivot to Asia' concept reflects this change. The altered US foreign policy in the Bush era was willing to compromise on many issues with China; however, it became more assertive under the Trump and Biden administrations.
- It must be added that the same statement applies to China as well: the launch of the Belt and Road Initiative and other Chinese initiatives affected the status quo in Europe, too. 'The pivot to Asia' basically tells us that the United States is not capable of protecting its economic and political interests in all regions with the same convincing power anymore.

The competition between China and the United States is often portrayed as a struggle between two giant states, while the interstate rivalry at the level of politics is complemented by the capitalist competition at the level of economics. These two competitions are not fought separately, but are closely intertwined.

It should be emphasized that there were attempts to counter the economic power of the United States. The most notable example was France in the 1960s, which lacked the economic power to do so, while Germany and Japan had the economic power but not the political will. China has both elements and, after the Global Financial Crisis (2008–9), was able to pool financial resources through its state-directed economy to expand globally. This was the moment it launched the Belt and Road Initiative and 16+1 cooperation.

When it comes to the final assessment of China's role in Central Europe and its intentions at the global level, we can see the following logic behind the development of relations between China and CEE:

- *Despite economic goals, China on collision course with the United States in Central Europe.* In the Central European region, China has no relevant geopolitical interests, and even its economic development interests are more related to the Western European region, which has benefited far more from cooperation with China than the Central European countries. China does not pursue a geopolitically motivated foreign policy in the region but is more interested in doing business than in engaging in long-term commitments. At the same time, the US global strategy puts the

United States on a collision course with China, whose rise is global, so the US response to it must logically be global as well.
- *Technology transfer from China suffers.* Therefore, certain elements of cooperation between China and CEE with a potential of high yields for both partners are viewed with suspicion. One area worth highlighting is the transfer of technology from China to these countries. Trade between China and Central European countries appears to be a smaller problem for the United States. Technological cooperation is a particularly sensitive issue, as the new Biden administration sees certain areas such as 5G networks, gears and artificial intelligence (AI) as strategically important to the geopolitical contest with China and discourages its regional allies from using critical Chinese technology. The irony of the situation is that if there is one area where the Visegrad countries could benefit significantly from relations with China, it is 5G and AI.
- *Rift among Central European countries regarding China policy.* Another issue that is more symbolic of US strategy is the search for an alliance with Central European countries on the situation of human rights and minority rights in China. Central European countries respond differently to this challenge: more pragmatic foreign policy strategies (see Hungary) are less likely to address these arguments against China because they realistically assess that they have no leverage over China and do not want to bear the financial burden of a foreign policy that would be sanctioned by China.

When it comes to the final assessment of Russia's role in Central Europe and its intentions at the global level, we can see the following logic behind the development of relations between Russia and CEE. In addition to the long-term strategic failure of Russia's invasion of Ukraine, which has created distrust of Russian intentions, Russia is a weak and declining economic power.

Even in the event that Russia manages to avert a sovereign default and a collapse of its currency thanks to its economic cooperation with China, it can either survive only as an economic satellite of China or experience a rapid decline, as economic sanctions affect not only trade but also technology transfer and capital. In essence, Russia has very little to offer to Central European countries, either technologically or economically, other than threatening them militarily or cutting off their access to energy. Had Russia continued its peaceful cooperation, it could have offered some degree of trade diversification. But that is no longer the case.

In contrast, the United States can offer Central European countries capital, technology, access to the institutions of the current world order and security guarantees. When it comes to the energy supply of Central Europe, it is almost impossible to replace Russia, but it can be done within a period of five to ten years if significant investments are made in the region to improve the energy infrastructure and develop energy production. It is obvious that all these steps are possible, but they will slow down economic growth in the region. The price of energy decoupling is high, and we doubt that the United States or the EU will pay the price that small Central European countries will have to pay for geopolitical superpower competition in the region.

7.3. The newcomer in the region: China

This section starts with a brief introduction to China and Central Europe's relations; first the emphasis is put on the shared history of socialism between 1949 and 1990, then it tries to explain why relations between the two regions were intensified again after a silence of almost two decades (1990–2008). There are four reasons how we can explain the refocusing of foreign policies:

- China's accelerated growth and the export orientation of its economy required ever greater internationalization and gave China the power to play a growing role in Central European economies in terms of trade, investment and technologies.
- Central European countries have reached a certain point in their economic strategy where their development cannot continue without further diversification of trade, investment relations and technology transfer, since their 'dependent economic model' depends only on Western capital and technology.
- In the wake of the Global Financial Crisis, further impetus for growth could not come from the West, but from the East. In 2009–10, the global economy was kept alive by China's demand and stimulus package, so the pivot to Asia – essentially, to China – was obvious to the leaders of Central

European countries. What seemed to be a relief for Central European countries could also be interpreted as a sign of a global power shift.
- The Obama and Trump administrations' refocused foreign policy approach – the Pivot to Asia – not only neglected Central European countries, but also devalued Europe as a whole in the grand strategy. It not only turned away the United States from Europe due to the 'Jacksonian revolt' of American foreign policy during the Obama and Trump administrations but it also accelerated the de-globalization in world economy.

All these elements forced Central European countries to look for other options in trade, investment and technology transfer, while de-globalization created a power vacuum in the Central European region that was not filled by any country for many years.

- The *EU* was apparently not prepared for any kind of geopolitical, let alone military, conflict in the region. Even before 2022, the reluctance to enlarge the EU to include the Balkans showed that the EU was not prepared to act as a political and economic superpower. The willingness to treat Ukraine as a potential EU member seems to be a delayed political gesture from the European Union since neither is Ukraine prepared for EU membership, nor will the EU accept a country in the middle of a military conflict with Russia as a member.
- The war with Ukraine showed that *Russia* wanted to fill this vacuum but did not have the power to do so. Obviously, Central European countries do not want this relationship with Russia either.
- The *United States* had the political, economic and military power but did not want to fill this vacuum – at least not until the end of the war in Ukraine. To date (22 October 2022), the United States seems to be mobilizing its resources to contain Russia, but the question remains as to what will remain from these commitments after the war is over in Ukraine.
- What *China* wants from the region is trade, the flow of investment and technology in both directions. China has neither the need, nor the will, nor the power (political and military) to act as a major power in the Central European region. Rather, what China needs is to open up new markets and internationalize its economy.

The next part of this section followed the story of Chinese opening up in a chronological order. Opening up to the world has always been seen as a must by Chinese reformers, while also being associated with bad experiences. The so-called treaty port industrialization of China – enclaves of the Chinese economy under foreign rule – was economically successful, but severely limited economic sovereignty and led to a one-sided development that created an asymmetrical dependence of the Chinese economy (Naughton 2007: 43). The overreaction came in the form of Mao's heavy industry and state-directed industrialization, which finds its precursor in Manchurian industrialization. This second type of industrialization was originally initiated by the Japanese state to exploit China's resources, focusing on heavy industry. The model was adopted by the Kuomingtang government and basically created the foundation on which Mao's Big Push industrialization was based. Treaty port industrialization could not solve the dilemma of modern China's economic development, namely, how to accelerate technological development without creating asymmetric dependence and increasing reliance on Western technologies and capital investment. The other problem of Mao's Big Push strategy was the unsuccessful modernization of agriculture, which was unable to provide sufficient food for the Chinese population.

The 'Open Door' policy is associated with China's leader Deng Xiaoping, who initiated the opening of the economy in 1978, initially in the form of special economic zones. The model successfully combined the positive elements of the two earlier types of industrialization:

- The 'Open Door' policy avoided excessive reliance on external capital and technology, thus reducing the leverage of foreign capital.
- The 'Open Door' policy was able to attract foreign capital without creating a 'dual economy' typical of emerging and developing economies where the newly created modern sector has almost no links to the traditional sector of the economy. The traditional sector provides cheap labour to the modern sectors, but this does not significantly increase domestic incomes and produces for the international market rather than the domestic market. China could avoid this trap, although there are large differences in levels of development within the country.

The 'go out' strategy initiated by the Chinese government in 1999 was the second phase of internationalization of the economy. In addition to these major concepts, the Chinese government also anchored the Chinese economy in the global economy by creating numerous institutional linkages. When looking at recent initiatives to make Chinese economy more international, the internationalization efforts of the Chinese currency since 2009, the launch of the 16+1 cooperation with Central and Eastern European countries (2012), the Belt and Road Initiative (2013), the establishment of BRIC bank, the New Development Bank in 2015 and the set-up of the Asian Infrastructure Investment Bank in 2016 can be mentioned as key pillars of this process.

The last stage in the history of the opening policy seems to be the implementation of the so-called 'dual circulation' strategy, which has become one of the main priorities in the government's fourteenth Five-Year Plan (2021–5). There are two main interpretations of this concept. It is a rebalancing strategy, which is a logical step in the catching-up process of China's economy, involving a shift towards higher value chains and GDP growth based more on services. At this stage of development, the emphasis is on technological development and indigenous innovation. The second explanation, which does not preclude the first, is that this is a response to the American decoupling from the Chinese economy – triggered by Trump's trade war and continued under the Biden administration amid growing great power rivalry between the United States and China. The disruption of global supply chains by the global pandemic and war in Ukraine was just the last straw.

In the next part of the section, we discuss the recent development in China–EU relations, and conclude that it is very difficult to form a common China policy at EU level for the following reasons:

- The EU still does not have a jointly exercised foreign policy. It is most likely it will not have any soon. The war in Ukraine and the differing responses show that the foundations for a common foreign policy in the EU are absent. If member states are not able to find a common voice in such an acute issue such as the Ukraine war, they for sure will not come up with a joint strategy on China.
- There are differences between the EU institutions in their attitude towards China. (Compare the European Commission and the European Parliament!) The set-up of EU institutions does not allow for the pursuit

of a responsibly conducted foreign policy. While the European Parliament has leverage in foreign policy, the members of the Parliament mostly pursue their own agendas motivated by domestic – EU and member state-level – politics.
- Western and Central European countries have different needs in terms of economic cooperation with China. Differences in China policy are very obvious when it comes to economic cooperation. While it is indifferent to Central Europe, whether or not China invests in Western Europe, Western multinational companies can lose markets in Central Europe, if Chinese companies become major investors in the region. In other words, multinational companies with headquarters in Western Europe are not interested in Chinese companies entering the markets of Central European countries.

The path that led to disillusionment with China most likely began with political scandals that drew the attention of the Central European public to political issues related to China. However, as we have already seen, political scandals were easily triggered when cooperation with China–CEE did not bring significant economic success in certain countries and did not provide these countries with real diversification opportunities in terms of trade, investment and technology. Certain countries (Slovenia and Hungary) were more successful, so political scandals did not take place there the way that they did in other, less successful countries such as Czechia, the Baltic countries and Poland. We investigated the question as to why certain countries were more successful than others based on Chinese investments in Central Europe while we used Dunning's classic framework, which divides the motivation for foreign direct investment into four categories:

- *Resource-seeking direct investments.* Central European countries are poor when it comes to natural resources. Poland is perhaps the only country where raw materials (copper) play an important role in the export structure. Slovakia, Slovenia and the Baltic countries export wood and wood products to China in a rather insignificant volume. Hungary is the least resource-rich country in the region and offers no natural resources to China. The only resource these countries can practically offer is relatively cheap labour, which is no less abundant in China than in these countries, meaning that the two regions compete rather than complement each other.

- *Market-seeking direct investments.* The markets of the countries are small – only Poland can offer a larger market – but even in this case we should add that the main attraction for China is the Single Market with about 448 million customers. In other words, it is highly unlikely that Chinese companies would target any Central European country, but the entire Single Market.
- *Efficiency-seeking investments* are typical when the division of labour between subsidiaries can contribute to better and more efficient production at the group level. Exploiting local advantages and combining local strengths or compensating for weaknesses are some reasons why multinational companies invest in other countries. Usually, this investment phase prevails when previous investments (market- and resource-oriented investments) can be reorganized, and in this way higher efficiency can be achieved. We have argued earlier that neither resource-oriented nor market-oriented investments are prevalent in China–CEE relations, so efficiency-oriented investments are not typical either.
- *Strategic asset-seeking direct investments.* Among strategic assets, technology, brands and land are worth mentioning. Regarding technology and brands, Western and Scandinavian countries are more attractive to Chinese companies than Central Europe. Although Italy does not score well in innovation, its classic luxury brands are very attractive to Chinese companies, something Central Europe can rarely offer China. Investments aimed at acquiring strategic locations (land, ports, etc.) are typical of Chinese investments in the world, but they are also not typical of the Central European region.

Looking at these four motivations, we can understand why the main targets of Chinese direct investment in Europe are not Central European countries, but Western Europe.

7.4. Russia: Behind the new Iron Curtain?

In this section we looked at the evolution of Russian foreign policy after 1991 to the present. The mainstream of analysts argues that Russian foreign policy can be divided into two phases after 1991. The first period is marked by Yeltsin's foreign policy, which was more pro-Western and aware of democratic deficits of the Russian political system, while the second phase would be the Putin era, which is anti-Western and, moreover, confrontational. At the same time, both presidents made efforts to restore respect for Russia as a major power in world affairs. From the Russian point of view, this respect was lost as a result of Russia's political and economic weakness after the collapse of the Soviet Union.

The four main political schools or currents of Russian political philosophy can be characterized as follows:

1. *The pro-Western idealists* who mainly contributed to the collapse of the Soviet Union believed in the market economy, democracy and self-determination, and therefore integration with the West seemed inevitable to them and was an integral part of their philosophy. Yeltsin and his government are perhaps the best example of this approach.
2. While representatives of the former group did not benefit financially from integration with the West, a powerful economic interest group also emerged, the *pro-Western pragmatists,* with a vested interest in maintaining relatively good relations with the West.
3. The *anti-Western pragmatists* – similar to the first group – try to maintain their influence on the values and norms that determine Russian politics and, consequently, foreign policy. The thinking of this group is based more on the old approach of 'realpolitik' in foreign policy, which generally does not believe in win-win situations, but in zero-sum games. The anti-Western pragmatists are also aware of Russia's weakness on many levels and therefore believe that Russia needs the West's financial support (capital, technology, etc.) to improve its relative position in the global economy and politics. Obviously, short- and long-term strategies are different, and it is a challenge for this group to separate long-term and short-term goals.
4. *Anti-Western ideologues* agree with the former group in their 'balance of power' approach, but are not motivated by economic gain; rather, they believe that ethnic, civilizational and religious aspects must also be part of the calculus. Today, Russian foreign policy is basically determined by anti-Western ideologues; their ideology was implemented with one significant change. In the original version of the ideology, China was often featured as a civilization whose rise threatens Russia,

while the current Russian foreign policy is built upon the assumption that the West cannot be defeated without a deep cooperation with China.

In this chapter, we also addressed a future scenario that envisions the rise of economic blocs, one in the West with the United States and the European Union as the main players in this bloc, and another in Eurasia with China and Russia as pillars of this bloc. The chapter focuses on the possible consequences of such a scenario for Central Europe. This hypothesis may seem extreme and overstretched, but it can predict the contours of the future geopolitical landscape.

We briefly looked at what would happen if this change were to take place, in the following order: (a) trading blocks, (b) independent technological ecosystems, (c) parallel financial worlds and (d) supply chains with substitute brands.

- *Trading blocs.* The share of China and Russia in the trade of Central European countries is small, but the structure of goods is also important. Before the war in Ukraine, we could argue that neither imports nor exports to Russia are important, but these countries depend on Russian energy and other raw materials. When it comes to replacing Chinese goods, it seems much easier because Chinese imports into the region are mainly ITC products, which are important products, but disrupting the flow of these products into the region is less of a threat to the region's daily activities.
- *Independent technological ecosystems.* In relation to Russia, there are fewer projects involving technology transfer from Russia in Central Europe than in relation to China. Chinese technology transfer involves much smaller projects, is broader in scope and offers greater long-term potential for the development of Central European countries as it relates to advanced communications technology. The nature of Russian and Chinese technology transfer is also different because it would be easier to substitute or not use Chinese technology, as Chinese companies offer existing technologies from other sources. If two economic blocs with more or less independent technological ecosystems were to emerge, with few transitions between the two systems, it could be strategically important to maintain compatibility with both blocs.

- *Parallel financial worlds.* Geographic proximity to Russia pushes these countries into a Western orbit. At the same time, cooperation with China in financing would be more attractive if the yuan's role as an international currency reserve were stronger. A look at the US dollar shows what the yuan lacks at the moment. In addition to convertibility, China must have a negative current account balance, which means that more money (yuan) is leaving the country than is coming in. And why? This is the only way foreign central banks can accumulate yuan on a significant scale. While the United States has run a current account deficit since the mid-1970s, China's balance has been positive since China began its reforms in the late 1970s. This is the point where cooperation between China and the CE region can develop, but we definitely do not see this potential in cooperation between Russia and Central European countries.
- *Supply chains with substitute brands.* American and Western companies leaving the Russian market are accelerating the building of substitutes for Russian brands and companies, a process that has always been part of Chinese economic development policy and is far less typical in Russia. This provides great business opportunities for Chinese companies that can replace Western companies in certain segments and provide Russia with products and services that embody key technologies. Russian companies have been integral to European supply chains, but far less so than Central European companies. Chinese companies could take advantage of this situation and benefit from Russia's decoupling from the West, but they are less likely to also transfer technology in the form of foreign direct investment.

The consequences of de-globalization trends for the Central European region are many, but when it comes to Russian influence in the region, Russia's political and economic influence is bound to decline. The systematic downgrading of Russian economic relations will most likely be an integral part of the long-term strategy for foreign trade and relations in the region, even though this is contrary to the economic interests of these countries. The foreign policy response of these countries remains varied and depends on factors determined by historical experience with Russia, geographic proximity to Russia, relations with Ukraine, economic dependencies on Russia in terms of trade and technology transfer, among others.

7.5. Germany and its European Union: Central European aspects

This section focuses on how the European Union and its leader Germany try to manage relations to Central European countries and get an answer to the question of why there is such a wide gap between Western and Central Europe with regard to the future of the EU. In this context, it is worth exploring the question of why the gap between Western and Central Europe is so wide with regard to the future of the EU. National identity and nation states are two concepts that seem to be more important for Central Europe than for Western European countries. This division of the continent can be explained by the late state formation and slower, dependent economic development in the Central European region, while the Western European countries were at the forefront of modernization and democratization, and many were countries that exploited the resources of other continents by force for centuries.

We also looked at the roots of tensions between Western and Central Europe. We highlighted three disputes: (1) migration policy, (2) the law-of-law challenges and (3) opposing views on integration:

- *Migration.* Anti-migrant policies are often explained by the rise of illiberal regimes in Central Europe. The narrative about the rise of illiberal regimes with authoritarian features is flawed. Rather, it is a culture war imported from the United States to Europe. Fukuyama traces the struggle between the ultra-liberal left, popularly termed 'wokism', and right-wing populist movements with their identity politics. In the twentieth century, political fault lines formed around economic issues, and political parties responded to these challenges. However, the collapse of the Soviet empire and the disappearance of the working class, whose rights had been protected by the social democratic parties, made it impossible for classical left-wing politics to continue. The so-called 'Third Way' reflected this ideological uncertainty. The movement, represented by Tony Blair, the British prime minister between 1997 and 2007, and the social democratic theorist Anthony Giddens, attempted to reconcile centre-left ideas with those of the centre-right, but was essentially a reaction to the end of classical social democratic politics. Giddens's 'Third Way' was never really successful, and the solution came from American left-wing movements that recognized that promoting the interests of marginalized groups such as women, ethnic minorities, LGBT people, immigrants, among others, was not a good idea. As these policies have proven successful, the American right has redefined its mission. While it protects traditional national identity, the policies it pursues are often linked to race, ethnicity and religion. The wrong conclusion drawn by many political analysts – including Fukuyama – is to equate the American right with Hungarian or Polish conservatism. On the one hand, it is an extreme generalization to lump Hungary and Poland together with Thailand or Turkey, but on the other hand, Hungarian and Polish economic policies are about the majority of the population, and the popularity of these governments, contrary to the opinion of liberal analysts, is not based on identity politics, but on comprehensive economic welfare measures that have improved the quality of life of citizens in these countries, aimed at improving the competitiveness of Hungarian and Polish businesses and increasing national ownership shares in banking, insurance, retail and other sectors. Identity politics cannot work in these countries the way it does in the United States, which is ethnically and culturally diverse, while Poland and Hungary are much more culturally and even ethnically homogeneous and have deeply rooted historical religions.

- *Rule of law.* The historical legacy of these countries – the Ottoman Empire in the south of the region, but especially the decades of communism – makes it difficult for these countries to address weaknesses in governance. Some argue that the ruling parties in these countries try to consolidate their rule by dismantling constitutional checks. In our view, these attempts are much more about strengthening these states, which in the 1990s and early 2000s were simply following policies dictated or recommended by Western multilateral organizations (IMF, EBRD, EU, etc.). In our view, the Global Financial Crisis in 2008–9 was the great dividing line for two reasons:
- First, these countries cannot rely on Western structures in crisis situations. Greece, which has suffered for years from the eurozone crisis, is the cautionary example that makes Central European countries hesitate when it comes to adopting the Euro and other federalist structures and solutions.

- Second, Germany's unwillingness to help Greece also called into question Germany's commitment to the European project. Until that point, the dominance of German companies in the region could be seen as an integral part of economic integration in the Single Market, but the absence of German aid exposes German economic policy and makes it look like an economic colonization of the region.
- *Opposing stances on integration.* The narrative that Central European countries are reluctant to integrate economically is false. If we look at the number of infringement cases in the Single Market, we find that only Poland has a number of infringement cases significantly above the EU average, while Czechia and Hungary are only slightly above average and all other Central European countries perform better than the EU average.

Against this backdrop, German criticism of Poland and Hungary, with their alleged rule-of-law deficits, seems to be less about genuine concerns about the state of the rule of law than about the relatively worse position of German economic actors in the region. In addition to the clash of German versus Central European interests, we believe that there are fundamental differences between the West and the East of the European Union, and these differences are long-term and will not disappear soon:

(1) *Europe's hierarchical dependencies* have always been an integral part of the region's development. The West is the core in the division of labour, and the East is the periphery of the continent, whose role is to serve as relatively cheap labour for Western European capital investment. Immanuel Wallerstein's theory of core and periphery abandons nations or countries as analytical units and does not use any other concept of political and power structures, relying, instead, on the economy or, more precisely, the 'world economic system', which, according to him, is divided into core, semi-periphery and periphery. Core countries are capital-intensive; workers here have high wages, and economies can be characterized by high-tech patterns. The Western European countries are core countries, while the Central European region belongs to the semi-periphery, which is less developed than the core and more advanced than the periphery. Periphery and semi-periphery countries are characterized by their dependence on core countries for capital and technology, and the fact that these countries provide labour and materials (Wallerstein, 2013: 12–18).

Of course, critics have often pointed out that the theory, which focuses on economics and ignores cultural and social factors, simplifies historical events, but we can use it as a basic framework to understand why the centralization of power and the strengthening of states in Central European countries inevitably lead to tensions with Western Europe, and why these moves run counter to the interests of Western European capital owners.

(2) *The delayed development of the region* and the very different historical experiences of the region also lead to a different concept of nation and nation state. For this reason, it is not natural for these countries to abandon sovereignty or the concept of the nation state so shortly after regaining sovereignty in the 1990s. As mentioned earlier, these countries are much more culturally and even ethnically more homogeneous than Western European countries, and for this reason identity politics does not work the way it can in the United States or Western Europe. It is a complete misreading of political events in Central Europe that right-wing conservative governments would engage in identity politics in the way that the American right has done in recent years; on the contrary, economic policies that affect entire societies are much more typical.

Therefore, we argue that the role of the European Union is less significant than one would assume based on the headlines about how and why Central European countries, especially Poland and Hungary, are being pressured by the European Commission or how debates with the EU are developing. The main player in shaping CEE–EU relations is Germany.

The second part of the section describes how Germany built an economic hinterland in Central Europe and how Central Europe makes attempts to decrease German economic and political influence. In the 1990s, Germany saw opportunities in the so-called emerging economies for two reasons. These countries were able to absorb Germany's overproduction and become promising markets for German products and services, while also offering skilled and relatively cheap labour.

The degree of economic colonialism is very much determined by the behaviour of local elites. While China opened its economy to defend its national interests, Central European elites served foreign interests in the 1990s. The real change took three decades, coming only after 2010 when conservative political forces in some Central European countries (especially Poland and Hungary) acted against these economic policies, which were based on adapting local economies to the needs of Western European (mostly German) companies.

These governments are the best examples of a new approach to Western and German capitalism. While accelerating economic development, these countries seek to weaken asymmetric dependence, with the following steps being typical:

- Concentration of national capital in the hands of (Hungarian, Polish, Czech, etc.) national capitalists,
- Strengthening of business associations and institutions representing national interests (trade unions, chambers of commerce),
- Strengthening national banks, partly by nationalizing them and partly by giving preference to national owners,
- Keeping infrastructure in public ownership and modernizing it on the basis of long-term national interests and not those of multinational companies,
- diversifying trade and investment relations (even if this is done at the expense of German companies),
- Reducing dependence on external financing by relying more on domestic bond buyers and reducing public debt.

We have seen that German interests are in many respects at variance with those of the Central European countries, as we have shown in the case of Poland and Hungary.

- The interests of German companies overlap – to some extent – with the interests of Polish and Hungarian nationals in terms of importing capital and technology, but beyond a certain point, more capital and technology only lead to deeper economic dependence on Germany.
- The strategy of German foreign policy is unclear for two reasons. Mrs Merkel's departure from office has left a void and ambiguity in German foreign policy. During her time as chancellor, Berlin was too cautious to fully embrace US leadership on Russia–China policy, while the new leadership appears to be abandoning the idea of 'European strategic autonomy'. In the context of the Ukraine war, it is clear that the phrase is elusive and has no real content. While Poland's fear of Russia leads the Polish leadership to join the mainstream of the EU and Germany's

Russia policy, Hungary sticks to following its own economic interests, and this pragmatic approach seems to make the country an outsider in European politics.
- German–Russia policy will soon change when the negative effects of economic sanctions backfire and it becomes clear that Russia as a nuclear power cannot be defeated in the same way as middle powers with conventional armies. That will be the point at which Germany's Russia policy will converge with Hungary's position on the war, and German foreign policy will be exposed, and it will become clear that the EU's common foreign and security policy serves only German interests.

7.6. The region as a pray of superpowers?

In the last section of this chapter we focused on the attempts of Central Europe to catch up with Western Europe and the results. We started with the sober remark that the influence of Germany, Russia and the United States has always been extremely high in the region and China has joined the 'club' of powers in the last decade that wield significant clout in the region. While the Soviet Union promised to lift the countries out of poverty after the Second World War (and failed), the European Union assured these countries that they would regain their sovereignty and become economically stronger. However, the performance of these countries after the collapse of the Soviet bloc fell short of their own expectations, and the process of catching up began but was never completed. The Global Financial Crisis in 2008–9 revealed the shortcomings of unilateral dependence on Western Europe, its capital and technology. And the crisis made clear that the catch-up model, 'the dependent model' of Central Europe, is exhausted and new engines of growth must be found.

We argued that the 'dependent model', was successful on many economic indicators: inflation and unemployment rates slowly declined after the initial shock of economic transition in the 1990s; foreign direct investment flowed into these countries and fundamentally reshaped their economic structure. Prior to 1990, these countries were dominated to varying degrees by heavy industry, which was replaced by manufacturing; the automotive industry in particular became a flagship industry in the Central European region. Foreign investment and the resulting exports restored equilibrium in the economy; newly created jobs in these industries generated ripple effects; higher wages boosted domestic demand and affected demand for domestically produced goods and services. So we can argue that the 'dependent model' was successful up to a point in the development of these countries. However, the Global Financial Crisis revealed the weaknesses of the model, which is not only dependent on external financing, but also on a region whose economic strength is relatively weaker.

After taking a closer look at the region's overreliances on the West – external sources, foreign companies, weak research and development performance, weak labour bargaining power – we highlighted five types of traps that slow down the region's catching up using the case of Hungary:

- *The trap of foreign ownership.* The share of Hungarian ownership improved dramatically between 2010 and 2020 in the energy, banking and media sectors. Although the share of Hungarian companies in these sectors exceeds 50 per cent, there are still business areas where foreign companies dominate. German capital leads in insurance, telecommunications, food retailing and construction.
- *The trap of the excessive role of multinational companies in Hungarian exports,* while the country lacks an adequate number of Hungarian small- and medium-sized enterprises. Export revenues are mostly generated by foreign companies (80 per cent), and only 20 per cent of export revenues are generated by Hungarian-owned companies.
- *The trap of negative profit transfer balance.* In 2021, foreign-owned companies in Hungary generated profits of EUR 8.2 billion, while Hungarian-owned companies abroad generated only EUR 1.8 billion. The balance was a deficit of EUR 6.4 billion. The same figure was EUR 23.2 billion in Poland, 11.8 billion in Czechia and 8.2 billion in Romania. In other words, these countries must embark on a phase of internationalizing their development externally, otherwise this asymmetry will persist.
- *The trap of duality.* Foreign companies in Hungary are more productive than Hungarian companies. Between 2010 and 2016, this ratio was 2.4, while in 2020 it dropped to 1.9. This still means that foreign firms are almost twice as productive as Hungarian firms. The catch-up process can be accelerated by more digitalization and innovation.

- *The trap of rural underdevelopment.* While GDP per capita in the capital Budapest is 151 per cent of the EU average, the same figure in Hungary's northern plains is 47 per cent. Eliminating or reducing these glaring inequalities is key to the economic development of these countries (Orban, 2022).

If we take a look at these challenges, we can claim that these traps can be found in each Central European country in varying degrees. If we also look at the inventory of possible solutions, we can understand that these steps to strengthen the domestic economy, in turn, harm the interests of German companies to varying degrees, putting these countries (especially those that have taken these steps, Poland and Hungary) on a collision course with Germany and German foreign policy interests.

In the next section we looked at two very different foreign policy responses of Central European countries (Baltic countries vs. Hungary) to understand how we get to so dissimilar an outcome:

The common features of Baltic foreign policy can be summarized in four points:

1. *Russia as the main threat.* Latvian, Estonian and Lithuanian foreign policymakers, unsurprisingly, see Russia as the main security challenge for their countries. The leaders of the three countries visited Ukraine twice in 2022 to express support and solidarity. The first visit was basically just hours before the invasion began on 24 February, and the second visit was in early May.
2. *The Russian ethnic minority as a security threat.* In these three countries, the Russian minority plays an important role in society to varying degrees. There are different approaches in the literature to the question of whether or not Russians pose a threat in these countries, but regardless of the answer, it is always a card that can be played by Russia.
3. *Proponents of NATO and EU integration.* Baltic countries are very small countries, and small countries have different priorities; their existence depends on cooperation with others. The degree of economic and political integration determines the possible number of countries in the world. The more successful the military alliances and the integration of the world economy, the more likely it is to form a new entity (country), as the cost of 'maintaining' countries and the intensity of security threats

becomes lower. We live in an age of de-globalization and more frequent military conflicts, so these countries subordinate any other foreign policy goal to strengthening economic and military security.

4. *China is seen as a threat.* Since this security can only come from NATO and the EU, other aspects of their foreign policy are aligned with US and EU priorities. For this reason, it is not surprising that these countries distance themselves from China, even though China poses no real threat to them.
5. *A foreign policy based on values.* This policy is at odds with their economic interests. However, security challenges are more important to them at the moment, so they subordinate their economic interests to security priorities.

Hungarian foreign policy is often described as the foreign policy of an 'illiberal, authoritarian state', but we have already pointed out that this misinterpretation is due to the following factors:

- The weak Central European states underwent a centralization process after 2008–9 to respond to the economic and social challenges posed by the Global Financial Crisis.
- This process is mainly aimed at eliminating or at least weakening the unilateral dependence on the West in the economic sphere.
- The restructuring process logically runs counter to the interests of multinational corporations, mainly from Germany, the United States, the United Kingdom, France, the Netherlands, Belgium and Austria.
- These policies are often contextualized as a 'culture war' that takes the form of identity politics in the West, while the reforms of these countries are often far-reaching social reforms.

The Eastern Opening Policy of the Hungarian government is an instrument to reduce dependence on the West for trade, investment and technology transfer. The strategy roughly defines the regions where greater economic cooperation is needed. Since then, several erroneous interpretations of the strategy have emerged. In the following points, we try to dispel doubts.

1. The goal of the strategy has always been to deepen economic cooperation with Asian countries and never political cooperation (i.e. copying solutions of authoritarian regimes).

2. At the same time, Hungarian foreign policy was never aimed at regime or system changes in these countries (such as China, Russia, etc.).
3. Despite increasing cooperation with the East, the policy of opening up to the East was never about replacing the West with another region, as the Hungarian economy is deeply embedded in European supply chains.
4. The policy of opening up to the East was never about a single country, but about diversifying trade and investment relations. It is also about cooperation with Japan, South Korea and India, among others.

Hungarian foreign policy is no different from that of the Baltic countries, as these countries pursue their own interests, and the type of interests they can pursue depends on the current circumstances. In this case, Hungary has the freedom to focus on its economic development, while the Baltic countries subordinate everything to security.

Bibliography

Adler, K. (2022, 27 June). Ukraine War: G7 Leaders Pledge Action on Russia – Do We Believe Them? Retrieved from: https://www.bbc.com/news/world-europe-61954441

Allen, M. A., Machain, Carla Martinez & Flynn, M. E. (2022, 25 January). The US Military Presence in Europe has been Declining for 30 Years – The Current Crisis in Ukraine May Reverse that Trend. *The Conversation*. Retrieved from: https://theconversation.com/the-us-military-presence-in-europe-has-been-declining-for-30-years-the-current-crisis-in-ukraine-may-reverse-that-trend-175595

American Enterprise Institute (2020). China Global Investment Tracker. Updated in 2020. *AEI*. Retrieved from: https://www.aei.org/china-global-investment-tracker/

Andrén, M. (2020). Europe of Nations, Europe without Nationalism. *History of European Ideas*, Vol. 46, 2020 – Issue 1: Special Issue: Transnationalism in the 1950s: Europe, debates and politics, pp. 13–24. Published online: 15 December 2020.

Asif, M., Adnan, M. & Ullah, I. (2019). USA's Pivot to Asia and China's Global Rebalancing through BRI. *Pakistan Social Sciences Review*, Vol. 3, no. 2, December, pp. 241–53. Retrieved from: https://pssr.org.pk/issues/v3/2/usas-pivot-to-asia-and-chinas-global-rebalancing-through-bri.pdf

Aslund, A. (2011). Lessons from the East: European Financial Crisis, 2008–2009. *Peterson Institute for International Economics*, Policy Brief, June 2011, Number PB11-9. Retrieved from: https://www.piie.com/publications/pb/pb11-09.pdf

Babones, S. (2017, 27 November). China's Bid to Buy Eastern Europe on the Cheap: The '16+1' Group. *Forbes*. Retrieved from: https://www.forbes.com/sites/salvatorebabones/2017/11/27/chinas-bid-to-buy-eastern-europe-on-the-cheap-the-161-group/?sh=4c57e4e83467

Bachrynowski, Sz. (2021). Where Are the Polish-German Relations Heading? The 30th Anniversary of the Treaty of Good Neighbourship and Friendly Cooperation. *Warsaw Institute*, Special Reports, 22 January 2021. Retrieved from: https://warsawinstitute.org/polish-german-relations-heading/

Baev, P. K. (2021). Russia and America's Overlapping Legacies in Afghanistan. *Brookings*, 18 August 2021. Retrieved from: https://www.brookings.edu/blog/order-from-chaos/2021/08/18/russia-and-americas-overlapping-legacies-in-afghanistan/

Bansal, R. & Singh, S. (2021). China's Digital Yuan: An Alternative to the Dollar-Dominated Financial System. *Carnegie Endowment for International Peace*, 31 August 2021. Retrieved from: https://carnegieendowment.org/files/202108-Bansal_Singh_-_Chinas_Digital_Yuan.pdf

Barboza, D., Santora, M. & Stevenson, A. (2018, 12 August). China Seeks Influence in Europe, One Business Deal at a Time. *New York Times*. Retrieved from: https://www.nytimes.com/2018/08/12/business/china-influence-europe-czech-republic.html

Beckley, M. & Brands, H. (2021, 1 October). The End of China's Rise: Beijing Is Running Out of Time to Remake the World. *Foreign Affairs*. Retrieved from: https://www.foreignaffairs.com/articles/china/2021-10-01/end-chinas-rise

Bello, W. (2017). Keynesianism in the Great Recession: Right Diagnosis, Wrong Cure. *Transnational Institute*, Finance Working Papers, Global Finance Series, February 2017. Retrieved from: https://www.tni.org/en/publication/keynesianism-in-the-great-recession

Berend T. I. (2011). Central and Eastern Europe in the World Economy: Past and Prospects. *Development and Finance*, no. 1. Retrieved from: http://www.ffdf.hu/en/2011-1/central-and-eastern-europe-in-the-world-economy-past-and-prospects

Bergmane, U. (2021). The Reset of U.S.-EU Relations with the Baltic States. *Baltic Bulletin*, 12 June 2021. Retrieved from: https://www.fpri.org/article/2021/06/the-reset-of-the-us-eu-relations-and-the-baltic-states/

Bermingham, F. (2021, 12 May). Germany 'Has All the Tools' to Whip Hungary into Line on Hong Kong, but Does It Really Want To? *South China Morning Post*. Retrieved from: https://www.scmp.com/news/china/diplomacy/article/3133097/germany-has-all-tools-whip-hungary-line-hong-kong-does-it

Bernstein, R. & Munro, R. H. (1997). China I. The Coming Conflict with America. *Foreign Affairs*, March/April 1997, pp. 18–32.

Bhusari, M. & Nikoladze, M. (2022). Russia and China: Partners in Dedollarization. *Econographics*, 18 February 2022. Retrieved from: https://www.atlanticcouncil.org/blogs/econographics/russia-and-china-partners-in-dedollarization/

Bialer, S. (1980). *Stalin's Successors: Leadership, Stability and Change in the Soviet Union*. New York: Cambridge University Press, p. 237.

Bibó, I. (1946). A kelet-európai kisállamok nyomorúsága. (The Miseries of East European Small States). Az Új Magyarország röpiratai. [New Hungary's Pamplets] Budapest, p. 116.

Biden, J. (2021). Remarks by President Biden on America's Place in the World. U.S. Department of State Headquarters, Harry S. Truman Building, Washington, D.C. Retrieved from: https://www.whitehouse.gov/briefing-room/speeches-remarks/2021/02/04/remarks-by-president-biden-on-americas-place-in-the-world/

Blanchard, B. & Tian, Y. L. (2020, 31 August). Czech Senate Speaker Will Pay 'Heavy Price' for Taiwan Visit, China Says. *Reuters*. Retrieved from: https://www.reuters.com/article/us-taiwan-czech-china-idUSKBN25R059

Blanchette, J. & Polk, A. (2020, 24 August). Dual Circulation and China's New Hedged Integration Strategy. *Center for Strategic and International Studies*. Retrieved from: https://www.csis.org/analysis/dual-circulation-and-chinas-new-hedged-integration-strategy

Brands, H. & Gaddis, J. L. (2021). The New Cold War: America, China, and the Echoes of History. *Foreign Affairs*, November/December 2021.

Brattberg, E. & Soula, E. (2018). Europe's Emerging Approach to China's Belt and Road Initiative. *Carnegie Endowment for International Peace*, 19 October 2018. Retrieved from: https://carnegieendowment.org/2018/10/19/europe-s-emerging-approach-to-china-s-belt-and-road-initiative-pub-77536

Brzezinski, Z. (1970). America and Europe. *Foreign Affairs*, Vol. 49, no. 1, pp. 11–30. Retrieved from: https://www.foreignaffairs.com/articles/europe/1970-10-01/america-and-europe

Brzezinski, Z. (1997). A Geostrategy for Eurasia. *Foreign Affairs*, Vol. 76, no. 5, pp. 50–64.

Burchard, H. (2022, 18 July). Germany's Scholz Urges EU to Deepen Unity in the Face of Russian Threat. *Politica*. Retrieved from: https://www.politico.eu/article/germany-scholz-urge-eu-deepen-unity-face-russian-threat/

Chalmers, J. & Emmott, R. (2021). Hungary Blocks EU Statement Criticising China over Hong Kong, Diplomats Say. *Reuters*. Retrieved from: https://www.reuters.com/world/asia-pacific/hungary-blocks-eu-statement-criticising-china-over-hong-kong-diplomats-say-2021-04-16/

Chang, G. G. (2001). *The Coming Collapse of China*. New York: Random House.

Chirathivat, S. & Langhammer, R. J. (2020). ASEAN and the EU Challenged by 'Divide and Rule' Strategies of the US and China: Evidence and Possible Reactions. *International Economics and Economic Policy*, Vol. 17, pp. 659–70. Retrieved from: https://link.springer.com/article/10.1007/s10368-020-00470-6

Churchill, W. (1930, 15 February). The United States of Europe. *Saturday Evening Post*, 15 February 1930.

Clinton, H. (2011, 11 October). America's Pacific Century. *Foreign Policy*. Retrieved from: https://foreignpolicy.com/2011/10/11/americas-pacific-century/

Coolican, S. (2021). The Russian Diaspora in the Baltic States: The Trojan Horse That Never Was. *LSE Ideas*. Retrieved from: https://www.lse.ac.uk/ideas/Assets/Documents/updates/LSE-IDEAS-Russian-Diaspora-Baltic-States.pdf

Council of the EU (2022, 26 July). Member States Commit to Reducing Gas Demand by 15% Next Winter. Press Release. Retrieved from: https://www.consilium.europa.eu/en/press/press-releases/2022/07/26/member-states-commit-to-reducing-gas-demand-by-15-next-winter/

Council of Foreign Relations (2021). China's Belt and Road. Implications for the United States. Independent Task Force Report No. 79. Retrieved from: https://www.cfr.org/report/chinas-belt-and-road-implications-for-the-united-states/download/pdf/2021-04/TFR%20%2379_China%27s%20Belt%20and%20Road_Implications%20for%20the%20United%20States_FINAL.pdf

Czak, Hans J. & Nur-tegin, Kanybek D. (2011). Big Bang vs. Gradualism – A Productivity Analysis. *EuroEconomica*, Vol. 29, Issue 3, pp. 38–56.

Daily News Hungarian (2022, 19 April), Hungary, Turkey set up Joint Economic and Trade Committee. Retrieved from: https://dailynewshungary.com/hungary-turkey-set-up-joint-economic-and-trade-committee/

Deme, D. (2022, 22 August). EUR 7.4 BN Battery Plant to be Built in Debrecen. *Hungary Today*. Retrieved from: https://hungarytoday.hu/eur-7-4-bn-battery-plant-to-be-built-in-debrecen/

Department of Defense (2018). A Summary of the National Defense Strategy of the United States of America. Sharpening the American Military's Competitive Edge. Retrieved from: https://dod.defense.gov/Portals/1/Documents/pubs/2018-National-Defense-Strategy-Summary.pdf

Deutsche Welle (2013, 20 May). Merkel's Cavalry and Orban's Tanks Occupy Touchy Territory. *Deutsche Welle*. Retrieved from: https://www.dw.com/en/merkels-cavalry-and-orbans-tanks-occupy-touchy-territory/a-16825787

Djordjevic, B. (2016). The Current Situation and Prospect of Policy Coordination of the Belt and Road between China and the EU. In *China-CEEC Cooperation and the 'Belt and Road Initiative'*. Edited by Huang Ping and Liu Zuokiu. China Social Sciences Press, Bejing, pp. 52–63.

Downs, E. (2022, 16 March). China-Russia Energy Relations: Will New Oil and Natural Gas Deals Help Russia Weather Economic Sanctions? Columbia, Center on Global Energy Policy. Retrieved from: https://www.energypolicy.columbia.edu/research/qa/qa-china-russia-energy-relations-will-new-oil-and-natural-gas-deals-help-russia-weather-economic

Duclos, M. & Wright, G. (2022, 25 January). Macron's Proposals on Russia Could Be Good for the West. *Institute Montaigne*. Retrieved from: https://www.institutmontaigne.org/en/blog/macrons-proposals-russia-could-be-good-west

Dugin, A. (2012). *The Fourth Political Theory*. London: Arktos.

Dunning, J. (2000). The Eclectic Paradigm as an Envelope for Economic and Business Theories of MNE Activity. *International Business Review*, Vol. 9, pp. 163–90.

Duss, M. (2022, 4 May). The War in Ukraine Calls for a Reset of Biden's Foreign Policy. America Can't Support Democracy Only When It's Convenient. *Foreign Affairs*. Retrieved from: https://www.foreignaffairs.com/articles/ukraine/2022-05-04/war-ukraine-calls-reset-bidens-foreign-policy

Czap, H. J. & Nur-tegin, K. (2011). Big Bang vs. Gradualism – A Productivity Analysis – A Productivity Analysis. *Euroeconomica*, Vol. 29, Issues 3. Retrieved from: https://www.researchgate.net/publication/227410005_Big_Bang_vs_Gradualism_-_A_Productivity_Analysis

Elyatt, H. (2022, 1 April). Russia and the West Are Battling to Get China and India to take their Sides in the Ukraine War. *CNBC*. Retrieved from: https://www.cnbc.com/2022/04/01/russia-and-the-west-battle-to-get-china-and-india-on-side-in-the-war.html

Energy Intelligence (2022, 15 June). Russian Energy Revenues Resistant to Sanctions. Retrieved from: https://www.energyintel.com/00000181-629c-dc60-afe3-eaffd9db0000

Euronews (2021). Hungary Only Nation Against EU Call for Israel-Hamas Ceasefire. Retrieved from: https://www.euronews.com/2021/05/18/eu-fms-due-to-discuss-political-solutions-to-end-israel-gaza-conflict-as-violence-surges-o

European Commission (2020). Report from the Commission to the European Parliament, the Council, the European Economic and Social Committee and the Committee of the Regions on the Impact of Demographic Change. Brussels, 16 June 2020. Retrieved from: https://ec.europa.eu/info/sites/default/files/commission-report-impact-demographic-change-17june2020_en.pdf

European Commission (2021). The 2021 EU Industrial R&D Investment Scoreboard. EU Publications. Retrieved from: https://op.europa.eu/en/publication-detail/-/publication/02ab5f6a-c9bd-11ec-b6f4-01aa75ed71a1/language-en/format-PDF/source-257925010

European Commission (2022, 27 January). EU Refers China to the WTO Following its Trade Restrictions on Lithuania. Press Release. Retrieved from: https://ec.europa.eu/commission/presscorner/detail/en/ip_22_627

European Council (2020). EU-China Summit via Video Conference, 22 June 2020. Retrieved from: https://www.consilium.europa.eu/en/meetings/international-summit/2020/06/22/

European Council (2022). EU-China Summit via Video Conference, 1 April 2022. Main results. Retrieved from: https://www.consilium.europa.eu/en/meetings/international-summit/2022/04/01/

European Union (2008). Consolidated Version of the Treaty on European Union – TITLE I: COMMON PROVISIONS – Article 1 (ex Article 1 TEU). *Official Journal*, Vol. 115, 09 May 2008, pp. 0016–0016. Retrieved from: https://eur-lex.europa.eu/LexUriServ/LexUriServ.do?uri=CELEX:12008M001:EN:HTML

Ewert, Insa (2019). China as a Dividing Force in Europe. *MERICS*. Short analysis. Retrieved from: https://merics.org/en/analysis/china-dividing-force-europe

Foreign Affairs Council (2016). Council Conclusions on Implementing the EU Global Strategy in the Area of Security and Defence. Retrieved from: https://www.consilium.europa.eu/media/22459/eugs-conclusions-st14149en16.pdf

Frost, F. (1997). United States-China Relations and the Clinton-Jiang Summit. *Parliament of Australia*, Current Issues Briefs 1997–1998. Retrieved from: https://www.aph.gov.au/About_Parliament/Parliamentary_Departments/Parliamentary_Library/Publications_Archive/CIB/CIB9798

Fukuyama, F. (1989). The End of History. *The National Interest*, no. 16 (Summer), pp. 3–18. Published By: Center for the National Interest.

Fukuyama, F. (2018). Against Identity Politics. The New Tribalism and the Crisis of Democracy. *Foreign Affairs*, September–October, pp. 90–115.

Galántai, J. (1974). *Magyarország az első világháborúban 1914–1918*. Budapest: Akadémiai Kiadó, p. 272.

García-Herrero, A. (2021, 1 September). What is Behind China's Dual Circulation Strategy? *China Leadership Monitor*. Retrieved from: https://www.prcleader.org/herrero

Gause, F. G. (2022). The Price of Order. Settling for Less in the Middle East. *Foreign Affairs*, Vol. 101, no. 2, March–April, pp. 10–21.

Gavin, F. J. & Poyakova A. (2022, 19 January). Macron's Flawed Vision for Europe. Persistent Divisions Will Preclude His Dreams of Global Power. *Foreign Affairs*. Retrieved from: https://www.foreignaffairs.com/articles/europe/2022-01-19/macrons-flawed-vision-europe

Gebert, K. & Guérot, U. (2012). Why Poland is the New France for Germany. Commentary. *European Council on Foreign Relations*. Retrieved from: https://ecfr.eu/article/commentary_why_poland_is_the_new_france_for_germany/

Gibelin, Th. (2018, 13 March). Central Europe and the European Economy. *VisegradPost*. Retrieved from https://visegradpost.com/en/2018/03/13/central-europe-and-the-european-economy/

Gilpin, R. (1976) *U.S. Power and the Multinational Corporation: The Political Economy of Foreign Direct Investment*. New York: Macmillan.

Global Times (2021a, 30 July). Yuan Expands in China-Russia Trade Amid US Financial Sanctions, 30 July 2021. Retrieved from: https://www.globaltimes.cn/page/202107/1230093.shtml

Global Times (2021b, 30 July). Yuan Expands in China-Russia Trade Amid US Financial Sanctions, 30 July 2021. Retrieved from: https://www.globaltimes.cn/page/202107/1230093.shtml

Global Times (2021, 29 September). China Ranks No.1 Globally in Outward FDI for the First Time, 29 September 2021. Retrieved from: https://www.globaltimes.cn/page/202109/1235451.shtml

Global Times (2022, 19 March). The US Should Match Words with Deeds in Implementing Consensus Reached by Two Heads of State. Retrieved from: https://www.globaltimes.cn/page/202203/1255265.shtml

Global Times (2022, 15 August). What Did Hungary Do Right When It Received the 'Biggest Ever Investment in Its History' from China? Global Times Editorial. *Opinion/Editorial*. Retrieved from: https://www.globaltimes.cn/page/202208/1272975.shtml

Gorenburg, D. (2019). Circumstances Have Changed Since 1991, but Russia's Core Foreign Policy Goals Have Not. *PONARS, Eurasia*. New Approaches to Research and Security. Retrieved from: https://www.ponarseurasia.org/wp-content/uploads/attachments/Pepm560_Gorenburg_Jan2019_0.pdf

Grant, W. & Wilson, G. K. (2012). *The Consequences of the Global Financial Crisis: The Rhetoric of Reform and Regulation*. Edited by Wyn Grant & Graham K. Wison, Chapter 12. Oxford University Press, pp. 226–46.

Guppy, D. & Sicong, X. (2020, 25 October). Guide to China's Dual Circulation Economy. *CGTN*. Retrieved from: https://news.cgtn.com/news/2020-10-25/Guide-to-China-s-dual-circulation-economy-US8jtau4h2/index.html

Hasselbach, C. (2022, 11 April). War in Ukraine: German Foreign Policy under Fire. *Deutsche Welle*. Retrieved from: https://www.dw.com/en/war-in-ukraine-german-foreign-policy-under-fire/a-61436299

High Representative of the Union for Foreign Affairs and Security Policy (2016). Implementation Plan on Security and Defence, Brussels, 14 November 2016. Retrieved from: https://www.consilium.europa.eu/media/22460/eugs-implementation-plan-st14392en16.pdf

Hill, F. (2016). Understanding and Deterring Russia: U.S. Policies and Strategies. *Brookings*, 10 February 2016. Retrieved from: https://www.brookings.edu/testimonies/understanding-and-deterring-russia-u-s-policies-and-strategies/

HIPA (2020, 11 February). 2019-ben is rekord értékű külföldi működőtőke-beruházás érkezett Magyarországra. *Hungarian Investment Promotion Agency*. Retrieved from: https://hipa.hu/2019-ben-is-rekord-erteku-kulfoldi-mukodotoke-beruhazas-erkezett-magyarorszagra

HIPA (2021, 25 January). A koronavírus járvány ellenére is a sikeres működőtőke beruházások éve volt 2020. *Hungarian Investment Promotion Agency*. Retrieved from: https://hipa.hu/a-koronavirus-jarvany-ellenere-is-a-sikeres-mukodotoke-beruhazasok-eve-volt-2020-

HIPA (2021, 31 December). Korea lett hazánk első számú befektetője 2021-ben. *Hungarian Investment Agency*. Retrieved from: https://hipa.hu/korea-lett-hazank-elso-szamu-befektetoje-2021-ben

Hooker, R. D. Jr. (2014). *The Grand Strategy of the United States*, INSS Strategic Monograph. Washington D.C.: National Defense University Press, October 2014. Retrieved from: https://ndupress.ndu.edu/Portals/68/Documents/Books/grand-strategy-us.pdf

House of Representatives (2017, 22 March). Hearing before the Subcommittee on Europe, Eurasia, and Emerging Threats of the Committee on Foreign Affairs.

Retrieved from: https://www.govinfo.gov/content/pkg/CHRG-115hhrg24752/html/CHRG-115hhrg24752.htm

Huang, E. (2022, 31 March). Take China and Russia's 'No Limits' Relationship with a 'Grain of Salt,' Says Former PBOC Advisor. *CNBC*. Retrieved from: https://www.cnbc.com/2022/03/31/take-china-russia-no-limit-relationship-with-grain-of-salt-li-daokui.html

Hungarian Central Statistical Office (2018) *Külföldi irányítású vállalkozások Magyarországon*, Budaepst, p. 5. Retrieved from: https://www.ksh.hu/docs/hun/xftp/idoszaki/pdf/kulfleany18.pdf

Hungary Today (2021, 22 March). Foreign Minister Slams EU Sanctions Against Myanmar, China, as 'Pointless and Harmful'. Retrieved from: https://hungarytoday.hu/foreign-minister-slams-eu-sanctions-against-myanmar-china/

Hungary Today (2022, 19 April). FM Szijjártó: Hungary-Turkey Cooperation Key Focus of Foreign Policy. Retrieved from: https://hungarytoday.hu/szijjarto-ankara-hungary-turkey-relations/

Hungary Today (2022, 17 June). Foreign Secretary Szijjártó: South Korean Company Makes Largest Investment of the Year So Far. *Hungary Today*. Retrieved from: https://hungarytoday.hu/foreign-minsiter-secretary-peter-szijarto-south-korean-investments-nyiregyhaza-hungary/

Hutt, D. & Turcsány, R. Q. (2020, 27 May). No, China Has Not Bought Central and Eastern Europe. *Foreign Policy*. Retrieved from: https://foreignpolicy.com/2020/05/27/china-has-not-bought-central-eastern-europe/

IMF (2021). World Economic Outlook Database, 2021 October Edition.

Institute of Economics of the Latvian Academy of Sciences (2022). Latvia's Foreign Affairs in 2021: Priorities and Achievements. *China-CEE Briefing*, Vol. 46, no. 4 (LVA). Retrieved from: https://china-cee.eu/wp-content/uploads/2022/08/2021er12_Latvia.pdf

Irinyi, K. (1973). *Mitteleuropa-tervek és az osztrák-magyar politikai közgondolkodás*. Budapest: Akadémiai Kiadó, p. 272.

John, A., Shen, S. & Wilson, T. (2021, 24 September). China's Top Regulators Ban Crypto Trading and Mining, Sending Bitcoin Tumbling. *Reuters*. Retrieved from: https://www.reuters.com/world/china/china-central-bank-vows-crackdown-cryptocurrency-trading-2021-09-24/

Johnson, D. D. P., Phil, D. & Thayer, B. A. (2016). The Evolution of Offensive Realism. *Politics and Life Sciences*, Vol. 35, no. 1 (Spring), pp. 1–26. Retrieved from: https://www.cambridge.org/core/journals/politics-and-the-life-sciences/article/evolution-of-offensive-realism/56B778004187F70B8E59609BE7FEE7A4#

Joint U.S.-Russian Declaration (2002, 24 May). *New York Times*. Retrieved from: https://www.nytimes.com/2002/05/24/international/joint-usrussian-declaration.html

Kallas, K. (2022, 9 March). Kallas to the European Parliament: We Need to Provide a Clear Hope for Ukraine's European Dream. Retrieved from: https://valitsus.ee/en/news/kallas-european-parliament-we-need-provide-clear-hope-ukraines-european-dream

Kauranen, A. (2022, 2 May). Finnish Group Ditches Russian-Built Nuclear Plant Plan. *Reuters*. Retrieved from: https://www.reuters.com/world/europe/finnish-group-ditches-russian-built-nuclear-plant-plan-2022-05-02/

Kavalski, E. (2020). How China Lost Central and Eastern Europe. *The Conversation*. Retrieved from: https://theconversation.com/how-china-lost-central-and-eastern-europe-142416

Kennedy, S. (2015, 1 June). Made in China 2015. *Center for Strategic and International Studies*. Retrieved from: https://www.csis.org/analysis/made-china-2025

Kobayashi, S., Baobo, J. & Sano, J. (1999). The 'Three Reforms' in China: Progress and Outlook. *Japan Research Institute*, RIM, September 1999, no. 45. Retrieved from: https://www.jri.co.jp/english/periodical/rim/1999/RIMe199904three reforms/

Koge, K. (2018). The Concept of 'Hedging' Revisited: The Case of Japan's Foreign Policy Strategy in East Asia's Power Shift. *International Studies Review*, vol. 20, pp. 633–60.

Komócsin, S. (2022, 18 August). Akkugyártó nagyhatalom lesz Magyarország, de nagy árat fizetünk érte. *Napi.hu*. Retrieved from: https://www.napi.hu/magyar-vallalatok/akkumulator-gyartas-kina-energia-kiszolgaltatottsag.758128.html

Komuves, A. & Emott, R. (2021, 20 May). Hungary to Block EU's Africa-Pacific Trade and Development Deal. *Reuters*. Retrieved from: https://www.usnews.com/news/world/articles/2021-05-20/hungary-to-block-eus-africa-pacific-trade-and-development-deal#:~:text=BUDAPEST%2FBRUSSELS%20(Reuters)%20-,foreign%20minister%20said%20on%20Thursday

Kornai, J. (1986). The Hungarian Reform Process: Visions, Hopes, and Reality. *Journal of Economic Literature*, Vol. 24, no. 4 (December), pp. 1687–737 (51 pages). Published by: *American Economic Association*.

Krastev, I. (2014, 3 March). Revisionism. Putin's Plan for Overturning the European Order. *Foreign Affairs*. Retrieved from: https://www.foreignaffairs.com/articles/russia-fsu/2014-03-03/russian-revisionism

Kratz, A., Zenglein, M. J., Sebastian, G. & Witzke, M. (2022). Chinese FDI in Europe. 2021 Update. Investments Remain on Downward Trajectory – Focus on Venture Capital. A report by *Rhodium Group and the Mercator Institute for China Studies*. Retrieved from: https://merics.org/sites/default/files/2022-04/MERICS-Rhodium-Group-COFDI-Update-2022-2.pdf

Kristof, D. N. (1993). The Rise of China. *Foreign Affairs*, November–December. Retrieved from: https://www.foreignaffairs.com/articles/asia/1993-12-01/rise-china

Lake, D. (1996). Anarchy, Hierarchy, and the Variety of International Relations. *International Organization*, Vol. 50, no. 1, pp. 1–33. Retrieved from: https://quote.ucsd.edu/lake/files/2014/07/IO-50-1-1999.pdf

Laris, M. (1999). In China, Yeltsin Lashes Out at Clinton. Criticisms of Chechen War Are Met with Blunt Reminder of Russian Nuclear Power. *Washington Post*, p. 35. Retrieved from: https://www.washingtonpost.com/wp-srv/WPcap/1999-12/10/123r-121099-idx.html

Lau, S. (2022, 11 August). Down to 14 + 1: Estonia and Latvia Quit China's Club in Eastern Europe. *Politico*. Retrieved from: https://www.politico.eu/article/down-to-14-1-estonia-and-latvia-quit-chinas-club-in-eastern-europe/

Lawder, D. (2019, 11 April). China Needs Open Capital Markets for Yuan to be Global Currency, IMF's Gopinath Says. *Reuters*. Retrieved from: https://www.reuters.com/business/china-needs-open-capital-markets-yuan-be-global-currency-imfs-gopinath-says-2022-04-26/

Le Corre, P. (2019). A Divided Europe's China Challenge. *East Asia Forum*, 26 November 2019. Retrieved from: https://carnegieendowment.org/2019/11/26/divided-europe-s-china-challenge-pub-80437

Lehne, S. (2019, 11 April). Europe's East-West Divide: Myth or Reality? *Carnegie Europe*. Retrieved from: https://carnegieeurope.eu/2019/04/11/europe-s-east-west-divide-myth-or-reality-pub-78847

Liao, J. C. (2021). How BRI Debt Puts China at Risk. 27 October 2021. *The Diplomat*. Retrieved from: https://thediplomat.com/2021/10/how-bri-debt-puts-china-at-risk/

Liimets, E.-M. (2022, 15 February). Overview of Estonia's Foreign Policy in 2021. *ERR News*. Retrieved from: https://news.err.ee/1608500846/liimets-overview-of-estonia-s-foreign-policy-in-2021

Lipton, D. & Sachs J. (1990). Creating a Market Economy in Eastern Europe: The Case of Poland. *Brookings Papers on Economic Activity*, no 1, pp. 75–133.

Liu, Z. Z. & Papa M. (2022, 7 March). The Anti-Dollar Axis. Russia and China's Plans to Evade U.S. Economic Power. *Foreign Affairs*. Retrieved from: https://www.foreignaffairs.com/articles/russian-federation/2022-03-07/anti-dollar-axis

Loong, L. H. (2021). The Endangered Asian Century. America, China, and the Perils of Confrontation. *Foreign Affairs*, July/August 2020, pp. 52–64.

Lopez G. (2022, 15 March). Europe Awakens to Superpower Potential after Ukraine Invasion. *Deccan Herald*. Retrieved from: https://www.deccanherald.com/opinion/in-perspective/europe-awakens-to-superpower-potential-after-ukraine-invasion-1091679.html

Lukyanov, F. (2021). EU-Russia Relations: What Went Wrong? *Modern Diplomacy*. Retrieved from: https://moderndiplomacy.eu/2021/03/09/eu-russia-relations-what-went-wrong/

Mackinder, J. H. (1919). *Democratic Ideals and Reality: A Study in the Politics of Reconstruction*. New York: Henry Holt and Company, p. 150.

Magda, I. (2017). Do Trade Unions in Central and Eastern Europe Make a Difference? Low Coverage and Greater Fragmentation Can Limit the Benefits of Trade Unions. Warsaw School of Economics and Institute for Structural Research, Poland. Retrieved from: https://wol.iza.org/uploads/articles/360/pdfs/do-trade-unions-in-central-and-eastern-europe-make-a-difference.pdf?v=1

Mair, S. (2021). Partners or Rivals? Dealing with Authoritarian Powers. In Günther Maihold, Stefan Mair, Melanie Müller, Judith Vorrath and Christian Wagner (eds), *German Foreign Policy in Transition*. Volatile Conditions, New Momentum. SWP Research Papers, pp. 116–19. Retrieved from: https://www.swp-berlin.org/publications/products/research_papers/2021RP10_GermanForeignPolicy.pdf

Mandelbaum, M. (1998). *The New Russian Foreign Policy*. Council on Foreign Relations Press, New York.

Maynes, C. W. (1999). US Unilateralism and Its Dangers. *Review of International Studies*, Vol. 25, pp. 515–18. British International Studies Association.

Mcfaul, M. (1999). What Are Russian Foreign Policy Objectives? Carnegie Endowment for International Peace. Retrieved from: https://carnegieendowment.org/1999/05/01/what-are-russian-foreign-policy-objectives-pub-424

McKinnon, R. I. (1992). *The Order of Economic Liberalization: Financial Control in the Transition to a Market Economy*. Baltimore: Johns Hopkins University Press.

Mead, W. R. (2017). The Jacksonian Revolt. American Populism and the Liberal Order. *Foreign Affairs,* March/April 2017.

Mearsheimer, John J. (2001). Great Power Politics in the Twenty First Century, in *The Tragedy of Great Power Politics*, Chapter 10. W. W. Norton & Company, New York and London, p. 371.

Mearsheimer, John J. (2021). The Inevitable Rivalry. America, China, and the Tragedy of Great-Power Politics. *Foreign Affairs,* November/December 2021, pp. 48–59.

Menon, S. (2022, 3 August). Nobody Wants the Current World Order. How All the Major Powers –Even the United States – Became Revisionists. *Foreign Affairs*. Retrieved from: https://www.foreignaffairs.com/world/nobody-wants-current-world-order

Milewski, J., Pomian, K. & Zielonka, J. (1985). Poland: Four Years After. *Foreign Affairs,* Winter 1986–1986, pp. 337–59.

Minami, T. & Inujima, A. (2022). Russia Boosted Yuan Holdings Over Dollar Just Before Invasion. *Nikkei Asia*. Retrieved from: https://asia.nikkei.com/Business/Markets/Currencies/Russia-boosted-yuan-holdings-over-dollar-just-before-invasion

Ministry of Foreign Affairs, Republic of Estonia (2020). Estonian Foreign Policy Strategy 2030. Retrieved from: https://vm.ee/sites/default/files/Estonia_for_UN/Rasmus/estonian_foreign_policy_strategy_2030_final.pdf

Mishke, J. & Umland, A. (2014, 19 April). Germany's New Ostpolitik. An Old Foreign Policy Doctrine Gets a Makeover. *Foreign Affairs*. Retrieved from: https://www.foreignaffairs.com/articles/western-europe/2014-04-09/germanys-new-ostpolitik

Moak, K. (2020, 14 September). Why 'Dual Circulation' Policy Makes Sense. *CGTN*, Opinion. Retrieved from: https://news.cgtn.com/news/2020-09-14/Why-dual-circulation-policy-makes-sense-TLSR4osXfi/index.html

Mobley, T. (2019). The Belt and Road Initiative: Insights from China's Backyard. *Strategic Studies Quarterly*, Vol. 13, no. 3 (Fall), pp. 52–72. Retrieved from: https://www.jstor.org/stable/pdf/26760128.pdf

Moitsugu, K. (2022, 7 March). China Calls Russia Its Chief 'Strategic Partner' Despite War. *ABC News*. Retrieved from: https://abcnews.go.com/International/wireStory/china-russia-chief-strategic-partner-war-83292299

Moldicz, Cs. (2021). *China, the USA and Technological Supremacy in Europe*. Series Editor E. Kavalski. London: Routledge, Rethinking Asia and International Relations, pp. 1–174.

Moldicz, Cs. (2022). Hungarian and Turkish Relations in the Light of the Russian and Ukrainian War. *China-CEE Briefing*. Retrieved from: https://china-cee.eu/wp-content/uploads/2022/07/2022er04_Hungary.pdf

Morillas, P. (2017). Shapes of a Union: From Ever Closer Union to Flexible Differentiation after Brexit. *CIDOB Barcelona Center for International Affairs*, Vol. 166, January 2017. Retrieved from: https://www.cidob.org/en/publications/publication_series/notes_internacionals/n1_166/shapes_of_a_union_from_ever_closer_union_to_flexible_differentiation_after_brexit

Munroe, T., Osborn, A. & Pamuk H. (2022). China, Russia Partner Up against West at Olympics Summit. *Reuters*, 5 February. Retrieved from: https://www.reuters.com/world/europe/russia-china-tell-nato-stop-expansion-moscow-backs-beijing-taiwan-2022-02-04/

Myant, M. (2018a). Dependent Capitalism and the Middle-Income Trap in Europe na East Central Europe. *International Journal of Management and Economics*, Vol. 54, no. 4, pp. 291–303. Retrieved from: https://www.sciendo.com/article/10.2478/ijme-2018-0028

Myant, M. (2018b). The Limits to Dependent Growth in East-Central Europe. *Régulation Review. Capitalism, Institutions, Power*, 24/2nd semestre/Autumn 2018: Capitalismes dépendants. Retrieved from: https://journals.openedition.org/regulation/13351?lang=en#tocto1n8

Myers, R. (1992). The Socialist Market Economy in the People's Republic of China: Fact or Fiction? The Australian University Canberra. Retrieved from: https://

openresearch-repository.anu.edu.au/bitstream/1885/145851/2/Morrison
%20Oration%2055.pdf

Naczyk, M. (2014). Budapest in Warsaw: Central European Business Elites and the Rise of Economic Patriotism Since the Crisis. Presented at the Conference: SASE 26th Annual Conference, 10–12 July 2014.

National Bank of Canada (2021). Geopolitical Briefing, 17 May 2021. Retrieved from: https://www.nbc.ca/content/dam/bnc/en/rates-and-analysis/economic-analysis/GeopoliticalBriefing_210517.pdf

Naughton, B. (2007). *The Chinese Economy: Transitions and Growth*. Cambridge, MA, London, England: The MIT Press.

Naumann, F. (1917). *Central Europe. A Translation of Christabel M. Meredith from the original German of Mittel-Europa by Friedrich Naumann, Member of the Reichstag*. New York: Alfred A. Knopf.

Nelson, J. (1993, 5 April). Clinton Sees New Partnership With Russia, Boosts U.S. Aid: Summit: America's Interests and Values Are Embodied in Yeltsin's Policies, the President Says. Assistance Package is Expanded to $1.6 Billion to Include Grain Sales. *Los Angeles Times*. Retrieved from: https://www.latimes.com/archives/la-xpm-1993-04-05-mn-19451-story.html

Orban, V. (2021). Hungary Has Vetoed the European Union's Joint Statement Regarding Missile Attacks on Israel. Retrieved from: https://miniszterelnok.hu/samizdat-no-8/

Orban, V. (2021, 19 June). Viktor Orban's Speech at the '30 Years of Freedom' Conference in Budapest, Hungary. Retrieved from: https://miniszterelnok.hu/viktor-orbans-address-at-the-conference-entitled-free-for-thirty-years/

Orban, V. (2022, 19 February) Victor Orban's Speech at the Annual Opening of the Hungarian Trade and Industry Chamber. Retrieved from: https://kormany.hu/beszedek-interjuk/miniszterelnok/orban-viktor-beszede-a-magyar-kereskedelmi-es-iparkamara-gazdasagi-evnyito-esemenyen

Ostry, J. D., Loungani, P. & Furceri, D. (2016). Neoliberalism: Oversold? *IMF Finance and Development*, Vol. 56, no. 2. Retrieved from: https://www.imf.org/external/pubs/ft/fandd/2016/06/pdf/ostry.pdf

Özer, D. A. (2022, 22 April). Turkey, Hungary Seek Diplomatic Solution, Cooperate on Ukraine War. *Daily Sabah*. Retrieved from: https://www.dailysabah.com/politics/diplomacy/turkey-hungary-seek-diplomatic-solution-cooperate-on-ukraine-war

Panitch, L. & Gindin, S. (2013). The Integration of China into Global Capitalism. *International Critical Thought*, Vol. 3, pp. 146–58.

Paulauskas, K. (2016). The Baltics: From Nation States to Member States. Institute for Security Studies Occasional Paper. No. 62. Retrieved from: https://www.iss.europa.eu/sites/default/files/EUISSFiles/occ62.pdf

Pe'er, I., Graham, N. & Bhusari, M. (2022). Strengthening Ties: China and the GCC. *Econographics*, 31 January 2022. Retrieved from: https://www.atlanticcouncil.org/blogs/econographics/strengthening-ties-china-and-the-gcc/

People's Bank of China (2021). Progress of Research & Development E-CNY in China. Report prepared by Working Group on E-CNY Research and Development of the *People's Bank of China*. July 2021. Retrieved from: http://www.pbc.gov.cn/en/3688110/3688172/4157443/4293696/2021071614584691871.pdf

Petersen, A. H. (2021). America's Hollow Middle Class. The Goods. *Vox*. Retrieved from: https://www.vox.com/the-goods/22166381/hollow-middle-class-american-dream

Pivak, V. (2021). Can the Yuan Ever Replace the Dollar for Russia? *Carnegie Moscow Center*. Retrieved from: https://carnegiemoscow.org/commentary/85069

Ponczek, C. B. (2022, 20 April). Poland and Hungary Part Ways on Putin. *CEPA*. Retrieved from: https://cepa.org/poland-and-hungary-part-ways-on-putin/

Poplavski, K. (2016). The Role of Central Europe in the German Economy. The Political Consequences. *Center for Eastern Studies*. Retrieved from: http://aei.pitt.edu/76457/1/raport_role-ce-in-german-economy_net.pdf

Portfolió (2021, 19 June). Kiderült, hogyan képzeli el az Európai Unió jövőjét Orbán Viktor. *Portfolió*. Retrieved from: https://www.portfolio.hu/gazdasag/20210619/kiderult-hogyan-kepzeli-el-az-europai-unio-jovojet-orban-viktor-488860

Posen, A. S. (2022, 17 March). The End of Globalization? What Russia's War in Ukraine Means for the World Economy. *Foreign Affairs*. Retrieved from: https://www.foreignaffairs.com/articles/world/2022-03-17/end-globalization

Poyakova, A. & Haddad, B. (2019). Europe Alone. What Comes After the Transatlantic Alliance. *Foreign Affairs*, July/August 2019, pp. 109–20. Retrieved from: https://www.foreignaffairs.com/articles/europe/2019-06-11/europe-alone

Pukhov, R. (2017, 11 December). Russia's Unexpected Military Victory in Syria. *Defense News*. Retrieved from: https://www.defensenews.com/outlook/2017/12/11/moscow-based-think-tank-director-russias-unexpected-military-victory-in-syria/

Putin, V. (2007, 10 February). Speech and the Following Discussion at the Munich Conference on Security Policy. Retrieved from: http://en.kremlin.ru/events/president/transcripts/page/358

PwC (2017). *The Long View.* How will the Global Economic Order Change by 2050? The World in 2050. Retrieved from: https://www.pwc.com/gx/en/world-2050/assets/pwc-the-world-in-2050-full-report-feb-2017.pdf

Quiroz-Gutierrez, Marco (2022). Crypto is Fully Banned in China and 8 Other Countries, January 4, 2022. *Forbes*. Retrieved from: https://fortune.com/2022/01/04/crypto-banned-china-other-countries/

Radin, A. & Reach, C. (2017). *Russian Views of the International Order. Building a Sustainable International Order*. A RAND Project to Explore U.S. Strategy in a Changing World, Santa Monica, CA: RAND Corporation.

Radio Free Liberty (2017, 8 August). Russia Steps Up Efforts to Cut Reliance on U.S. Dollar, Payments System. *Radio Free Liberty*. Retrieved from: https://www.rferl.org/a/russia-steps-up-efforts-cut-reliance-us-dollar-visa-payments-system-mastercard/28664423.html

Raik, K. (2022). The Contours of a New Western Russia Strategy. *Estonian Foreign Policy Institute*, Brief, May 2022. Retrieved from: https://icds.ee/wp-content/uploads/dlm_uploads/2022/05/ICDS_EFPI_Brief_The_Contours_of_a_New_Western_Russia_Strategy_Kristi_Raik_May_2022-1.pdf

Ramo, J. C. (2004). The Beijing Consensus. *The Foreign Policy Centre*. Retrieved from: https://fpc.org.uk/wp-content/uploads/2006/09/244.pdf

Reisinezhad, A. (2020). The Dutch Disease Revisited: Theory and Evidence. *HAL Open Science*, halshs-03012647. Retrieved from: https://halshs.archives-ouvertes.fr/halshs-03012647/document

Reuters (2020, 6 May) Czechs Sign Joint 5G Security Declaration with United States, 6 May 2020. Retrieved from: https://www.reuters.com/article/us-czech-usa-5g-idINKBN22I33O

Reuters (2022a, 12 August). China's CATL to Build $7.6 bln Hungary Battery Plant to Supply Mercedes. *BMW*. Retrieved from: https://www.reuters.com/business/autos-transportation/chinas-catl-build-new-756-bln-battery-plant-hungary-2022-08-12/

Reuters (2022b, 12 August). Mercedes Benz becomes First Partner of CATL's New Hungary Battery Plant. Retrieved from: https://www.reuters.com/business/autos-transportation/mercedes-benz-catl-battery-plant-hungary-will-help-reach-production-goals-2022-08-12/

Richardson, J. (2020, 20 December). China's BRI Will Go from Strength to Strength, Redrawing Global Petrochemicals Map. *Independent Commodity Intelligence Services*. Retrieved from: https://www.icis.com/asian-chemical-connections/2020/12/chinas-bri-will-go-from-strength-to-strength-redrawing-global-petrochemicals-map/

Rohac, D. (2022, 17 April). Germany Has a Hungary Problem. Berlin's Complicity with Viktor Orbán Imperils European Unity against Russian Aggression. *Wall Street Journal*. Retrieved from: https://www.wsj.com/articles/germany-has-a-hungary-problem-nato-russia-ukraine-invasion-foreign-policy-europe-11650225015

Rosen, D. H. (2021). China's Economic Reckoning. The Price of Failed Reforms. *Foreign Affairs,* July/August 2021, pp. 20–9.

Rosenstein-Rodan, P. N. (1961). Notes on the Theory of the 'Big Push'. Economic Development for Latin America. *Proceedings of a Conference held by the International Economic Association, Editor: Howard S. Ellis.*

Rossatom (2022). History of Cooperation. Retrieved from: https://rosatom-centraleurope.com/rosatom-in-country/history-of-cooperation/

Rumer, E. (2019, 5 June). The Primakov (Not Gerasimov) Doctrine in Action. *Carnegie Endowment for International Peace*. Retrieved from: https://carnegieendowment.org/2019/06/05/primakov-not-gerasimov-doctrine-in-action-pub-79254

Rumer, E. & Sokolsky, R. (2019). Thirty Years of U.S. Policy Toward Russia: Can the Vicious Circle Be Broken? *Carnegie Endowment for International Peace*. Retrieved from: https://carnegieendowment.org/files/RumerSokolsky_USRussia_final_web.pdf

Ryan, M. & Timsit, A. (2022, 25 April). U.S. Wants Russian Military 'Weakened' from Ukraine Invasion, AUSTIN Says. *The Washington Post*. Retrieved from: https://www.washingtonpost.com/world/2022/04/25/russia-weakened-lloyd-austin-ukraine-visit/

Salamon, R. (1995). *The Transformation of the World Economy*. New York: St. Martin's Press, p. 238.

Schliephake, C. V. & Beaven, W. (2022). Primacy of EU Law and Poland's Constitutional Court. Cautrecacas. *Competition and EU Law Blog*. Retrieved from: https://www.cuatrecasas.com/en/global/article/eu-primacy-of-eu-law-and-polands-constitutional-court

Scholz, O. (2022, 17 July). Die EU muss zu einem geopolitishen Akteur werden. *Frankfurter Allgemeine*. Retrieved from: https://www.faz.net/aktuell/politik/die-gegenwart/scholz-zum-ukraine-krieg-eu-muss-geopolitischer-akteur-werden-18176580.html?GEPC=s3

Schulhof, V., van Vuuren, D. & Kirchherr, J. (2022, February). The Belt and Road Initiative (BRI): What Will it Look Like in the Future? *Technological Forecasting & Social Change*, Vol. 175, p. 121306, Elsevier. Retrieved from: https://reader.elsevier.com/reader/sd/pii/S004016252100740X?token=1F59522CDA1394E2290FABC76E4FDA68BD23D7877F716695F64567B9EFCA9EFC303414F6BBA7F07689B0165589500D3F&originRegion=eu-west-1&originCreation=20220406111517

Schultz, K. (2002). The Historic Czech Delegation to Taiwan: When a Small Democracy Stands up to China's Intimidation. *Global Taiwan Brief*, Vol. 5, Issue 18, pp. 12–16. Retrieved from: https://globaltaiwan.org/wp-content/uploads/2020/09/GTB-PDF-5.18.pdf

Schutte, G. R. (2021). The Challenge to US Hegemony and the 'Gilpin Dilemma'. *Revista Brasileira de Política Internacional*, Vol. 64, no. 1, o. e004, 2021. Centro de Estudos Globais da Universidade de Brasília. Retrieved from: https://www.redalyc.org/journal/358/35866229004/html/

Schweller, R. & Pu, X. (2011). After Unipolarity: China's Visions of International Order in an Era of US Decline. *International Security*, Vol. 36, no. 1, pp. 41–72.

Shapiro, J. (2021, 22 April). Biden's Everything Doctrine. The Mantle of Global Leadership Doesn't Fit a Foreign Policy for the Middle Class. *Foreign Affairs*.

Retrieved from: https://www.foreignaffairs.com/articles/united-states/2021-04-22/bidens-everything-doctrine

Shea, J. (2009). 1979: The Soviet Union Deploys Its SS20 Missiles and NATO Responds. Video Lecture by Jamie Shea, Deputy Assistant Secretary General for Emerging Security Challenges. Retrieved from: https://www.nato.int/cps/en/natohq/opinions_139274.htm

Shead, S. (2022, 3 June). Russia Says It Will Remove Dollar Assets from Its Wealth Fund. *CNBC*, 2022, 3 June. Retrieved from: https://www.cnbc.com/2021/06/03/russia-to-remove-dollar-assets-from-national-wealth-fund.html

Sherman, E. (2022, 2 May). Russia's Move to Gold May Jolt Your Company. *Forbes*, 2 May 2022. Retrieved from: https://www.forbes.com/sites/zengernews/2022/05/02/russias-move-to-gold-may-jolt-your-company/?sh=5044a83872e6

Shortridge, A. (2021). The U.S. War in Afghanistan Twenty Years On: Public Opinion Then and Now. *Council on Foreign Relations*, 7 October 2021. Retrieved from: https://www.cfr.org/blog/us-war-afghanistan-twenty-years-public-opinion-then-and-now

Silverstein, K. (2019). As China's 'Belt and Road' Initiative Replaces U.S. On Global Stage, The Implications For Energy And Trade. *Forbes*, 5 December 2019. Retrieved from: https://www.forbes.com/sites/kensilverstein/2019/12/05/as-the-us-becomes-isolationist-china-is-becoming-globalist-the-implications-for-energy-and-trade/?sh=2397c23019f4

Smitt, E. (2022, 17 February). U.S. Army Troops Arrive in Poland to Reassure Allies. *New York Times*. Retrieved from: https://www.nytimes.com/2022/02/17/us/politics/us-troops-ukraine-russia.html

Stam, C. (2018, 21 June). Germany Earned €2.9 Billion from Greece's Debt Crisis. *Euroactive*. Retrieved from: https://www.euractiv.com/section/economy-jobs/news/germany-earned-2-9-billion-euros-from-greeces-debt-crisis/

Stent, A. (2020). Russia and China: Axis of Revisionists. Global China: Assessing China's Growing Role in the World. *Brookings*. February 2020. Retrieved from: https://www.brookings.edu/research/russia-and-china-axis-of-revisionists/

Tachikava, T. (2021). China-led Economic Zone Composed of Belt and Road Participants. *Kyodo News*, 16 April 2021. Retrieved from: https://english.kyodonews.net/news/2021/04/d86e736c918c-focus-yuans-promotion-to-key-currency-eyed-amid-chinas-rapid-growth.html

Tagliabue, J. (1983). West Germans Protest Nuclear Missiles for 4th Day. *New York Times*, p. 9, 5 April 1983. Retrieved from: https://www.nytimes.com/1983/04/05/world/west-germans-protest-nuclear-missiles-for-4th-day.html

Than, K. & Hovet, J. (2020, 30 July). Auto Industry Set to Put Brakes on Central Europe's COVID-19 Recovery. *Reuters*. Retrieved from: https://www.reuters.com/article/us-easteurope-economy-automotive-analysi-idUKKCN24V0QT

Tilles, D. (2021). Kaczyński, Le Pen, Orban and Other Leaders Meet in Warsaw to Reject EU's 'Social Engineering'. *Notes from Poland*. Retrieved from: https://notesfrompoland.com/2021/12/05/kaczynski-le-pen-orban-and-other-leaders-meet-in-warsaw-to-reject-eus-social-engineering/

Torreblanca, J. I. (2021). Technology. In *European Council on Foreign Relations & Stiftung Mercator: The Power Atlas. The Seven Battlegrounds of the Networked World*. Edited by Mark Leonard, December 2021. Retrieved from: https://ecfr.eu/special/power-atlas/technology/

Trump, Donald J. (2019). Press Release – U.S.-Poland Joint Declaration on 5G Online by Gerhard Peters and John T. Woolley. The American Presidency Project. Retrieved from: https://www.presidency.ucsb.edu/node/333992

Turcsany, R. Q. (2016). China-CEE Cooperation in the 16+1 Platform and His Role in the Belt and Road Initiative. In *China-CEEC Cooperation and the 'Belt and Road Initiative'*. Edited by Huang Ping and Liu Zuokiu. China Social Sciences Press, Bejing, pp. 13–26..

United States – Slovak Republic (2020, 23 October). Joint Declaration on 5G Security. Media Note, Office of the Spokesperson, 23 October 2020. Retrieved from: https://2017-2021.state.gov/united-states-slovak-republic-joint-declaration-on-5g-security/index.html

van der Leyen, U. (2022, 1 March). Speech by President von der Leyen at the European Parliament Plenary on the Russian Aggression against Ukraine, Brussels. Retrieved from: https://ec.europa.eu/commission/presscorner/detail/en/speech_22_1483

Vaski, T. (2021, 25 May). Hungary Supports Belarus' Ban from EU Airspace Over Ryanair Hijacking. Retrieved from: https://hungarytoday.hu/hungary-belarus-ban-european-union/

Vinokurov, E. (2020, 21 February). Russia and Middle East Need International North-South Transport Corridor. Valdai Discussion Club, Expert Opinions. Retrieved from: https://valdaiclub.com/a/highlights/russia-and-middle-east-need-international/

Voa News (2022, 5 May). Putin Apologizes to Israel for Lavrov's Anti-Semitic Remarks. *Voa News*. Retrieved from: https://www.voanews.com/a/putin-apologizes-to-israel-for-lavrov-s-anti-semitic-remarks/6559586.html

Wall Street Journal (2016). 'China's Offensive in Europe': Is There a Master Plan in Beijing? 22 June 2016. Retrieved from: https://www.wsj.com/articles/BL-CJB-29345

Wallace, W. & Zielonka, J. (1999). Misunderstanding Europe. *Foreign Affairs*, November–December 1998, pp. 65–9.

Wallerstein, I. (2013). Structural Crisis, or Why Capitalists May No Longer Find Capitalism Rewarding. In Immanuel Wallerstein, Randall Collins, Michael Mann, Georgi Derluguian and Craig Calhoun, *Does Capitalism Have a Future?* Oxford University Press, Oxford, pp. 8–26.

Wang, H. (2016). A Deeper Look at China's 'Going Out' Policy. *CIGI Commentary*, March 2016. Retrieved from: https://www.cigionline.org/static/documents/hongying_wang_mar2016_web.pdf

Westad, Odd Arne (2019). The Sources of Chinese Conduct. Are Washington and Beijing Fighting a New Cold War? *Foreign Affairs,* September/October 2019, pp. 86–95.

Wilson, E. (2022). BRI: Have We Passed Peak China? *Euromoney*, 6 February 2022. Retrieved from: https://www.euromoney.com/article/29ppq3xrh5p5bxgoh9dz4/opinion/bri-have-we-passed-peak-china

World Intellectual Property Organisation (2020). World Intellectual Property Indicators 2020. Retrieved from: https://www.wipo.int/edocs/pubdocs/en/wipo_pub_941_2020.pdf

World Intellectual Property Organisation (2021, 8 November). World Intellectual Property Indicators Report: Worldwide Trademark Filing Soars in 2020 Despite Global Pandemic, 8 November 2021. Retrieved from: https://www.wipo.int/pressroom/en/articles/2021/article_0011.html

Xinbo, W. (2022). Where will the International System Head Post Russia-Ukraine Conflict? *Global Times*, Opinion/Viewpoint. Retrieved from: https://www.globaltimes.cn/page/202206/1267498.shtml

Xinhuanet (2020, 7 September). Czech Senate Speaker's Taiwan Trip 'Boyish Provocation': Czech President. Retrieved from: http://www.xinhuanet.com/english/europe/2020-09/07/c_139349344.htm

Xuetong, Y. (2022). Becoming Strong. The New Chinese Foreign Policy. Foreign Policy. *Foreign Affairs*, Vol. 100, no. 4, pp. 40–7.

Yao, K. (2020, 15 September). What We Know about China's 'Dual Circulation' Economic Strategy. *Reuters*. Retrieved from: https://www.reuters.com/article/china-economy-transformation-explainer-idUSKBN2600B5

Zielonka, J. (2019). The Mythology of the East-West Divide. *Eurozine*, 5 March 2018. Retrieved from: https://www.eurozine.com/mythology-east-west-divide/

Zuokui, L. (2016). *Europe and the 'Belt and Road Initiative': Responses and Risks*. China Social Sciences Press, Beijing.

Zwetsloot, Remco, Corrigan, Jack, Weinstein, Emily, Peterson, Dahlia, Gehlhaus, Diana & Fedasiuk, Ryuan (2021). China is Fast Outpacing U.S. STEM PhD Growth. Center for Security and Emerging Technology. Data Brief. Retrieved from: https://cset.georgetown.edu/publication/china-is-fast-outpacing-u-s-stem-phd-growth/

Index

5G technology 7

American–European relations 5
American hegemony 3
anti-Western idealists 80
anti-Western ideologues 81, 158
anti-Western pragmatists 80, 158
asymmetry of power 5, 26, 149

balance of power 77, 81–2, 158
bargaining power 7, 115, 137, 167
Beijing Consensus 5
belt and road initiative 1, 6, 12, 21–2, 26, 29, 39, 52, 56, 61–2, 66, 147–8, 150, 155
Biden administration 23, 40, 53, 57, 85, 151, 155
big bang transformation 130–1
Big Push industrialization 55, 154
Brexit 51–2, 95, 100, 102, 128
Budapest–Belgrade railroad 70

CEE–EU relations 109, 164
Central Europe 1, 3, 5–8, 10–15, 17–26, 28, 30, 32, 34, 36, 38, 40, 42, 44, 46–7, 49–50, 52, 54, 56, 58–62, 64–6, 68, 70, 72–3, 75–80, 82, 84–90, 92, 94, 96, 99–104, 106–10, 112–18, 120, 122, 125–32, 134–40, 142, 144–52, 154, 156–62, 164, 166, 168, 170
CE region 5–6, 37, 42, 93, 160
China–EU relations 58
China policy 6, 15, 18, 37, 57, 59, 61, 70, 123, 151, 155, 156, 165
Chinese economic reforms 4
Chinese economy 23, 40, 50, 52, 54–7, 84, 86, 154–5
Chinese yuan 19–21, 69, 93
Cold war 3
Crimean Peninsula 45, 91, 112
culture war 143, 169

de-globalization 52, 63, 95, 142, 153, 160, 169
democratization 10, 25, 37, 99, 161
Deng Xiaoping 50, 55, 154
dependent model 11, 50, 126, 128, 131, 133, 137, 146, 166, 167
developing economies 5, 55, 154
development traps 7, 137
differentiated integration 102
digitalization 6, 67, 138, 167

E7 countries 132
Eastern Opening Policy 143, 169
Eastern Treaties 110
economic colonialism 114, 164
economic influence 23, 47, 67, 75, 95, 160
economic sanctions 45, 89, 94, 123, 166
economic superpower 54, 153
efficiency-seeking investments 72, 157
emerging economic blocs 6, 87
emerging economies 21, 114, 164
energy infrastructure 47, 90, 152
energy production 47, 94, 152
European allies 51, 140
European Commission 10, 13, 15, 23, 29, 42, 57, 59, 60, 89–90, 97, 103, 106–9, 136, 155, 164
European integration 32–3, 61, 109, 111, 126
European Union 6–9, 11, 12, 26, 27, 30, 33–4, 42, 51, 54, 58, 62, 66, 73, 75, 78, 86–7, 89, 94, 99–103, 105, 107–9, 111, 113, 115–17, 119, 121–3, 125, 128, 141, 149, 153, 159, 161, 163–4, 166
Eurozone crisis 1, 34, 63
ever closer union 6, 99–100

financial crisis 1, 5, 23, 33, 35, 39, 51, 102, 105, 125, 127–9,

131–3, 143, 146, 150, 152, 162, 166, 167, 169
financial infrastructure   53, 67, 91, 92
financial order   31, 91
financial system   19, 20, 31, 33, 88
Five-Year Plan   57
foreign direct investment   53, 59, 71, 88, 95, 131, 133, 156, 160, 166
foreign exchange reserve   69
foreign trade   46, 88, 95, 160
free markets   4, 22, 148
Fudan   70, 92

G-7 countries   5, 9
geographical proximity   75, 113
geopolitical environment   5, 21
global economy   35, 39, 51, 53, 56, 64, 80, 146, 152, 155, 158
globalization   26, 36, 51–3, 61, 64, 95, 110
global pandemic   5, 21, 52, 53, 57, 125, 155
global strategy   40, 150
gradual transformation   130
gross domestic product   7

heavy industry   55, 131, 154, 166
hierarchical dependencies   108, 163
human rights   41, 44, 58, 111, 120, 141, 151

independent technological ecosystems   3, 88, 91, 159
industrialization   54–5, 154
integration process   14, 102, 126, 127
interdependence   3, 42, 61
intergovernmental approach   101–2, 126
international institutions   52–3
internationalization   19–21, 50, 56, 67, 69, 93, 127, 145, 152, 154–5
international trade   19, 52, 69, 83, 91, 95
investment relations   11, 14, 42, 50, 116, 125, 144, 152, 165, 170
Iron Curtain   6, 7, 75, 157
Israel-Palestine ceasefire   7, 121

Jacksonian revolt   51, 153

Kuomingtang   55, 154

laissez-faire   70
liberalization   69, 93, 130

market-seeking direct investments   72, 157
migration   161
military power   47, 54, 149, 153
modernization   10, 26, 36, 37, 55, 76, 90, 99, 110, 129, 154, 161
multilateral organizations   105, 162
multilateral trade   52
multinational corporations   51, 143, 169

national banks   116, 165
national interests   11, 114–16, 164, 165
NATO   1, 4, 6, 10, 25, 27, 31, 42–5, 51, 77, 79, 81–2, 84, 86–7, 97, 110, 112, 116, 140–2, 168, 169
neoliberal   4, 5, 35, 68, 134, 146

Obama administration   44
One-China   15, 70
open door policies   6, 54

parallel financial infrastructures   6, 91
parallel financial worlds   160
Paris Agreement   53, 111
partnership agreement   70
Pax Americana   9
peaceful cooperation   3, 47, 152
periphery   108, 163
Pivot to Asia   5, 29, 46, 146, 150, 152
political integration   142, 168
populist movements   52, 104, 161
practical union   101
PRC   49, 57
production costs   113
profit transfer balance   138, 167
pro-Western idealists   78–9, 158
pro-Western pragmatists   79, 158

raw materials   10–11, 53, 62, 70, 72, 76, 89, 94, 156, 159
rebalancing strategy   57, 155
re-polonization   133
rule-of-law   103, 105–6, 163
Russia's foreign policy   75, 140
Russian diaspora   139
Russian Empire   139
Russian energy   53, 88–9, 118, 159

Russian natural gas   97
Russian oil   85, 89–90, 97

Second World War   28, 30, 31, 46, 53,
    110, 116, 125, 139, 145, 166
Securities and Exchange Commission   68
semi-periphery   108, 163
shift of global power   148
small states   99
social development   13, 99
Soviet bloc   3, 4, 109, 125, 166
Soviet era   107
Soviet Union   11, 22, 25, 30, 32, 42–3,
    49, 64, 75–8, 96, 110, 125, 139,
    149, 158, 166
state-directed industrialization   154
strategic autonomy   123
superpower competition   47, 152
supply chains   6, 10, 25, 57, 59, 88, 93, 94,
    113, 144, 155, 159, 160, 170
supranational   100, 127

Taipei   15, 41, 70
technological sovereignty   6, 90
technology transfer   9, 47, 50, 70, 90, 91,
    95, 143, 151–3, 159–60, 169
trading blocs   159

transatlantic partnership   111
trans-pacific partnership   53
trap of duality   138, 167
trap of foreign ownership   138, 167
Treaty on European Union   100
Trump administration   36, 38, 51, 111

Ukraine war   23, 42, 46, 53, 59, 64, 83,
    84, 91, 93, 95, 123, 149, 155, 165
underdevelopment   138, 168
US foreign policy   5, 7, 12, 18, 20, 24–5,
    29, 33, 37, 112, 140–1, 149, 150

Visegrad countries   3, 6, 25–6, 40–1,
    97, 146, 151

Wallerstein, Immanuel   108, 163
Wang Yi   70
war with Ukraine   54, 153
Washington Consensus   4, 5, 131
world economy   35, 37, 52, 76, 79, 86,
    142, 145, 153, 168
World Health Organization   53

Xi Jinping   3

Zero-Covid policy   53

www.ingramcontent.com/pod-product-compliance
Lightning Source LLC
Chambersburg PA
CBHW052118300426
44116CB00010B/1709